# Professional Identity Crisis

# Professional Identity Crisis

## *Race, Class, Gender, and Success at Professional Schools*

*Carrie Yang Costello*

Vanderbilt University Press

Nashville, Tennessee

© 2005 Vanderbilt University Press
All rights reserved
First Edition 2005

10 09 08 07 06 05  1 2 3 4 5

Printed on acid-free paper.
Manufactured in the United States of America

Library of Congress Cataloging-in-Publication Data

Costello, Carrie Yang, 1964–
Professional identity crisis : race, class, gender, and success at
professional schools / Carrie Yang Costello.— 1st ed.
    p. cm.
Includes bibliographical references.
ISBN 0-8265-1504-5 (cloth : alk. paper)
ISBN 0-8265-1505-3 (pbk. : alk. paper)
1. Professional education—Social aspects—United States—Case studies.
2. Socialization--United States--Case studies. I. Title.
LC1059.C75 2005
378'.013'0973--dc22
2005005463

# Contents

# Acknowledgments

Producing a research-based book is an interesting found experiment in the development and maintenance of social networks. There are numerous people to thank, first of all the many professional students and professors at U.C. Berkeley who allowed me to observe them and who spoke with me at length about matters both fascinating and uncomfortable. Without their generosity of spirit, this project would have been impossible.

Next I must thank the many readers of the many incarnations of this manuscript: Kim DaCosta, Troy Duster, Kristin Espinosa, Laura Fingerson, Evelyn Nakano Glenn, Arlie Hochschild, Jean Hudson, Jennifer Jordan, Jerry Karabel, Miki Kashtan, Steve McKay, Ellie Miller, Stacey Oliker, and Karolyn Tyson. I've alphabetized you in honor of your helping give order to relative chaos.

My work was buttressed by institutional support. I am grateful to have received funding in the form of a U.C. Berkeley Vice Chancellor for Research Fund Award and a Dean's Dissertation Fellowship. I also appreciate having been given opportunities to present papers on materials that appear in this book at meetings of the American Sociological Association, the Society for the Study of Social Problems, and Sociologists for Women in Society.

I thank my family, Pekka and Nina, for keeping me from imbalance, and my parents, siblings, and assorted friends for good measure. And finally, I thank my former attorney colleagues who kept saying of my writing, "This isn't law, it's *sociology*," for setting me on the path to a very satisfying career.

# 1 The Professional School Experience
## An Informal Introduction

Professional schools are an important gateway to success in contemporary U.S. society. Once, their doors were not open to all. They excluded women, denied entry to people of color, and set admission quotas for Jews. But today, all are welcome to apply—the criteria for acceptance are based on qualifications, not demographics. And it is a qualified group indeed that is granted admission to America's prestigious professional schools. Students entering professional schools have impressive collegiate grade-point averages. Most of them have scored well on standardized tests such as the GRE, MCAT, or LSAT. They come with impressive letters of recommendation and extensive records of extracurricular activities. Today's matriculants may be of diverse races, genders, and class backgrounds, but their resumes are uniformly exemplary.

Unfortunately, their equivalent earlier accomplishments do not translate to equal levels of professional success. A quick look at earning disparities between men and women in the professions makes this clear: in 2000, the median net income for a U.S. male physician was $195,000, while for a female physician it was $120,000; the median salary in 2002 for male attorneys was $69,680, while for females it was $50,648; and the median income for male social workers in 2003 was $54,290, compared to the median female income of $43,510 (Women Physician Congress, 2003; Dugan, 2002; Linsley, 2003). Individuals who face more than one demographic hurdle are particularly challenged; for example, data indicate that nearly 100 percent of female African American attorneys leave their first law-firm job within eight years (Blumenthal, 2004).

There is a large body of literature exploring how the workplace produces patterns of social inequality, but this does not explain the fact that patterns of race, class, and gender stratification appear starting in the first days of professional schooling.[1] The disproportionate success of white males from class-privileged backgrounds is a matter of substantial controversy within the professions. Some conservative individuals claim that academic competition at professional schools ensures that the "smartest" rise to the top. These individuals argue that the greater tendency of white men to excel is explained by affirmative action policies that grant less "smart" people of color admission to elite schools. Professionals of a liberal bent dismiss such explanations angrily. They believe that white men achieve disproportionate success because women and people of color face a conspiracy to discriminate on the part of biased professors, administrators, and employers. The problem with these lay theories is that they are both incorrect: the conspiracies they posit do not exist.

The theory that inappropriate affirmative action explains the underperformance of "nontraditional" professional students can be disproved in a number of ways. Students of color are not showered with undeserved grade-point averages by liberal college administrations, so such students' college success cannot be explained by affirmative action. Students who are members of underrepresented minorities are sometimes beneficiaries of affirmative action in professional school admissions—but at other schools there is no affirmative action, and students of color underperform in comparison to their white peers at both sets of institutions.[2] Moreover, other "nontraditional" groups of professional students who do not do as well as their traditional peers, such as students with evangelical religious commitments, have never been the subjects of affirmative action policies, so their failure to be high achievers can hardly be explained away by affirmative action.

The theory that a conspiracy to discriminate explains the better grades and career outcomes of class-privileged white men is equally unconvincing. White males outperform other professional students even in classes run by feminist, antiracist social work professors. Although incidents of overt and intentional discrimination do occur at professional schools, they are fairly infrequent, while the underperformance of women and students of color is pervasive. And white men outperform other students even on exams where their names are concealed under blind grading policies meant to ensure nondiscrimination, belying the theory that a conservative cabal creates the disparities.

What then can explain "nontraditional" students' failure to reach the same level of success as their "traditional" peers at professional schools? This is the question that led me to begin the research this book presents.

Before I begin formally to present my solution to the puzzle of the underperformance of "nontraditional" students, I offer the cases of five of the students who graciously allowed me to observe and interview them as they experienced their first year of professional school.[3] I met these students at U.C. Berkeley's Boalt Hall School of Law and School of Social Welfare while attending classes with them as a participant observer. I believe that it would be useful for the reader to come to understand, at least in part, how different students experienced the first year of professional school.

## Brian

Brian was a confident and articulate white man in his midtwenties. (I have changed all students' names to protect their confidentiality.) On the day we met for our interview, he was wearing a pair of khaki corduroys, a snowy white, unadorned T-shirt, and an elegant European watch with a curved face. Brian had always excelled academically and expected even before entering college to pursue either an MBA or a JD.

Brian conveyed to me that he was very happy with his decision to attend law school. He found the work challenging and interesting and felt that as long as he put in the necessary preparation time, he did well in class, both when volunteering to speak and when called upon by a professor. He told me that when he was called upon to answer a question, "I think there is a moment of pause, and then I feel a natural stress reaction. But I have done an enormous amount of public speaking in the past, and so I am very comfortable doing that." If a professor chose to debate a point he had made, Brian found that he enjoyed rather than dreaded the occasion, because, as he put it, "I have always been a hard debater." Being rational by nature, Brian felt an affinity for the rational gamesmanship of debating.

Brian not only performed well in class, he also received excellent grades. He faxed copies of his grade reports to the law firms to which he had applied for a summer associate position and received phone calls "the very next day from firms that were interested," a response he felt was gratifying personally but rather unfair generally. The unfairness Brian perceived to arise from the fact that "as far as testing knowledge of the law, at most this accounts for 50% of the grade," the other half of the grade being determined by "a certain writing style," which Brian felt he was fortunate to possess, since it was not something taught in class. Many of the students around him were not so fortunate, and he deemed it sad that their lower grades "undermined their sense of well-being or sense of self-confidence."

Still, Brian was clearly enjoying his success at law school. He felt sympathy for students who were unable to get the high grades he had received, and yet he simultaneously felt that his success reflected his intelligence, work habits, verbal abilities, and interests. While some students complained that the reading load was too long and boring, Brian said, "By and large I feel fortunate in that I do find it very compelling, interesting reading. I enjoy it and it moves fairly quickly."

Brian was sanguine about the likelihood that he would make a good lawyer and that he would do good as well, helping society through corporate law practice:

> I believe I have a core set of beliefs, which I will not compromise. I think I will generally contribute to social well-being and the general good. I will employ my legal skills to facilitate—I plan to go into corporate law—facilitating business transactions both in that context and hopefully in pro bono work, so that at the same time I will be able to help people achieve their own goals.

When considering his future legal career, Brian enjoyed a sense of moral comfort as well as confidence in his skills.

Because of his ability to prepare quickly for class, Brian found that he had time for recreation, often going out to bars or even getting away for the occasional weekend of snowboarding and camping. He engaged in these activities with his numerous new Law School friends, whose company he enjoyed even more that he had that of his pre–Law School friends, because he felt he was more similar to the friends he had made at law school. Brian felt that he and his Law School friends were "the focused type: we work hard when we are working—and then we go play." All in all, Brian was excelling academically and enjoying himself personally. After a brief period of adjustment in which, he says, "I was not sure what was acceptable behavior," Brian settled comfortably into the life of a successful law student.

## Jasmine

A very different first-year law student, Jasmine, was a petite, energetic Filipina who had blunt-cut, shoulder-length hair and an urbane and fashionable style. She was more casual and colloquial in her speech than Brian was. Like him, Jasmine had a history of excellent academic performance, and her academic success had defined her within her Filipino American community in Los Angeles:

> I'm the first person from my community to go to graduate school. Law school is a big deal to them, to everybody, so I know I have to do a lot of representing for them. And when I go back, they look for a lot of leadership in me. It feels good, but it's a lot of responsibility; . . . it's a burden I take on.

Like Brian, Jasmine had dreamed of going to law school for a long time, but unlike him, she has found the transition to law school challenging:

> When I was little, it was for some reason always a plan that I had that I was going to go to law school. I think I was six when I started writing letters to all the top law schools—I was kind of crazy. And then I started working with kids and my life was really revolving around juveniles and stuff like that, and it was really clear that what I wanted to do was be a juvenile-court judge, and that's the reason I stay here, because seriously, if I didn't know, I would not be able to continue this.

Jasmine was uncomfortable at law school for multiple reasons—ideological, emotional, academic, social, and personal.

One cause for Jasmine's discomfort was that she was not receiving training in the areas of law which interested her. "I feel the classes aren't relating to what I want to do; it's boring," she told me. The courses seemed framed to train students to meet the needs of wealthy adults rather than of underprivileged children. She needed to rationalize the effort she put into studying what seemed to her tangential matters:

> I think there's a system, and a system runs what's happening in society and how the law works. Being in law school means learning the system, how to work the system. There are a lot of things I see that should be changed in the system, but at the same time I need to understand where it's at in order to move it.

Jasmine's relationship to the law she was studying was much more alienated than Brian's was: while Brian approached the law uncritically as something in which to immerse himself so that he could excel, Jasmine adopted a critical stance toward the law as something she wanted to master without internalizing its values, so that she could change it (and not vice versa).

A central problem Jasmine saw was that the law seemed to her coldly rational, lacking in empathy. She felt that law professors did not train students to show empathy or respect for clients: "The teachers don't want to focus on that. . . . I think there's a lot of human relations avoided at times. They don't teach lawyers people skills here." As a result of what seemed to her their rationalist bias, Jasmine felt that judges reached unjust decisions in many of the cases she read.

> I have to suppress my emotional side to do legal analysis. Sometimes it's hard to understand why judges do certain things, and then you have to look at the law and the statutes and consistency, and all that stuff plays a big part in why they're doing it, but a lot of times if you look at the individual case it doesn't make any sense.

While the law as she was learning it in class seemed coldly unempathetic, Jasmine felt that her empathy and people skills were the assets that would serve her best in being a good juvenile-court judge: "While I recognize the rational part, especially being a juvenile judge, I'll really recognize the emotional part; I recognize where these kids are coming from, so I think I'll make a good judge." Jasmine was clinging tightly to her empathetic understanding of justice and her sense of mission—but in this she felt no support from professors and little from classmates.

Jasmine was not enjoying herself socially at law school in the way Brian was. When I asked her if she had made many friends, she replied, "Depends on what you call friends. I know a lot of people." She was disappointed with the Law School social milieu, describing it as "a very high-schooly atmosphere" characterized by competition, cliquishness, and emotional immaturity. Everyone seemed to be intelligent, but Jasmine felt that there was more to life than being smart, and many students seemed to her to be sheltered, self-centered, and disturbingly indifferent to social justice.

Jasmine had been a rhetoric major at a reputable college, and she said she was confident she could handle law school intellectually. Nevertheless, her first-semester grades were below average. She was having some difficulty coping with not getting the good grades she was accustomed to. She rationalized others' better performance by stating that the high scorers were not smarter than she was or more apt pupils of the law, but that "they really work their butts off," which is something she did not wish to do. Still,

Jasmine was concerned about her underperformance and avoided looking at her grades for weeks:

> It was probably my old fears coming out, about always looking at grades, and I didn't want it to hold me back from learning now, from wanting to be at school, because I think a lot of people maybe get discouraged and they just feel like they want to fall back, because what's the point? I don't want to pressure myself like that.

Jasmine did not suggest that her underperformance had anything to do with her personality or style. Nonetheless, it was clear that much of her discomfort at law school arose from issues of style and identity, and that being a law student precipitated a sort of identity crisis for her that Brian never encountered. She struggled to put this into words:

> Even in my first semester here at law school, it was like, What am I doing here? I was fighting against a lot of, "I'm not like these people, I don't want to do that.". . . Throughout the whole law-school process— I'm expecting it, I guess I surrendered to it—there's just a lot of identity finding, a lot of changing.

That Jasmine's very sense of self was changing during law school raised the distressing possibility for her that she might become someone the present Jasmine would not admire. She was worried that she might "lose" herself and had felt herself "on the edge" of just giving up and becoming a corporate lawyer, although for the time being, at least, she had reaffirmed her sense of mission in serving underprivileged youth.

Attending law school had already had a curious effect on Jasmine's identity: she had developed a sort of split personality. Her entire self-presentation varied according to whether she was at school or at home with her Filipino community in Los Angeles:

> In the legal culture . . . you have to adopt a different way of being, a different vocabulary and way to carry yourself . . . you have to in order to—that's how I got this far. And when I go home, if I act the way I do here, if I speak the legalese, they won't get it. So I have to go back to the different way and rechange the way I talk and everything.

When moving between the two environments, Jasmine experienced an awkward period of transition:

Sometimes it's weird where I'll go home and my cousins and my friends say, "What did you say? What?" When I go home, it's always, "You're kind of whitewashed." And when I come here, I have to get back my law style.

This split identity allowed Jasmine to exist in two disparate worlds without having to choose between them, but it was not an easy way to live.

Both Brian and Jasmine had been very successful college students, yet Brian was doing well and enjoying himself at law school, while Jasmine was not. What distinguished the two to cause them to have such disparate experiences during their first year of law school? Brian was a white man, while Jasmine was a woman of color. Jasmine had an empathic orientation, while Brian was oriented toward rationality. Brian spoke in hyperarticulate academic prose; Jasmine spoke colloquially. Jasmine had a strong liberal ideology and intended to pursue social justice aims, while Brian held basically libertarian views and intended to become a corporate attorney.[4] Which of these factors, if any, contributed to the difference in their experiences? Does being a "nontraditional" professional student per se doom a person to underachievement? To help answer this question, allow me to introduce Miki.

## Miki

A student at the U.C. Berkeley School of Social Welfare who was also pursuing a joint degree in public health, Miki was a Hawaiian-born woman of Japanese descent, vibrant, in her midtwenties, with a style simultaneously scholarly and funky. Academically energetic, Miki double-majored in college in psychobiology and Asian/Pacific Islander studies and intended to go to medical school after completing her MSW and MPH degrees. Her career goal, she told me, was "to work in a community clinic doing either OB/GYN prenatal stuff, or pediatrics work in the 'hood."

Miki was doing well academically and felt that the social welfare program "actually seems easier than undergrad." Nevertheless, she found herself at first having to adjust to a pedagogical style that was "different from what I expected." Because she was used to the teaching style of the biological sciences, Miki was expecting to memorize theories and formulae, but instead the professors said, "These are the theories you are reading; what do you think of these theories and how do you think you can apply them?"

When I asked whether this difference in pedagogical styles had made her uncomfortable, she replied:

> No, it's just different, and sometimes I have to remind myself that, yes, I am learning, because I can't spit out a formula. But I like it, on the other hand, just because it allows me to be more creative; if I can master these techniques, I'll have an arsenal to use later. In a sense there is more room for creativity and more room to be just more subjective.

Miki might have needed to adjust to the different style of social work scholarship, but that she did this successfully was evident in her excellent first-semester grades.

Miki found it easy to speak in class, and she participated in discussions often. As she said, "I don't really have a problem speaking in class; in fact, I'm sure sometimes the professors would like me to shut up." She felt comfortable that her liberal views were in the program's mainstream, although the consensus seemed so strong that sometimes, she felt, "it gets boring not fighting someone." At such times, Miki would call up an old conservative investment-banker friend to debate with because, she said, with a certain chagrin, "it grounds me." Rather like Brian, Miki did not find the workload onerous and was able to complete all her course work and still have time to play with her dog and two cats or to see a movie.

If Brian was rationally oriented and Jasmine was emotionally oriented, Miki felt herself to be balanced between the two. Her desire for this balance was reflected in her pursuit of dual degrees: "Part of the reason I'm doing the MSW/MPH is because I like to jump between the empathic and rational, and part of the reason I double majored in Asian/Pacific Islander studies and psychobio was to be able to keep between the two." If forced to choose, Miki said, "I guess I would probably be more comfortable in the emotional side." She experienced no mismatch between her emotional orientation and the social work training she was receiving.

Miki felt aware of being a woman of color in the social welfare program, but not uncomfortably so. She did not resent being asked to "give the Asian perspective" on a particular issue:

> I do feel like there is a certain expectation to represent "your people," but I just took a thousand Asian-American studies classes in college, and I know a lot about the research, so I guess in a sense I put myself

in that position. I don't feel there's ever been a time when someone said, "Well, Miki, you're Asian, why don't you tell me?" I think it's because from the get-go, if there's something I know about APIs, I'll raise my hand and say, for example, "Hmong don't have a written language, so of course they're illiterate." So, then, I guess when there are questions, people naturally say, "Do you know?"

Rather than feeling stereotyped by being asked questions about Asian/Pacific Islander cultures, she felt that her academic expertise was affirmed.

Miki, in short, was as comfortable, confident, and successful in her professional program as Brian was in his, indicating that status as a woman of color does not doom a professional student to underperformance. But Miki is an MSW student rather than a law student, and social work is a traditionally feminine profession. Do all women do as well as she has in the social welfare program? Let me answer by introducing Charmaine.

## Charmaine

Charmaine, a single mother of two children, described her background as "multicultural: my mother is Caucasian with Indian, and my father is black with Indian." In her early thirties, she seemed both mature and youthful, accustomed to responsibilities but playful in her fashion statements, which included a dramatically pierced tongue. When her parents divorced when she was seven, Charmaine's standard of living fell sharply, and she lived for years in poverty. She was a former client of social workers and was proud to be on the other side of the fence.

Unlike the other students I have introduced, all of whom had prior records of uninterrupted academic success, Charmaine dropped out of high school when she became a mother at seventeen. She got her high school equivalency degree so that she could get a job "doing data entry, clerical, stuff like that," and after a while she decided to try to get an associate's degree.

You know, I was happy at that time, like, doing what I was doing, but I saw that a degree could help me with raises and things like that. By the time I finished my associate's, I saw the utility in getting the bachelor's, and at the time that I finished the bachelor's, I started thinking maybe I wanted to take a different turn, and I don't want to work in the "nine to five" for the rest of my life, so I had to begin thinking about, well, what interested me?

Having worked her way up from equivalency to community college to state college, Charmaine decided to apply to a professional program in social work as "kind of a culmination of my own desires." While her ability to work her way up from high school dropout to professional school matriculant while supporting two children is testimony to her perseverance and intelligence, Charmaine did not have a background similar to that of the other students I have introduced, who had always excelled academically and assumed from an early age that lives as professionals lay ahead of them.

In some ways, attending the social welfare program was a powerfully positive experience for Charmaine. Having been a client of social workers, she said it was a vindication of sorts for her to be able to win admission into an MSW program. Equally empowering was the insight into her own experience that Charmaine acquired as she learned social welfare theory:

> The more I learn about the basis of how policies and system structures are developed and become intact, I'm able to reflect back on why some of the things happen the way they happen, and why things happened for us the way they did, and it's like, well, because that's what they think, . . . and it's very enlightening, and it's very empowering to me, because I feel that the best way to overcome a lot of things is to understand the view from why the whole thing developed that way. I mean, I don't just see my education as a book-smarts thing—it's very much an integration of myself into learning and resynthesizing everything, and gaining this knowledge that I really have this desire to use, to help other people, and to help myself.

Attending the social welfare program was bringing about positive changes in Charmaine's life—and yet these changes were painful to manage.

Not only were Charmaine's career goals, social status, and class aspirations changing, but so was her style of self-presentation and way of looking at the world.[5] While empowering, these changes made it difficult at times for Charmaine to be sure who she was and where her affiliations lay. On the one hand, she felt tied to people from the impoverished, largely African American and Latino neighborhood where she had lived most of her life. She said that with friends from that community, "I'm able to be myself, truly be myself," because "we know each other; we know where we're coming from." On the other hand, Charmaine felt that at Berkeley, "things could be misconstrued to the nth degree." These comments would seem to indicate that she felt an affinity for her community of origin and alienated from the School of Social Welfare.

Yet comments Charmaine made at other points in our interview contrast sharply with her comments about being her true self only back home. When I asked how members of her community of origin reacted to her being admitted to a professional program, she said:

> In their day-to-day lives of putting food on the table and things like that, they don't know from this. Going here is like going to school. Me and my mom were just laughing about this it's just under the same heading. They don't know an AA, BA, MA, PhD. It means nothing to them, and it has nothing to do with putting food on the table for that day or a lot of other things that could be happening.

This statement would seem to indicate that it was from her community of origin that Charmaine was feeling alienated. A fact she disclosed later in the interview made this point even more clear. When I asked how people from her home community reacted to her choice of a career in social welfare, she replied solemnly:

> I don't discuss it. It wouldn't be something we would discuss, because they would have the conception of, "She's a social worker!" It has a bad connotation where I come from; . . . they cut your benefits, or things like that.

Charmaine had chosen a professional career path that she could not discuss with the community she came from. She felt that her old acquaintances could not understand the person she was now. Yet she simultaneously held the contradictory feeling that only "back home" could she "truly" be herself. Like Jasmine, she was suffering a crisis of identity.

To the extent that Charmaine desired to change from the kind of person who had needed to rely on social services as a client to the kind of person who serves others in a professional capacity, it would seem that she paid the price of her identity crisis willingly. But there were other ways in which she felt uncomfortable in her program that were solely negative. Central among these was her feeling that the professors and students around her, who were supposed to be educated and sensitive, held stereotyped beliefs about people living in poverty.

It makes me so irritated when I feel that the well-to-do are making broad, sweeping generalizations about those of us who come from a poor background, and they're wrong. That infuriates me! Let me bump that up from irritated to infuriated. Yes, I have heard folks here say things that . . . I just see red, because I really feel it bespeaks that you didn't take the time to get out to know people, and you just have assumptions about them.

It was disturbing to Charmaine that an attitude toward the poor which she felt was personally insulting was held by people whose profession was aimed at serving impoverished clients.

Another reason Charmaine felt uncomfortable in the social welfare program was, she said, that

there are so few people of color here, and you can define that however you want to define it, whether you're talking black, Latin, and so on. I was struck by that from about the first week. I was kind of uncomfortable with that, because the question comes up for me, "Well, are you telling me that there are just not enough of these people that cut the mark?"

At times, Charmaine presented herself to me as a person who wouldn't let her underrepresented minority status upset her, as when she stated: "I think anyone would have to look around and say, there are not too many people who look like me here. Whether I let it bother me, I can't really say that it bothers me, but I'm aware of it." At other times she admitted to feeling "intense rage" about it. When I raised the question of whether she had a disability, she laughingly listed her rage. While Charmaine presented this as a sort of joke, it was accurate in a way: she was disabled from concentrating on her studies when she was raging at racism and classism in the program, and she was disabled from integrating into the profession when it inspired her ire instead of her respect. If being a professional involved feeling superior to the poor or accepting racial disparities, then Charmaine wanted none of it.[6]

Although the students in the social welfare program are predominantly female, I met many women who, like Charmaine, were uncomfortable there—sometimes feeling positively challenged but more often negatively so. What, then, of the men in the program? At the time of my research, less than one-quarter of the students in the U.C. Berkeley School of Social Welfare were men. Would their status as a numerical minority predispose them to feel uncomfortable, like Jasmine and Charmaine, rather than comfortable, like Brian and Miki? To suggest an answer, let us consider Peter.

## Peter

Peter was a married white man in his early twenties. His look, when I met him for our interview, was reminiscent of Brian's: he was wearing khaki pants with a white button-down shirt. Unlike Brian, however, he wore a small stud earring in one ear. Like Brian, he was very articulate, although his voice was softer, and he never cut me off in conversation the way Brian sometimes did; instead, he listened to me sensitively, making constant eye contact, leaning toward me, and nodding to show that he was following me. His manner was sufficiently "feminine" that when I first met him, I assumed he was gay. Yet there were also very masculine aspects to his personality.

Peter described himself to me as a "fiscally conservative liberal" and as a "Democrat who dresses like a Republican." Unlike Miki or Charmaine, Peter was part of the 15 percent of his class in the management track of the social welfare program. (In contrast to the program in general, the management track was dominated by men.)[7] Peter said of his decision to apply to the management track:

> Most people who decide to pursue a career in this area are interested in providing direct services, and I understand the appeal of being able to provide individual, face-to-face assistance to people in need. That's what lies at the core of social service work, and I do not denigrate it in any way—I have the highest respect for direct service providers. But I feel that my talents lie more in the area of ensuring that an organizational structure exists which can ensure that the client population is given swift and appropriate assistance, and that the social workers within the organization face the fewest institutional barriers to being able to provide that assistance.

Peter was a predominately rational person, and when speaking of the organization in which he did his clinical work, he sounded dry and business-like, using phrases such as "the integration of rehabilitative services" and "the way the funding structure gets operationalized." But there was more to Peter than a rational affinity for cost-benefit analyses. He was also a committed Christian who, after rededicating himself to attending church, felt pulled toward public service on religious grounds. He explained to me: "I do feel that I have been called. It was a powerful experience for me when I came to understand this pull as a calling, and to realize that I need to use the abilities that I have to benefit those who have been less fortunate." Peter's parents found his feeling of having been called hard to accept—"They have the typical bourgeois aspirations for me that most middle-class parents have"—but for him, it was the feeling of fulfilling his calling that gave his professional career choice meaning.

Peter was satisfied with his choice of schools, and comfortable in his program. His grades were excellent, and he found the program easy: "Since the course work has not been challenging, I've come to realize that it is up to me to challenge myself intellectually." He was working many hours on his reading and at his clinical placement, but he found he was still able to relax and listen to music, or to spend some unstructured time with his wife.[8] Peter was also comfortable with his peers, whom he described as "caring and dedicated." When I asked if he ever felt uncomfortable being in a minority as a male, he replied:

> Oh, far from it. I have been very comfortable here. I have always been
> a person who has had many female friends, and I have no problem
> being in a majority female setting.

Nor did Peter ever feel that others "poorly judged" him for being a straight white male.

Peter, in short, was socially, academically, and morally quite comfortable in the social welfare program. He said that he supposed he was successful at professional school because of his good preparation and because of following his calling. He certainly did not attribute his success to being male (or middle class, straight, and white, for that matter), yet his comfortable integration in the social welfare program was shared by most of his male peers, but by only about one-third of his female peers.

## Patterns

Throughout the two years of my research, I encountered many first-year professional students who, like Brian, Miki, and Peter, were comfortably integrated into their law or social welfare programs. Students such as these felt that they were "just going to school" and attributed their success meritocratically to their abilities and efforts. I encountered many other students, however, whose experiences were similar to Jasmine's and

Charmaine's. These students had a lot on their minds besides "just going to school": they were having problems integrating into their professional programs that were related to issues as fundamental as their sense of self. Many were worried that they might lose important aspects of their self-definition, such as their ideological commitments, their capacity for empathy, or their community loyalties. Some were struggling with finding themselves in their programs through personal growth—a process that, while positive, precipitated an identity crisis. The students facing these difficulties while trying to integrate into their professional programs were generally suffering academically, because they were preoccupied with issues other than "just going to school."

This is the phenomenon that my book explores: the place of identity in the professional socialization process. My basic thesis is this: students such as Brian, Miki, and Peter enjoy a consonance between their personal identities and the professional roles they encounter in professional school. They are thus able to internalize the role of lawyer or social worker easily, in a process so smooth as to be imperceptible to them, and they are able to focus on the intellectual tasks of professional school with little distraction.

Students such as Jasmine and Charmaine, however, suffer from a mismatch between the personal identities they possess upon entering their professional programs and the professional roles those schools proffer. They are therefore unable to internalize these roles without suffering a jarring dissonance between their personal identities and their fledgling professional identities. This dissonance presents a problem, because to be successful as professionals, students must internalize an appropriate professional identity. It also leads to a secondary problem, in that seeking to find a way to manage or resolve their identity dissonance distracts these students from focusing on their studies. My research aims to explore how the problems of identity dissonance disadvantage professional students in comparison to their identity-consonant peers.

# 2 Who Are You?

## Identity Theorized

As many scholars who study the professions have noted, one of the characteristics that distinguishes the professions from other occupations is that their members are expected to develop professional identities. For example, before I entered the profession of sociology, I had a number of other occupations, including working in food service and practicing as an attorney. I did not merely work as an attorney, I *was* an attorney, in the sense that being a lawyer was an important part of my self-concept. In contrast, working in food service did not come to define who I was.[1] Moreover, once I stopped working in food service, that chapter in my life was closed—I don't conceive of myself as an "ex-food-service worker." On the other hand, even though I am not practicing law, I remain an attorney, both formally and internally. Joining a profession altered my identity in a deep and enduring way.

Before we examine the issue of acquiring a professional identity, we need to understand what identities are. What identities do people hold, and how can we tell? One profitable way to approach these questions is to consider cases that test the boundaries of identity—for example, where a person is of mixed racial background—and then see what answers various theories provide, and how satisfying these answers are.

## Formal Identification

The simplest way to guess what identities a person has is to employ formal definitional rules. When considering race and ethnicity in the United States, it immediately becomes evident that we apply a patchwork of rules to label people of mixed racial backgrounds. In the case of people with partial African American heritage, we apply the "one-drop rule" inherited from our history of racial slavery, which holds that any person with known African ancestry is "black," no matter how fair his or her skin (Malcomson, 2001). In contrast, regulations require that people with partial Native American heritage obtain a federal Bureau of Indian Affairs Certificate of Degree of Indian Blood; if they cannot formally prove sufficient Native ancestry (typically one full-blooded grandparent), they will not be considered tribal members and cannot benefit from any Bureau of Indian Affairs programs (Jaimes, 1992). In the case of people of mixed Asian American heritage, there is no clear rule, which makes formal identification difficult. This makes plain one problem with using a formal definition of identity: it is arbitrary and varies across designations.

Another problem with using formal identification schemes to determine identity is that people may not agree with the formal schemes that are supposed to apply to them. Omi and Winant (1994) claim that social structures *do* determine identity. They say that the "identification of individuals and groups in racial terms" is "shaped by actually existing race relations," which vary by time and location (11). For example, they state, the identities of "quadroon" and "octoroon" are no longer found in the United States because there is no fractional titration of racial privilege in such terms today, and individuals who would once have been so labeled today identify simply as light-skinned blacks. But the identification issue is not that simple, as the highly charged community debates over whether African Americans of mixed heritage should identify as multiracial on the U.S. Census illustrate (Dalmage, 2000; Kertzer et al., 2001). Some African American leaders have argued that it is racially disloyal and self-deluding for people of mixed African American heritage to abandon the tradition of identifying simply as African American. Other activists of mixed racial backgrounds argue just as strongly that it is a moral duty to subvert the logic of the one-drop rule by claiming one's multiracial heritage.

Consider another liminal identification issue: the question of whether a person of mixed Jewish heritage will be considered a Jew. The customary identification rule within Jewish tradition is that a person is Jewish if his mother's mother was a Jew. Yet in the United States, so many people of mixed Jewish descent who were Jewish through their father's line rather than their mother's defiantly self-identified as Jewish that Reform and Reconstructionist congregations altered the rules of descent to include these individuals (Telushkin, 1991). This makes it quite clear that formal identification by others often does not match actual experienced identity—that, in fact, formal identification may follow rather than determine experienced identity. Formal, structural sociological theories of identity are problematic because they cannot explain variation in identity or agency in identity choice.

## Conscious Identity

If formal identification fails to satisfy us, let us examine conscious self-identification as our means of defining identity. It is clear that people can choose how to identify, sometimes in opposition to formal rules—and not only in cases of identities "on the borderline," but also under circumstances where others would expect their identities to be simple and unquestioned. Consider, for example, the contemporary phenomenon of transgenderism. Transgendered individuals assert a gender identity that conflicts with others' expectations. In our society, we have a rule that genitals determine gender identity. When a person feels female despite having male genitalia, or feels male despite having female genitalia, this subverts our genitals-determine-gender rule, and many people find it disturbing.[2] When conscious self-identification replaces formal rule-bound identification, the agency involved brings all formal social rules into question, which perturbs people. This is understandable because by our nature we need social norms. Without them, we slide into the confusion of what Durkheim called "anomie," a normless anarchic state (1951 [1897]). On the other hand, without social change, a society stagnates. The assertion of new ways to identify keeps a society dynamic.

Many resist the idea that our identities could be socially fixed by the accident of birth. It seems distinctly un-American—counter to our ideals of freedom and self-determination. We are strong believers in individual agency, and we want our identities to be something we choose to enact—or choose to disavow, alter, conceal, or reformulate. For example, criticizing the idea that racial identities are fixed and unalterable, Sarah Willie states that "race is relational, situational, and interpersonally dynamic," and thus "race and racial identity become another site of human agency, a characteristic or fact that individuals can and often do manipulate, despite its extraordinary power to proscribe social life" (2003:6). For example, a person might speak standard, Anglo-accented English in the company of white people, and regional, black-accented English in the company of African Americans, to gain the respect of each group.

The acknowledgment of human agency in the enactment of identity is important. However, the belief in individual autonomy can be taken too far. There are limits to our ability to alter our behavior. Our agency is constrained by the extent to which we are consciously aware of our raced/gendered/classed behavior. Consider, for example, how many people can hear others' accents but are unaware of their own. A person cannot manipulate an accent of which she is unaware.

## Habitus

The fact is, our identities are like icebergs. The large bulk of them lies invisible to us below the surface of consciousness, while only a small part of them are perceptible to our conscious minds. Sociologists refer to the nonconscious bulk of identity as "habitus," a medical term imported into sociological usage by Pierre Bourdieu (1990, 1977). According to the standard definition by Loïc Wacquant, habitus is constituted by "cognitive and corporeal schemata of perception, appreciation and action that agents engage in their practice" (1990: 401). Since this definition is rather opaque, let us consider the elements of habitus using concrete examples.

The first element of habitus is made up of an individual's unconscious assumptions about the way the world works—what the Germans call a *weltanschauung*, a worldview. An example might be the belief that people get what they deserve (unsurprisingly held much more frequently by those occupying positions of privilege than by the disadvantaged). A related example would be a belief about whether one will be treated with social respect. When approached by a figure of authority, does a person automatically act deferential, defiant, or unconcerned? This behavior turns on his nonconscious assessment of the social respect he is due. Calling such assessments "beliefs" is somewhat misleading, because rarely do people examine such assumptions or even realize they hold them. An individual simply assumes that when he speaks, people will listen—or that they won't. And because worldviews are understood in moral terms, when we subject a person's worldview to challenge, she is likely to take umbrage and feel upset.

The second element of habitus is taste. Tastes constitute a surprisingly large part of identity. For example, think of what you can tell about a person just by being informed that he loves Wonder Bread, or curried goat, or a neat single-malt scotch. Does an individual prefer baroque chamber music, progressive country, ambient new age, New Jack R&B, Indian tabla drumming? Tastes mark generational, ethnic, class, and subcultural identities.

We may be quite conscious of our tastes—especially, in the United

States, when it comes to consumer products—but at other times our tastes seem so completely natural, we assume they are universal. For instance, consider how you would react if you were asked to close your eyes and open your mouth, and someone popped a large cooked tarantula inside. Would you feel nausea, revulsion, a desire to rinse contamination out of your mouth? Would the sensation of the little hairs on its legs against your tongue horrify you? Roasted tarantulas are considered delicious in Thailand (see Menzel and D'Aluisio, 1998), and they are quite nutritious. Sensations of disgust, however natural they may feel, are purely cultural constructs—signs of our U.S. identity, just as enjoying tarantulas is a sign of rural Thai identity.

That violating our sense of taste can lead us to sensations of nausea and disgust brings us to the third, and to my mind most fascinating, element of habitus: embodied identity (or, to use Bourdieu's term, a "bodily hexis"). Experience shapes the body and how it is used—for example, when an American who is accustomed to sitting on a chair at a table travels to Japan and is expected to kneel on a tatami, she is likely to find it uncomfortable and awkward. Few Americans may consciously think of being adapted to chair sitting as constituting part of their American identity, but this is the case.

Embodied identity is also evident in gestures and in what we term "body language." A person who is angry will often make a rude gesture at his antagonist, but depending on his cultural affiliations this may be a raised middle finger (in the United States), a raised pointer (in Turkey), or a thumbs up (in Iran). The polite degree of personal space between self and other unconsciously assumed by an individual also varies by cultural identity. For example, in interactions between North and South Americans, it is common for the South American to keep advancing while the North American keeps backing up as each tries to maintain a polite social distance and wonders why the other is acting so strangely (Axtel, 1997).

We are very good at reading social information from another's stance, expression, and gestures. We use this skill to make snap judgments of the people we encounter in everyday life. We can watch a computerized stick figure walk and infer that the model for it was an urban African American male. Gay men may speak of having "gaydar," but all of us have similar expertise at recognizing particular bodily signs and gestures. We can catch a small flinch and worry, "Abuse survivor?" We may see a remarkably neat signature and surmise, "She went to Catholic school." We can see wide hand gestures and say to ourselves, "Italian." We may see a man hold his cigarette with his pinkie finger out and think, "Gay."

A fascinating fact about embodied identity is that while we may be very good at recognizing and reading it in others, we rarely notice it in ourselves, and when we do we are likely to find that it is remarkably resistant to manipulation. Like the other elements of habitus, embodied identity exists below the level of consciousness. I can illustrate this point with an exercise I use in my class on the sociology of gender. I call for one male and one female volunteer to come up to the stage. Then I ask each to pretend that he or she is a member of the other gender, and to walk across the room. Very campy, exaggerated performances ensue, to general laughter. Then I tell my two volunteers to try again, but this time to imagine that they have to rescue their child from Nazis or kidnappers or terrorists, and that to do so, they have to pass convincingly as a member of the other gender. The volunteers try again with serious expressions of concentration on their faces—but with unconvincing results. In other words, they find their gendered style of walking intransigent, not open to easy agentic manipulation.

As another example of the resistance of embodied habitus to change, consider people who undergo a sex-change procedure. Unlike my student volunteers, a person who, say, has sex reassignment surgery to go from male to female status clearly has a longstanding and strong motivation to learn to embody the chosen sex. Yet all that desire and commitment is often insufficient without professional retraining. For instance, at my own university, the College of Health Sciences runs a voice clinic that treats male-to-female transsexuals, providing long-term individual therapy to teach patients how to produce the vocal pitch shifts, intonations, and conversational deference that are expected of women in the United States.

A final element of nonconscious habitus is an individual's emotional identity. People have different emotional orientations—some are empathic, while others fail to notice emotional cues. The degree to which an individual is emotionally warm or cool is shaped by his race, gender, class, religion, sexual orientation, and many other characteristics. For example, our society associates a rational, emotionally controlled orientation with being white, male, upper class, Protestant, and heterosexual (see, e.g., S. Williams, 2001). Being emotionally demonstrative is devalued by those of privileged status in our society—while having emotional warmth is expected in those of lower status. Like all elements of habitus, our emotional orientation feels natural to us, at least if we are adults (boys who are told not to cry do not experience the repression of tears as natural at all). To continue using gender as an example, while a man may be aware that he would be better treated by his wife if he could cry while confessing an infidelity, or while a woman may want very much not to cry when reprimanded during a business meeting, their conscious desires may have little influence over whether the tears come.

Having examined various ways to talk about identity, let us summarize. Formal identifying schemes, while simple to apply objectively, often fail to capture the subjective reality of identities. Asking individuals to identify themselves reveals conscious identity, which is open to agentic manipulation. This is important, since it acknowledges individual self-determination. But it is equally important to remember that the bulk of identity likes below the level of consciousness, in habitus. Our assumptions and worldviews, our tastes, our postures and gestures, and our emotional orientations make up the main mass of our identities, and yet we are generally unaware of them. The invisibility of habitus and its resistance to conscious manipulation create a problem for people working to alter their identities—such as students at professional schools.

Let us consider for a moment how the various identity schemata apply to professional students. Formally, all a student need do to acquire a professional identity is graduate from the appropriate professional school and pass any required certifying exam. Being formally certified as a member of a profession, however, is still insufficient for acceptance by employers, peers, and clients. The Cinderella story of the 2001 film *Legally Blond*—in which success is achieved at Harvard Law School by a ditzy, overdressed Valley Girl who can't go anywhere without her beribboned dog—is a fairy tale. A certified professional school graduate who cannot "walk the walk and talk the talk" will not seem like a true professional to others and will not be successful. Consider whether you would be likely to return to a therapist who giggled during your confession of sexual difficulties, or to an attorney who burst into tears when her objection was overruled. Professional labor requires an appropriate emotional orientation, such as caring from a therapist or aggression from a litigator (Hochschild, 1983). It requires a suitable, subjectively internalized professional identity.

Part of the successful expression of an appropriate professional identity is a matter of conscious identity. An individual must want to embrace the professional role to internalize it in identity, and if he chooses instead to reject it, he embraces his agency and his other loyalties at the price of professional success. But most professional students do consciously wish to embrace their profession. The hitch for many is that their habitus presents a problem of which they are unaware. Being unaware of a conflict between their chosen professional role and their nonconscious identities, students cannot choose to try to resolve it. And even if they are made aware, for example, that they are displaying too much or too little deference to clients, they will find this problem difficult to address because of the resistance of habitus to conscious manipulation.

To put what I am saying another way, individual agency in working to become a successful professional is limited by structural forces that are internalized in the form of habitus. An important caveat here is to beware the presumption that this means professional students' lives are structurally predetermined—that their destiny to succeed or fail is set by their race, class, and gender. Agency is real and important, although constrained, and many students succeed despite the structural forces arrayed against them. Moreover, identities are not uniform and there is a great deal of individual variation in how people experience their genders, religious identities, ethnicities, and the like, and thus in how their identities will interact with a new professional identity.

## Managing Multiple Identities

### *Metaphors*

We all have multiple identities—religious, ethnic, gendered, political, sexual, familial, and so on. What we need now to address is how these multiple identities interrelate. Several metaphors can help us understand alternative theories of how multiple identities mesh. Let us start with a naïve vision. The naïve image of selfhood is that all of one's identities are smoothly incorporated into a seamless whole, like ingredients mixed together in just the right proportions to create a unique cake of selfhood. Neither the individual nor others can see the differentiated ingredients in his wholeness, any more than we can taste the baking soda or eggs in a cake.

In another vision of integrated multiple identities, the self is like the elephant in the old canard about the blind men and the elephant. Just as one man felt the elephant's trunk and said, "It's a snake," another felt its side and said, "It's a wall," while a third felt its leg and said, "It's a tree," so will different people see us differently, although we are unified and coherent entities. For example, in a setting in which Sunan is the only Asian individual in the room, people perceive her as Asian. In an all-Asian setting, Sunan's Thai identity may be prominent. In an all-Thai setting, Sunan's race and ethnicity are not salient, but her identity as a Muslim probably is. At the day-care center, people may see Sunan as the mother of twins, while at the doctor's office, she's seen as an asthmatic.

What's important in the elephant vision is that while different people in different contexts see very different things when they look at Sunan, the disjunction is in the eyes of the beholders. Sunan herself is many things at once, all her identities woven together to form an integrated, unriven, seamless self. But while we tend to imagine our identities as integrated into one coherent whole, sociologists have long noted that this is not the case (Dunn, 1998). Identities often conflict, as they may do as we acquire new identities over time. Such is likely to be the case, for example, if a man leaves a position in upper management to become a househusband.

Employing the metaphor that is least simplistic, disjunctures between a person's various identities are not illusions in the eyes of beholders but intrinsic to selfhood in complex societies. In this third vision, the self is like a room full of furniture. Each piece of furniture is an identity—some central to the room of the self, and some less so. Some identities are always found in the room, like grandma's rocking chair, but others are more like a trendy zebra-striped footstool: unlikely to be there in ten years. Most people keep their gender identities for life, but other identities are explicitly self-limiting (such as "newlywed" or "middle-aged") or likely to be abandoned (as anyone who has the name of his favorite band tattooed on his back at age eighteen is likely to discover to his chagrin). And just as the expansion of global markets has given us an ever increasing breadth of choice in buying furniture, the loosening of traditional ties now allows us to alter and add to our identities with ever greater ease (see Giddens, 1991).

What's useful about the image of the roomful of furniture is that it makes clear than not everything is likely to match. Just as grandma's rocking chair and the trendy footstool coexist awkwardly, so can one's religious identity and one's sexual identity, or one's racial identity and one's professional identity. We may acknowledge the clash or be oblivious to it, but the mismatch is there. And when you look at the living rooms of real-life friends, you're likely to see numerous mismatches of style and color. Sometimes the mélange comes across as graceful, sometimes it's disharmonious, but in either case, it's normal. Our furnishings and our selves are accreted idiosyncratically, and while "redecorating" our identities may be exciting, clashes are inevitable.

### Identity Consonance and Dissonance

I have developed a concept of identity consonance and dissonance that I explored through my field research.[3] I use these terms to describe the experience of acquiring a new identity, and how it feels when the new identity blends smoothly with other personal identities versus how it feels when they clash. My hypothesis is that the process of integrating a new identity into previously internalized identities goes smoothly when one's personal identities are consonant with the new role, while the process is a traumatic one when one's personal identities are dissonant with the role. Considering professional socialization specifically, integrating new professional identities into personal identities is an easy process for people whose personal identities are consonant with their new professional role, but traumatic for those whose personal identities are dissonant with it.[4]

As I have described, each of an individual's multiple identities is composed of a variety of conscious and nonconscious elements, such as ideologies, postures, and tastes. A proposed professional role also contains components such as worldviews and emotional orientations that must be incorporated for the individual to acquire a new professional identity. If a substantial number of the professional role components are in conflict with components of the individual's personal identity, she will experience identity dissonance as she attempts to incorporate and integrate her new professional identity.[5] While identity-consonant students incorporate their new professional identity smoothly and nonconsciously, identity-dissonant students experience an identity crisis that may cause them to feel uncertain about their values, ambitions, abilities, affinities, and their very self-worth. Moreover, identity-dissonant students must manage not only their internal anxieties but also the reactions of significant others to the alteration of their identities.

Identity dissonance is uncomfortable, and people try to avoid the distress it entails (see Collins, 2002). The experience of this discomfort at the conscious level has been well documented by social psychologists, who term it "cognitive dissonance" (the phrase on which my "identity dissonance" is based).[6] In general, students I observed who were experiencing identity dissonance suffered from a general sense of anxiety—a worrisome feeling that all was not well in their lives, although they often could not put a finger on why. They also endured an identity crisis in the classic sense, often being preoccupied with questions such as Who am I? What are my ideals? and What are my priorities? Because in our society we associate such self-questioning with adolescence, many students experienced professional school as infantilizing, complaining that the atmosphere was "high-schooly" and the people immature. Finally, identity-dissonant students tended to suffer from feelings of inauthenticity, recognizing that they were attempting to play a role rather than doing something that came "naturally" (as behaviors arising from habitus feel).

Individuals experiencing cognitive dissonance seek to reduce their discomfort by bringing their discordant beliefs into alignment. Identity dissonance is more difficult for subjects to cope with than the narrower problem of cognitive dissonance because so much of identity dissonance is nonconscious and hence opaque to the sufferer. Professional students cannot consciously devise strategies to deal with difficulties whose nature they cannot perceive. They develop coping mechanisms haphazardly at best.

However haphazardly derived, coping mechanisms that deal with identity dissonance by working to resolve it into identity consonance offer students the greatest relief. Identity dissonance is eliminated most smoothly when a student alters his personal identity so that it no longer strongly conflicts with his fledgling professional identity (causing him to become one of those people whose friends say, admiringly or disparagingly, "Professional school really changed him").

Another coping mechanism that resolves dissonance is for the student to reject the proposed professional role rather than to incorporate it as identity. She might do this consciously and cleanly by dropping out of the professional program, but the number of students who follow this route is few—the retention rate at professional schools is much higher than that at colleges.[7] Alternatively, she could defiantly continue to display components of identity which conflict with the professional role while she attempts to complete the professional program (for example, she might arrive at her moot court argument wearing a veil or a latex miniskirt). More typically, a student may reject the proposed professional role unconsciously and passively by attempting to avoid professional school settings and interactions whenever possible, and by role playing in professional socializing situations that he cannot avoid.[8] If the student copes by rejecting the proposed professional role, whether consciously or not, she will be able to achieve only marginal professional success.

Alternative methods for managing identity dissonance attempt a compromise between resolving identity dissonance in favor either of a student's personal identities or of his fledgling professional identity. These approaches allow professional students to maintain both conflicting identities, but at the cost of prolonging the discomfort of the dissonant state. One coping mechanism which allows a student to retain both identities involves an attempt to segregate personal and professional identities (e.g., by choosing to become a "good" priest with a secret gay life). While this solution allows the new professional, like the law student Jasmine discussed in Chapter 1, to have it all, it requires the constant management of valued and conflicting elements of the self, which puts the student in the difficult position of living with a split personality. Another available compromise is for the professional student to partly alter his conflicting but valued personal identity, reducing but not eliminating the experience of identity dissonance. A final compromise solution is for the student to attempt to maintain both identities and to deny that the dissonance between them presents a problem.[9]

Professional students may employ more than one dissonance-management strategy at a time, as MSW student Charmaine did: she sought to alter her personal identities at some points, seeking to become a powerful and insightful social worker rather than a disempowered, uncomprehending client, while at other times she rejected the professional role as objectionably racist and classist and resisted professional socialization. Of course, these two strategies were contradictory, leading Charmaine to feel unsure of where her "true self" and true loyalties lay. Professional students generally experience identity dissonance not on a rational level but at the deepest levels of the self in the nonconscious arena of habitus, and they do not construct their responses to identity dissonance on a rational level, either.[10]

Students confronted by the need to internalize a professional identity that conflicts with one or more of their personal identities always find the experience of identity dissonance difficult to cope with. But for a subset of students, the process of resocialization, while painful, is also experienced as significantly empowering—commonly because the fledgling professional identity is more socially valued than the personal identity it is displacing. I term this experience *positive identity dissonance*. For others, the chafing of their nascent professional identities against their valued personal identities is without benefit. I term this (sadly more common) experience *negative identity dissonance*.

## Professional Identity Theorized

Now that we have a grasp of the concepts of identity and identity dissonance, let us turn to the specific question of how professional identity is understood by social scientists. Concern with the importance of identity is often branded a contemporary or faddish phenomenon, but in fact it has a long history within the sociology of the professions. It is important to engage with this history, and to acknowledge the longstanding concern with issues of professional success and selfhood. In 1939, T. H. Allen wrote:

> The professional man is distinguished by the . . . fact that he does not give only his skill. He gives himself. His whole personality enters into

his work. It is hardly possible to be satisfied with a doctor or a lawyer unless one likes him and respects him as a man. (328)

Allen's focus on the centrality of the professional's identity led him in the 1930s to the following insight:

The mistrust of women doctors, which is not yet quite overcome, was probably due to the feeling that they had not yet had a chance to imbibe [professional] traditions. During their training they were kept on the fringes of the medical community, while, in addition, the influences of home and school, which had long been directed to producing in boys the virtues demanded by the codes of professional ethics, had ignored the girls or even fostered in them quite different qualities. Any member of the working class who aspires to professional status has to fight against the same difficulties and the same suspicions. (328–329)

We can see in these comments that social scientists long ago recognized that women and people of working-class backgrounds would be disadvantaged by their identities and would tend not to achieve the levels of success of their privileged male peers.

Among scholars in the sociology of the professions, the adoption of a professional identity is generally held to be necessary for both ethical and practical reasons. According to Eliot Friedson (1994), the internalization of professional norms and ethics in professional identity allows professionals to regulate themselves effectively, assuring that they do not abuse the autonomy they are granted. More generally, because professional work is cognitive and hence difficult for others to observe or evaluate, having a strong professional identity is necessary for professionals to behave with the authority, confidence, and professional demeanor that convinces others of their competence (see, e.g., Cassell, 1998; Freedman and Holmes, 2003; Grove, 1992). Hence, even if a student at a professional school absorbs all the knowledge and skills presented, that student will not be successful as a professional unless she or he also develops a professional identity.

Over the course of more than sixty years of sociological writing on identity and the professions, theoretical paradigms have come and gone, and with them approaches to identity. In the 1950s, identity was viewed through the lens of structural functionalism and its ethos of conformity. The structural functionalists focused on the process of professional socialization in professional schools, through which students were believed to learn the professional role and adopt a professional identity. I have done the same. But rather than treating the students as already deeply socialized into a variety of personal identities, under structural functionalism "students have often been portrayed as empty vessels ready to be filled with approved knowledge and values—unformed social actors who are rendered competent by the training process" (Atkinson, 1983: 229). This structural functionalist treatment of professional students as virtual *tabulae rasae* ignores the power and persistence of other personal identities that may be in conflict with professional roles.

Another weakness of structural functionalist theory is that it treats professional roles and professional identity as identical. Professional roles are reified and presented as monolithic in character, and professional identities are treated as objective Durkheimian social facts.[11] As Talcott Parsons put it:

> When a person is fully socialized in the system of interaction it is not so nearly correct to say that a role is something an actor "has" or "plays" as it is something that he *is*. It follows from this that the crucial components of that aspect of the structure of personality which interpenetrates with systems of social interaction are *the same* as those composing social systems. (Parsons and Bales, 1955: 107, emphasis in original)

Hence, Parsons states, studies of socialization "demonstrate . . . uniformity in the 'character structure' of those who have been socialized in the same cultural and institutional system" (Parsons, 1949: 37). In structural functionalism, structure determines identity; Parsons claimed that there was a perfect correspondence between objective roles ("social structure") and subjective identity ("personality structure") (Parsons and Bales, 1955: 107). How such perfect socialization occurred was never adequately theorized. Moreover, all professionals should have the same identity under this formulation—a counterfactual assumption. Structural functionalism is a framework that approaches identity as a matter of formal identification, and thus one cannot use it to explain diversity, conflict, social change, or, most basically, human agency.

When structural functionalism fell from academic grace in the 1960s, symbolic interactionism replaced it as the theoretical framework through which identity was—and is—most often approached by sociologists.[12] Where structural functionalism assumed a unity of intention between professional students and socializing agents, symbolic interactionism posited conflict, and where the functionalists saw a unitary professional identity, symbolic interactionists saw multiple identities. Moreover, where structural functionalists saw roles as being internalized almost unconsciously into identity, symbolic interactionists conceived the socializee as a conscious agent in the process: "A status, a position, a social place is not a material thing to be processed and then displayed; . . . it is . . . something that must be enacted and portrayed, something that must be realized" (Goffman, 1959: 75).

In the structural functionalist view, professional roles and professional identity are objective and subjective expressions of the same system. In symbolic interactionist theory, there is a spectrum of positions between external role and internal core, and the contents of those positions can vary greatly. Symbolic interactionists distinguish between "role," "identity," "master identity," and "true self" (Kleinman, 1981). For example, one role is that of patient. Visiting her physician, a woman adopts the identity of patient and attempts to play the role as she understands it. This identity, "patient," is far from the woman's sense of her "true self," which can best be represented by her name, for example, "Tonya." Professional identity is an example of a master identity, such as "doctor," which lies closer to the core of self than the identity of "patient" because of its social significance.

In symbolic interactionist accounts, professional identity is not necessarily a self-concept but a representation of the self to others. Professional identity is "asserted," "claimed," and "secured." While a professional student may be "converted" to a new view of himself, this occurs only after the student "rehearses" and "portrays" the professional role to others, "realizing" a professional identity by "mastering performance situations" (Loseke and Cahill, 1986: 245). The theatrical metaphor is so prominent in the accounts of symbolic interactionists, with their references to audience, costume, identifying props, and backstage actions, and above all to playing roles, that their view is often termed "the dramaturgical perspective" (Kollock and O'Brien, 1994: 127).

The symbolic interactionist views identity as a conscious phenomenon over which an individual has agency. This makes the perspective a definite improvement on the structural functionalist approach. However, as I have discussed, viewing identity as a conscious choice is problematic because it does not address the bulk of identity that exists at the nonconscious level of habitus, in tastes, worldviews, embodied identity, and emotional orientation, all of which are resistant to conscious manipulation.

Academic interest in the topic of professional identity saw a sharp rise beginning in the 1980s with the ascendance of identity politics, which links the assertion of identities with the empowerment of social groups (Hall, 1993; Hekman, 2004). Scholars influenced by identity politics view having a clear and positive identity as an essential sociopsychological achievement for both individuals and social groups (see, e.g., Helms, 1990; Meyer, Whittier, and Robnett, 2002). This perspective is often evident in the very titles of articles written by sociologists influenced by identity politics, for example, "The Construction of Identities as a Means of Survival: Case of Gay and Lesbian Teachers" (Dankmeijer, 1993); and "Women Lawyers and the Quest for Professional Identity in Late Nineteenth-Century America" (Drachman, 1990). Professional identity is often cast as something which must be "claimed" in a political/personal "struggle" against stereotypes, as individuals and groups seek to "construct" a "usable form of professional identity" (Walkowitz, 1990: 1051–1056).

Writings on professional identity from the perspective of identity politics tend to begin with the classic sociological insight that what it has historically meant to be a "professional" is not only to have expertise, autonomy, or the other typically cited formal characteristics, but also to be male, white, heterosexual, "able-bodied," and so on (see, e.g., Hughes, [1945] 1994). Hence, the content of a professional identity is typically imbued with the values of the dominant white male culture (Gilkes, 1982). Admitting individuals who are "other" in some central element of their identities (e.g., African American, female, deaf) to the professions is believed to lead inevitably to a disabling conflict in identity. For example, women engineers are said to experience this conflict daily in deciding how to dress, appearing "unprofessional" if their dress is feminine and displeasingly "unfeminine" if it is not (Carter and Kirkup, 1990).

Social scholars inspired by identity-politics theory generally have policy-oriented goals aimed at reducing social inequality. They present three positive solutions to conflicts between professional identity and some aspect of personal identity, each of which suggests the limits of identity-politics theory. The first is the creation of a new professional role that does not conflict with personal identity. This is typically portrayed as occurring through a cultural and political social movement, as when early women lawyers created clubs to "nurture" their emerging new role, which would balance the feminine self-concept of being "modest, sentimental, and caring" with the professional expectation that one be "assertive, rational, and objective" (Drachman, 1990: 2414). While this solution might work in the long run, I view it as the solution least helpful to individual professional students faced with identity dissonance that they must resolve. Roles are much larger than the individual and are slow to change; the individual professional needs an immediate resolution to his identity dissonance.

The second approved solution presented by social theorists of identity politics is to consciously resist professional socialization in order to retain a primary identity that is in conflict with the dominant cultural values that professional schools seek to inculcate in students. Cheryl Townsend Gilkes calls individuals who follow this strategy, such as a group of African American women she studied, "rebellious professionals" (1982: 289). As I show in the chapters that follow, few identity-dissonant professional students whom I observed manage their dissonance in this manner, which requires great self-confidence in the face of powerful socializing pressures.[13] The literature provides support for my findings, indicating that when the values of incoming professional students conflict with the common values of the profession, the individuals are likely to change much more than are the institutions. For example, interest in pro bono work and in social reform decrease markedly over the course of law-school socialization (Granfield, 1992; Erlanger and Klegon, 1977). This is because the professional habitus of the attorney is formal, disinterested, and oriented away from an ethic of care to an air of command (Erlanger and Klegon; Hochschild, 1983). This finding belies the feminist prediction that the entry of women into law would swiftly transform the profession (see Rosenberg, Perlstadt, and Phillips, 1991).

The third approved solution according to social theorists of the identity-politics camp is for the nontraditional professional to "refuse to choose." For example, Paula S. Derry studied psychotherapists who became mothers, who are assumed to experience a conflict between professional and maternal identity, faced with a choice between being "uncommitted" professionals or "bad" mothers. Derry found that "professional identity is neither unaffected nor does it become secondary" to maternal identity, but that psychoanalyst/mothers "realign" their identities (1994: 160).[14] What authors of this camp downplay in their desire to advocate having it all is the nagging discomfort of maintaining conflicting identities, which I attempt to capture in terming it "identity dissonance."

Scholars influenced by identity politics ignore an alternative solution to conflicts between professional and personal identities: the adoption of the professional identity and the displacement of the conflicting personal identity, thereby resolving identity dissonance into consonance. This approach is rarely the focus of studies by social scientists influenced by identity politics, because it is viewed negatively (see, e.g., Wijeyesinghe and Jackson, 2001). Nevertheless, this politically incorrect fourth solution was quite prevalent among the professional students I studied. It is, after all, the resolution of identity dissonance at which professional socialization is aimed. Moreover, the resistant solutions to resocialization pressure advocated by those who embrace identity politics assume a conscious model of identity. The issue of the nonconscious nature of identity at the level of habitus is ignored once again. The overwhelming majority of the professional students I studied did not devise conscious strategies to defuse an acknowledged problem with conflicting identities. Instead, they haphazardly arrived at coping mechanisms to manage a difficulty whose nature they could not articulate.

In considering the scholarly literature on professional identity, in sum, we can see that structural theories conceptualize identities formally and thus ignore diversity, agency, and social change. Symbolic interactionist accounts contribute important insights into the production of identity through interpersonal interactions, and allow for—in fact, valorize—individual agency. When inflected by the policy aims of identity politics, they also emphasize the production of identity as a focus of collective action with important implications for social equality. But most empirical research on professional identity gives short shrift to the study of conflicts and changes in nonconscious identity, which is problematic. The problem arises not just from theoretical frameworks, but also from methodology. After all, how can research subjects talk about matters of which they are unaware? I knew I would have to deal with this problem when planning how to carry out my own study.

# 3   Research Contexts
## *How and Where to Look*

To study professional identity and success at professional schools, I knew I would need to employ several research methods. Of course, I wanted to interview professional students, so that I could learn about their subjective experiences with the socialization process and ask them about how they were conscious of their identities. (My interview questions can be found at www.uwm.edu/~costello.) I also wanted to respectfully observe students' individual agency in action. But I knew it would be insufficient to rely on interviewee reports to understand the socialization process and to learn about professional students' identities, because so much of identity is comprised by habitus, which is nonconscious and hence "unspeakable," although it is revealed by subjects in their practice (Bourdieu, 1977). Ethnographic fieldwork would allow me to develop insight into unarticulated aspects of the socialization process. I also knew that methodologists consider it necessary to observe the interaction of subjects and their environments to reach valid conclusions about how institutions influence individuals (Rubin, 1981). Finally, I wanted to document and analyze the messages sent by the professional school settings themselves.

I accordingly chose to employ a variety of research methods. I engaged in more than four hundred hours of participant observation, conducted seventy-two in-depth, semistructured interviews, and took more than 250 photographs of the professional school settings. Because I practice a research approach that Michael Burawoy calls "reflexive science" (1988) and Pierre Bourdieu terms "phenomenological" (1977), I also spent a great deal of time taking notes on my presuppositions, my interpretation of my ongoing findings, and my own possible influence on the social world I was observing.

My basic research aims were to examine both sides of the socialization equation: the "input" of professional socialization and the "product" of professional identity. I began my research by studying the input—the socializing messages conveyed to professional students regarding professional roles, which students are expected to internalize as a professional identity. I investigated the socializing messages sent by three sources: the professional school settings, professors, and professional student peers. In studying the school settings, I documented the built environments, décor, and landscaping photographically. When studying the professors, I examined not only the explicit verbal instruction they gave regarding the ideological orientations of their professions, but also the socializing messages sent by their pedagogy and their habitus. And in studying peers, I observed how professional students served as reference points and role models for one another during the professional socialization process. I observed students in the classroom, noting not only their words but also their manner of speech, gesture and stance, dress, and style, which would allow me insight into their habitus. I also observed students outside the classroom, as they interacted in and with the libraries, hallways, courtyards, and (women's) bathrooms.[1]

Once my study of the input of professional socialization was established, I began my research into the effects of professional socialization: the shifts in identity that were its products. First, I observed outward, "objective" alterations in appearance, demeanor, and behavior. For example, a trend toward more conservative haircuts among first-year professional students could well indicate that students were being resocialized toward a more conservative self-concept. Next, I studied the subjective experience of the resocialization process through interviews, focusing on the experiences of identity consonance or dissonance. For example, what would it feel like to be a liberal activist who has chosen to go to business school to learn to manage nonprofit organizations, only to receive constant socializing messages that the appropriate habitus for an MBA is conservative and profit-oriented? I also wished to explore how professional students coped with identity dissonance. Would our liberal activist business student be more likely to alter her self-concept, to resist professional socialization, or to seek to maintain two dissonant identities? And what would be the consequences of each response? Finally, I studied the academic implications of identity consonance and dissonance. Would identity-dissonant professional students indeed face more barriers to academic success than did their identity-consonant peers?

My research goals established, I needed to select my research settings. My hope was to select two sites that would provide a good variety of contrasts, a choice that would lead to the richest data. I decided to choose a school of social work and a law school, because the two professions are very different. Law is an old and hallowed profession whose practitioners have traditionally been white men of the upper classes, and whose clients have traditionally been of a similarly privileged background. Social work is a less prestigious profession, established in the twentieth century, whose practitioners have traditionally been white women of the middle class, and whose clients have come from underprivileged backgrounds.

It was my intention to study as many personal identities as possible. Race, class, and gender would be my major focus, since these are conceptualized as the "big three" of U.S. social stratification. But I also intended to study sexual orientation, identity as a person with a disability, political identity, religious identity, and familial identity. It was clear that I would need to locate professional schools with diverse student populations to be able to accomplish all this. Therefore, I selected the schools of law and social work at the University of California, Berkeley.

I believed it was important to select two schools within the same university so that I could control for a number of extraneous factors that might otherwise confound my findings. If I were to find significant differences between the two schools—for example, in the resources expended upon them, or in the demographics of their students, or in their prevailing political atmospheres—I could be sure that these could not be accounted for by regional differences or differences in the resources available at two universities. In addition, I desired to select a law school and school of social work that were both considered Top 10 schools. (Within the professions, with their orientation toward prestige, reference is usually made to Top 10 schools rather than to representative schools in determining norms and trends.) During the time that I carried out my research, U.S. News and World Report included both U.C. Berkeley schools on its definitive Top 10 lists.[2] And of those top schools, Berkeley had the greatest degree of diversity among its students.

The relatively high degree of diversity at U.C. Berkeley's School of Social Welfare and Boalt Hall School of Law did indeed allow me to observe and interview students from a wide range of backgrounds. Nevertheless, in conducting my interviews, it was necessary for me to oversample from student groups whose relative numbers were few and who had personal characteristics associated with identities I hoped to study: students of color, men at the School of Social Welfare and women at Boalt Hall School of Law, students with strong religious commitments, students with disabilities, students from lower socioeconomic class backgrounds, LGBTI students, students with strong political ideologies, and students with spouses and/or children.[3] The resulting demographics of the interview subjects, as indicated by self-identification, are summarized in Table 2.1.

**Table 3.1. Demographics of Interview Subjects**

|  | Law (N = 35) | Social Welfare (N = 37) |
|---|---|---|
| Male | 15 | 13 |
| Female | 20 | 24 |
| White | 17 | 11 |
| African American | 4 | 5 |
| Asian American | 4 | 5 |
| Latino/a | 2 | 2 |
| Native American | 1 | 2 |
| Mixed race | 3 | 6 |
| "Other" (by self-description) | 4[a] | 6[b] |
| Strongly conservative | 3 | 3 |
| Strongly liberal | 8 | 5 |
| Strongly Christian | 2 | 4 |
| Strongly Catholic | 1 | 2 |
| Strongly Jewish | 0 | 4 |
| Lower-class origin | 12 | 16 |
| Has spouse/child | 9 | 10 |
| LGBTI | 3 | 9 |
| Disabled | 3 | 4 |

a. 2 Indian, 1 Bengali, 1 "unknown"
b. 5 Jewish or Semitic, 1 African

# The Research Settings

## Physical Settings

People are constantly subject to the socializing influence of their surroundings, although typically few of us are aware of this (McDowell, 1999). For example, call to mind the sets of the classic sitcoms *The Honeymooners* and *The Cosby Show*. Comparing the two, it is easy to see that the sets of the Cramden and Huxtable houses are constructed to signify very different class standings. Now imagine that we could assign two children to live in the two houses. A child who grew up fixing his breakfasts in the simple kitchen of the Cramden house would be likely to develop a working-class habitus, while a child raised to fix herself breakfast in the well-stocked and well-appointed Huxtable kitchen would be likely to develop an upper-middle-class habitus. Still, if we were to ask these two individuals, "How are you socialized by your kitchen appliances and decor?" we would likely receive blank stares in reply.

Sometimes a setting is sufficiently remarkable that its socializing import does register consciously. For example, my parents once lived in a house that had formerly been a funeral home. Every time my mother bathed in the six-foot-long bathtub, she was aware that she owed its generous size to its having formerly been used to prepare bodies for burial, and this generated in her a heightened sense of her own mortality that she discussed with me years later. But my mother has never remarked that the house conveyed class messages through its spaciousness and architectural detail, because these characteristics were unexceptional to her. In a similar fashion, some aspects of the two professional school settings I studied were remarkable enough that students noticed their socializing effects. But these aspects were the tip of the iceberg.

I gathered voluminous data on the built environments at the schools of law and social welfare, only a taste of which I will present here, although I have published some additional information elsewhere (Costello, 2001). The Boalt Hall Law School setting is characterized in general by an atmosphere of gender, race, and class privilege. The importance of those within is proclaimed in a bombastic inscription on the school's exterior:

> You will study the wisdom of the past, for in a wilderness of conflicting counsels, a trail has there been blazed. You will study the life of mankind, for this is the life you must order, and, to order with wisdom, must know. You will study the precepts of justice, for these are the truths that through you shall come to their hour of triumph. Here is the high enterprise, the splendid possibility of achievement, to which I summon you and bid you welcome.[4]

The stately halls, lobbies, and courtyards of Boalt Hall are austere, free from "feminine" touches such as plants or curvaceous ornamentation, and constructed to give off a sense of power and money through the liberal use of marble, gold-leaf lettering, and fine-grained woods. The hallways of the original building core are wainscoted with a rich honey-toned wood called *terminalia superba*, which was imported at significant cost from the west coast of Africa (Epstein, 1997: 207; photographs of the settings may be found at www.uwm.edu/~costello). Financial prowess is literally written on the classroom walls, halls, foyers, cafe, library collections, and individual study carrels, which bear the names of the patrons (almost universally with male, WASPish names) who donated the funds to renovate that space: the "Brobeck, Phleger, and Harrison Lecture Hall," the "Charles A. Miller Lobby," the "Robbins Collection." There are occasional portraits of legal dignitaries, almost all white-haired white men, and a lone abstract marble sculpture of a bear, the emblem of the University of California.

The Law School facilities include many spaces meant to provide student comfort, from courtyards with umbrella-shaded tables to a smart cafeteria named the Belli Commons. From the Belli Commons emanate socializing messages that shape the content of student tastes—a central component of habitus. At times, classical music plays softly from ceiling speakers. The food sold is light and European in character: soups and salads, croissants and bagels, and pizzaioli and sandwiches. Foods that might otherwise be pedestrian are given an upper-crust flavor. For example, no white bread is served; a student patron may select any bread he likes, so long as it is focaccia, whole wheat, sourdough, or baguette. Similarly, the beverage menu contains Italian sodas and cappuccinos, lattes and doppio espressos, but not 7-Up or coffee. The menu trains law students to adopt the upper-middle-class tastes they will be expected to display as lawyers.

The Law School seems a place constructed by and suited to wealthy white men; others may consciously or subconsciously feel like interlopers, as is illustrated by this quote from an interview with Cheryl, an African American women of lower-middle-class origins:

> At first I used to feel weird walking around the halls, like I didn't belong. I couldn't really believe I was here. Now I'm used to it, but sometimes I still kind of look around myself and think, "You really did it, girl," and it's sort of weird, but good.

In fact, I observed that most entering law students initially acted self-conscious and artificial around the school; I also observed that this self-conscious "stagey" behavior persisted longest in students of color and those with evident working-class backgrounds.

At the School of Social Welfare, a person who climbs the grand staircase of Haviland Hall enters a large foyer of gracious proportions—and coated with peeling paint. When originally occupied by the School of Education in 1924, Haviland Hall was probably quite lovely, but now its corridors look like those of poorly maintained public schools and government facilities everywhere: bland beige walls, ceilings of hung acoustical tile, flickering

fluorescent lights, assorted mismatched pieces of furniture, and ugly linoleum floors.[5] Students at the School of Social Welfare are socialized by these
corridors to understand that they, like their clients, will need to conserve
scant resources.

The facilities provided for student comfort are few and spartan. There
is no cafe at the School of Social Welfare—only four vending machines
covered with iron grating, as if theft and vandalism were to be expected.
There are no courtyards at Haviland Hall, no inviting patio tables or exterior benches to entice students into lingering to engage in casual study and
social chat. Students do study and socialize, but the absence of facilities that
encourage hanging out on campus leads social work students to engage in
these activities off campus in a more directed fashion. As a result, while law
students tended to speak of "living at the Law School," social welfare students often spoke of "having a life" and hence doing their business at school
and then departing.

After being socialized to see the conditions of Haviland Hall as normative, social welfare students came to see luxurious school settings as sinfully
materialistic. I overheard two of them discussing their impressions of the
richly appointed library at U.C. Berkeley's Haas School of Business. "Can
you believe the designer light fixtures and those chairs with the tapestry fabric?" asked one. "I can't believe with homeless people right down the street
they put so much money under their khaki butts," replied the second.

### Classroom Settings

Within these disparate facilities, I attended three core first-year
classes at each school. (I also visited a variety of upper-level classes, but I
focused on first-year classes because professional socialization is most intense at the beginning of a professional program.) At the School of Social
Welfare, I felt it was important that I sit in on the class entitled Introduction
to the Field and Profession, which is attended by all first-year students.
Fortunately, I did not have trouble getting permission from all involved
to do so. This class, taught by Professor Lipman, aimed, according to the
syllabus, "to introduce entering Masters students to the profession of social work and the field of social welfare, by exposing [them] to core ideas
and controversies."[6] (I discuss the classes and professors I mention here in
greater detail in the following chapter.)

In addition to the Introduction class, I wished to attend one of the four
sections of Foundations of Social Work Practice, and one of the seven area-

specific sections of the Social Work Practicum. Intended as a complement to the Introduction to the Field and Profession, Foundations of Social Work Practice introduced, according to the syllabus, the "knowledge, processes and skills needed for effective social work practice." The Introduction is supposed to address academic controversies; the Foundations course, the theory of practice. I attended Professor Dunn's section of Foundations of Social Work Practice, which met from noon to two. Students often brought their lunches to class.

If the Foundations classes are intended to teach the theory of practice, the Practicum is intended to guide the MSW student as she actually enters the field. It is through the Practicum that students explore potential field-work placement sites, prepare to interview for clinical placements, learn what to expect to encounter during their fieldwork, and discuss issues that come up once the placements begin. Each Practicum section is geared to-ward a particular area of practice, such as mental health or gerontology. I attended Professor Alverson's section, which was a Child and Family Practi-cum intended specifically for students whose educations were being funded under California Title IV-E. These students understood that they were required to serve the state for two years after graduating, usually in Child Protection Services, in exchange for their educational subsidies.

At Berkeley's Boalt Hall School of Law, the three first-year classes that I attended were Contracts, Property, and Torts. I will note the schedule for these courses because it illustrates how many things at the Law School seemed arbitrary and confusing. I attended Professor Hoffert's Contracts class, which met from 8:45 to 10:00 on Tuesdays and Thursdays; Professor Santana's Property class, which met on Mondays, Tuesdays, and Thursdays from 3:00 to 4:25; and Professor Tate's Torts class, which met on Mondays, Wednesdays, and Thursdays from 1:55 to 3:00 (and woe betide the student who believed that 2:00 to 3:00 was a more rational time slot—Professor Tate was not tolerant of tardiness).

Of the first-year law classes, only Introduction to Legal Research, Writ-ing, and Advocacy, which prepares students for moot court, is practice oriented. All the substantive law classes are abstract and theoretical. As described in the "Announcement of the School of Law, University of Cali-fornia, Berkeley," Contracts concerns "the law of contracts, dealing with the problems of formation, performance, remedies and termination"; Prop-erty is "an introduction to the law of real property, including the topics of adverse possession, possessory estates in land, future interests, marital property, landlord-tenant law, concurrent estates, easements and covenants, and land-use planning"; and Torts conveys "the law of civil injuries, including both intended and unintended interference with personal and property interests as well as liability without fault." If these descriptions seem rather dry and technical, and you wonder how you would enjoy sitting in on these classes, you may imagine my initial ambivalence. After all, I had attended their equivalents when I was a law student.[7] Fortunately, I found that my alternative focus during this second immersion in law school made the experience fascinating.

# 4   Role Models

## *The Socializing Influence of Professors and Peers*

On the first days of professional schooling, the students I encountered paid attention to the people they met. As they shook hands with their classmates, they eyed their clothes and took note of their manner, probably wondering whether they fit in and hoping to make some friends. But most of all, they focused on their professors. These were the individuals responsible for training and evaluating them, whom they consciously viewed as role models. Professorial approval would be necessary to the students' professional success and self-esteem, and the students paid scrupulous attention to professors' every early word and gesture.

## Professors

When scholars in the area of sociology of the professions write about professional socialization, they usually focus on the messages professors convey when they speak of the requisite cognitive skills and ideological orientations of the professions. This is also how professors I observed generally understood themselves to function as professional socializers.[1] Yet the professional identities which students must internalize are comprised only in part of conscious, cognitive elements. They are largely comprised of habitus—tastes, worldviews, postures, and emotional orientations. These are conveyed in part via verbal communication, but not directly—for example, the appropriate class habitus is implied when a law professor speaks of a hypothetical lawyer as buying a Mercedes, or a social welfare professor speaks of a hypothetical case worker as "parking her Civic." Professional school professors also embody the appropriate demeanor in their styles of dress, mannerisms, and tastes, serving as model individuals who fulfill professional roles.

## *Professorial Appearance*

**At the School of Law:** I sat in on three first-year core classes as a participant observer in both professional school settings. The classes I regularly attended at Boalt were Professor Roger Hoffert's Contracts class, Professor John Santana's Property class, and Professor Norman Tate's class on torts. Professor Hoffert was a white man of middle years and impressive stature, whose lack of concern with fashion trends was evident in his unstyled brown hair and large, unfashionable rectangular glasses. While he seldom wore suits, Professor Hoffert's garments could hardly be described as casual; a typical outfit consisted of a light blue button-down shirt, a crimson conservatively-patterned tie, gray wool slacks, and a navy blazer with brass buttons. This dignified style of dress added to Professor Hoffert's impressive air of authority.

Professor Hoffert's standard of dress was fairly typical of the Boalt faculty, and deviations from this standard conveyed messages to students. For example, Professor Tate dressed far more casually than did Professor Hoffert. On the very first day of class, when most professors (and students) were unusually attentive to and sharp in their dress, Professor Tate wore his standard outfit: a plaid button-down shirt and a pair of khaki pants. It was evident from his demeanor and comments that Professor Tate wished to project a chummy manner so that students would find him approachable.[2] I was interested to observe that, rather than giving him a good reputation among students, Professor Tate's casual attitude and dress were disrespected by the law students. I discussed Professor Tate's reputation with a third-year student who stated that while in his estimation, Professor Tate could "hardly be dumb" since he was a successful law professor, students tended to see him as "not terribly smart." The student attributed this reputation to what he deemed Professor Tate's ill-advised attempt to act like "just one of the guys." Professor Tate's reputation provides evidence that law students are socialized to associate authority, intelligence, and hierarchy, and to link all of these with "professional" dress.

The professionally attired Professor Hoffert is an example of the type of professor students came to consider highly intelligent and admired from a position of social distance. But Professor Hoffert was an ideal-typical respectable law professor not only because he wore a navy blazer, but also because he was an older white male of moderately conservative bent. Professors who deviated from this demographic norm were at a disadvantage in ensuring student respect, and they almost always sought to compensate for their demographic failings by dressing to a higher standard.

Professor Santana provides an example of this phenomenon. He deviated from the professorial archetype through his youth (he was in his early thirties), his Latino ethnic background, and his liberal politics. To compensate, Professor Santana dressed in smart professional apparel, such as a tailored charcoal tweed jacket, pleated olive wool slacks, a dress shirt, and a fashionably patterned silk tie whose colors coordinated exactly with the charcoal and olive of his jacket and slacks. Professor Santana, who dared to wear a short ponytail, was perhaps atypical in his fashionable approach to outdressing his older and more conservative while male peers. A more common and less controversial approach would be simply to wear a suit, since suits are considered more formal than the blazer and tie favored by many male professors. Professor Shen, an Asian male, favored this path, wearing a charcoal suit, white dress shirt with fine gold stripes, and gold "power tie" on the day I sat in on his class.

That students received the message that they should try to compensate for their youth and any other "undesirable" characteristics, such as female gender, nonwhite status, and so on, by dressing to a strict standard became evident during the annual interview seasons. When dressing professionally for job interviews, the students I observed at Boalt attired themselves in a rigidly conformist uniform of conservative black suit and starched white dress shirt or silk blouse. The uniformity, somber nature, and expensive cut of these suits gave me the disquieting impression that the Law School had been transformed during the interview season into an exclusive funeral parlor.

Female law professors faced the particular problem of distinguishing themselves from the Boalt support staff. Most professors at Boalt were male, and most secretaries female. That the female professors attended carefully to their attire so as to distinguish themselves from support staff was made vividly clear when the Boalt fire alarm went off at 8:15 one morning. At that hour, classes were not yet in session, and the majority of the people who exited the Simon tower with me were faculty and staff. I found myself standing between a group of chatting female secretaries and an aloof female professor. The secretaries were all dressed to a moderately high standard of feminine office dress: they wore floral skirts or print dresses, carried small, delicate purses, and wore accessories such as high heels and pastel sunglasses. Professor Susan Hilliard, in contrast, wore a sharply tailored brown pantsuit, a silk blouse in a subtle taupe shade, a scarf in subdued hues, and flat pointy-toed leather shoes; rather than a purse she carried a soft leather attaché case with a laptop computer protruding from it.

The richer, subtler fabrics worn by Professor Hilliard evoked a higher class status than that of the secretaries. Her pantsuit ensemble also gave a much more androgynous impression than did the outfits of the support staff. Since the ideal-typical law professor, as already noted, is male, and since femininity is associated with lower-status secretarial work, Professor Hilliard sought on the one hand to downplay her femininity to give an authoritative impression. On the other hand, Professor Hilliard did not walk out when the fire alarm rang dressed in a sports jacket and tie. Because she remains a woman, and because our culture stigmatizes women who appear unfeminine or "butch," Professor Hilliard was caught in a double bind, appearing unlawyerly if she seemed too feminine and unappealing if she appeared too masculine. Like other female attorneys, she dressed at the androgynous midpoint between the poles of masculinity/professional authority/butch unattractiveness and femininity/unprofessional lack of authority/heterosexual appeal.

Female law students were quickly socialized to apply the solution of androgynous dress to the double bind faced by females in the legal profession. Female first-year students swiftly adopted an androgynous style of attire. Expressed through the student standard of dress, which was far below the high standard displayed by the faculty, the androgynous style of female law-student dress consisted typically of a neat pair of jeans or slacks, a plain sweater or shirt, a simple hairstyle, and minimal jewelry or makeup.[3]

**At the School of Social Welfare:** Whereas the Law School has a faculty defined by an ideal-typical older white male majority, against which younger, female, nonwhite, or otherwise "other" faculty appear as nonideal, the School of Social Welfare has a more diverse faculty. As a result, while the Law School faculty attire was patterned as a norm and deviations therefrom, the dress of the faculty at the social welfare program could be more closely described as variations on a general theme. That theme was referred to by the social welfare faculty by the evocative sobriquet "calculated casual."

The three social welfare classes I regularly attended were Professor Robert Dunn's Foundations of Practice class, Professor Joe Lipman's Introduction to the Profession (attended by all first-year students), and Professor Marjorie Alverson's Child and Family Practicum. Professor Dunn was a white man of middle years, much like Professor Hoffert of the Law School, and in fact he too wore unfashionable, large rectangular eyeglasses. Yet the impression given off by each man's appearance was quite different. Professor Dunn wore a beard, and his clothing adhered far less to the corporate standard. A typical outfit consisted of a white shirt with thin brown stripes, pants of a mushroom hue, a dark brown belt, light brown shoes, and argyle socks in navy and beige. I wrote in my notes of this outfit, "Nothing really matches although all is neat and pressed." Whereas Professor Hoffert's navy blazers were meant to give a straightforward impression of authority, Professor Dunn's outfits carried two meanings: through their lesser formality they conveyed both a casual attitude and less hierarchical social distance, and through their neat pressing they conveyed that Professor Dunn had taken care in his dress. This is the aim of calculated casual attire: to dress in a moderately informal manner to put clients or students at ease, and yet to make it clear that this dress is professional because it is carefully selected and presented. While it might look to someone from the legal realm that social welfare professors could wear whatever they want, this impression is quite false; for example, old jeans, low-cut dresses, or unkempt clothing would be as unacceptable if worn by a social welfare professor as they would be if worn by a law professor.

Professor Lipman's style of dress provoked in his students an interesting reaction. He was a sharper dresser than Professor Dunn; in addition, his beard was more neatly trimmed and his round wire-rimmed glasses more fashionable.[4] An outfit typical for Professor Lipman consisted of a French blue button-down shirt, well-cut khaki pants, and a cordovan leather belt and shoes. Students responded to his higher standard of dress in a bifurcated fashion: first, they treated him as having greater authority than the average professor, and second, they felt less warmly toward him. While students at the Law School came to feel that liking a male professor on a personal level was irrelevant to feeling respect for him as a good teacher, students at the School of Social Welfare came to feel that their desire for all professors to be likable was legitimate.

I interpret the contradictory response to formal attire at the School of Social Welfare as a product of social work's status as a "feminine profession." In the "masculine profession" of law, the cultural values associated with masculinity and professionalism are congruent: masculinity and professionalism are both associated with characteristics such as power, rationality, dominance, aggression, and competence. But in the "feminine profession" of social work, the cultural values are conflicted: femininity is associated with values such as affection, caretaking, and attraction, while professionalism remains associated with the traits listed for masculinity. In the realm of attire, the congruent masculine and professional values of the law lead to a simple relationship where, at least for men, there is a clear ideal: the students are socialized to associate high formality in dress with high professorial competence. But the conflicting values within the profession of social work make it less clear what the ideal degree of formality of dress should be.

One can easily argue that the ideal degree of formality in attire for social welfare professors should be set at the point where perceived competence and perceived likability intersect. A moderate level of formality is associated with moderate perceived competence and moderate perceived likability. This is the aim of the calculated casual dress code: to carefully dress down so as to maximize both one's perceived competence and one's approachability. But note that the consequences of going above or below this midpoint are different: it is one thing to appear a highly competent but unlikable person and another to appear a very amiable incompetent. Professor Lipman, who dressed above the standard, was more highly respected than his average peers, although not as well liked. He served as a role model for students for the interesting possibility that they might gain professional prestige by straying outside professional norms.

The option of dressing at a level of formality higher than the standard was less positive for female professors because the consequences of appearing unlikable were much worse. Women in our society always face disapproval for appearing unempathetic, but in a profession that is described as the science of giving care, lack of empathy is viewed as highly unacceptable. Professor Alverson provided a classic example of a response to the conundrum of wishing to appear very competent without appearing cold: she adopted an approach to her appearance that I referred to rather sarcastically in my notes as "extremely calculated casual."

Professor Alverson, a white woman with attractive silvery hair, wore ensembles that were never formal but always carefully put together. For example, one day she wore a flowing green dress with an "ethnic" print evocative of African or Native American motifs, together with a soft vest in coordinating shades of green, black, and gold. Her suede shoes had low heels and were ornamented in coordinating tones of green, gold, and purple at the heel and toe. She also wore gold dangly earrings incised with a tree-and-moon pattern, and several green cloisonné bangle bracelets. Her pantyhose were sheer and her makeup light. To give another example, one day Professor Alverson wore a silk blouse in an Indian print. While Indian blouses were fashionable that year, most were loose and unstructured and rather sloppy looking, while Professor Alverson's was neat in cut, with a sharp collar, shoulder pads, and silk-covered buttons. She wore brown pleated trousers, brown low-heeled pumps, silver earrings in the shape of starfish, and several silver bangle bracelets.

Besides always being carefully selected to look simultaneously informal and highly put together, Professor Alverson's garments and accessories sent tasteful messages of cultural sensitivity. Her third-world-evocative prints signified ethnic sensitivity, and her earrings usually gave off a subtle political message, as did the tree-and-moon earrings that employed symbols of feminist spiritual practices, or the starfish earrings that quietly evoked nature and conservation. Professor Alverson took at least as much care in selecting her outfits as did Professor Hilliard at the Law School, because in their different ways female professors at both schools needed to balance signifiers of power with feminine attractiveness or care in their attire.

Interestingly enough, we can see that issues of dress in both schools were much more complicated for female than for male professors, even though law is considered a masculine profession and social work a feminine one. In fact, it was for male professors at the School of Social Welfare—for the men in the traditionally feminine profession—that the issue of professional dress was simplest. So long as a male professor wore a clean shirt that was not a T-shirt and pants that were not jeans, he appeared to be a competent professional.

Students at both schools learned a great deal about their respective professions simply by observing how their professors dressed. The higher standard of professional dress at the Law School socialized law students to expect to be accorded higher social status as attorneys than the social work students were socialized to expect from the lower standard of professional dress in their program. Students at both schools saw that professional dress excluded strong cultural gestures—a professor might wear a cowry-shell necklace but not flying dreadlocks, or wear a black turtleneck but not visible tattoos or piercings. And students in both programs learned similar messages about the gendered world of their prospective professions. Picking out an outfit (and by extension, daily life in general) was simpler for male than for female professors, although for different reasons. Women at the Law School learned that they must dress to look powerful without coming across as unattractively masculine. Women at the School of Social Welfare learned that they must dress to look competent without appearing to be cold or insensitive.

## Professorial Habitus

**At the School of Law:** As in the matter of dress, in general the habitus of the law professor is straightforward: law professors radiate an aura of authority. Arrogance appears not to be considered unseemly, and all the professors I observed at Boalt exuded supreme self-confidence. Students accepted and responded to this authority immediately and unquestioningly in the case of archetypical white male professors such as Professor Hoffert, although they displayed a certain degree of resistance to the authority of others, such as Professors Hilliard or Santana. For example, I noted that while all the law professors I observed displayed their dominance by controlling conversations—interrupting others but refusing to be interrupted themselves —students were more likely to display irritation at Professor Santana's interruptions than at Professor Hoffert's (although such displays were the exception to the rule in any case).

Professorial competence was evinced verbally. Law professors' speech was characterized by a formidable vocabulary, WASP patterns of grammar, long and complex sentences, and the tendency to impress by sprinkling their speech with Latin phrases.[5] For example, Professor Hoffert avowed: "Should you find yourself before a court, you will be expected to cite the Restatement rule; the opposing party may claim that the Restatement 2nd does not constitute binding authority, and he will be correct, but you will be very glad indeed to have the Restatement behind you." As another example, Professor Santana proclaimed: "This is a case of *damnum absque injuria*: the court holds that future wells drilled or pumped after the decision which negligently caused subsidence can lead to recovery, but not in the instant case due to *stare decisis* reliance." Aside from the Latin phrases, these sentences may not seem very different from those I have written that appear around them, but consider that the professor's sentences were spoken, not written. Conventions for written and spoken English are different, so that "good" written English is typically much more formal than spoken English; the professors at the Law School spoke in a way that most people can only write. This demonstrated the capacity to think on one's feet that they asserted was a professional necessity.

In addition to authority and verbosity, the speech of the law professors I observed was characterized by a light, bantering tone. The substantive material of the law might be heavy, but the emotional tone of the legal professional habitus is light. One aspect of being able to think on one's feet is apparently the capacity for stand-up humor, and professors displayed a dry and sarcastic wit. There was a somewhat sadistic edge to this humor, which was often deployed at the students' expense, enhancing professors' dominance in the classroom. To give just one example, Professor Hoffert was leading a Contracts class on the law of offer and acceptance. He constructed a hypothetical situation in which a student played a representative of the university, seeking to retain a law professor by offering him more money.

Playing the professor, Professor Hoffert accepted the student's offer by saying, "Very well, but your offer must take the following form: I want to see you outside my door Monday morning at 9:00 A.M. sharp with the money in your mouth, on all fours." The class roared with laughter.

Law professors' demeanor tended away from empathy and toward being thick-skinned. A correlate of the masculine qualities of power and authority is the quality of toughness. Among the general public, toughness is usually understood in physical terms; physical strength is decentered in the intellectual world of lawyers, but mental and emotional toughness is highly valued. The professor and Contracts class all laughed at the image of the student begging on all fours like a dog, and they expected him to grin and bear it rather than express hurt feelings and expect to be "coddled."

From the perspective of the lawyerly habitus, being called "sensitive" is more insult than compliment. Because of this, law professors were openly hostile to what was termed "being P.C."—the politically correct demand for sensitivity to the feelings and needs of minorities and women. This is by no means to say that the law professors I observed countenanced discrimination. They universally voiced support for antidiscrimination laws and regulations and made gestures toward inclusiveness such as devising hypothetical scenarios with lawyers who were female, people of color, or both. But any proposal which could possibly be construed as limiting free speech in order to protect the feelings of some aggrieved group was met with great hostility.

The typical characteristics of the law professor's habitus—an aura of authority, grandiloquence, and the devaluing of emotional sensitivity—were most easily displayed by WASP male professors, because they are congruent with WASP male roles. Professors who were not white or male displayed the same characteristics in their habitus, but this did not seem as natural to their students. I overheard students claiming that Professor Santana's particularly intense verbosity was "overcompensation," although I presume that if he spoke in a style more typical of Latino Americans he would have been perceived as an inferior professor. More simply, I heard Professor Hilliard referred to as a "bitch" for her failure to display the level of emotional sensitivity students expect in a woman.

**At the School of Social Welfare:** As in the case of professorial dress, the habitus of the professors in the School of Social Welfare was more complex than the law professors'. The social work professors I observed combined displays of empathy with signifiers of competence and rationality. They shared with the law professors a WASP-like habitus yet spoke frequently about diversity and cultural sensitivity.

The social welfare professors I observed projected authority that ema-nated from an air of competence rather than of egotism. While the law professors I observed sought to dominate and control discussion, the profes-sors of social work sought to lead and guide discussion. The social welfare professors avoided interrupting students who were speaking and in general assumed a more egalitarian relationship to their students than did law pro-fessors, but it was still clear that they had authority, and that students were expected to defer to it.[6]

In addition to authority, a primary component of the social welfare professor's habitus was the demonstration of empathy. "Insensitivity" at the School of Social Welfare was as stigmatized as "oversensitivity" was at the Law School. Social work professors demonstrated their sensitivity to stu-dents by maintaining eye contact and leaning in toward students who were speaking to them. They were solicitous of students who came to speak with them before or after class, and to demonstrate empathy they would briefly touch the shoulder of a student who seemed anxious. When a student was speaking, not only would the professors not interrupt, but they would em-ploy active listening techniques to indicate that the student had their full attention. For example, Professor Dunn would nod, stroke his beard, and murmur an occasional "mm-hmm" while a student was speaking. When she finished, he would sum up the student's points and seek affirmation that he had correctly understood, and then murmur "Good, good," or "Okay," or "Thanks for bringing that up," before moving on to another student.

The social welfare professors' need to balance sensitivity and author-ity produced a habitus that seemed less easy for students to read than the straightforward dominating habitus of the law professors. Social welfare professors seemed concerned that their professional sensitivity might be construed as unprofessional lack of authority; I observed two different (fe-male) social work professors telling their students, "I am not your mother."[7] However, during my interviews it emerged that the more common problem was that many social work students construed professorial assertions of au-thority as demonstrating an intimidating lack of empathy. The social welfare students were no less cowed by their professors than were the law students, despite the contrasting professorial comportment.

The habitus of the social welfare professors was serious in its emotional tone. Unlike the law professors, the social welfare professors engaged in little bantering or sarcasm, although they did engage in some light self-dep-recating humor, as when Professor Alverson, reading aloud the notes she wrote on the bottom of the blackboard for students who could not see them, disparaged her compacted handwriting, saying, "Hmm, what language is this in?" But the sadistic humor favored by law professors ran counter to the sensitive mien of the social welfare professors, who would never engage in a joke at the expense of a disadvantaged other.

The professors at Haviland Hall had an interesting relationship to the concept of political correctness. Certainly they agreed with its principles: that hurtful speech was unacceptable and that the disempowered should be given a voice. The fear that any humor at the expense of others, however light and teasing, could be experienced as cruel lay behind the universally serious mien of these professors of the science of caring. Yet as academics, social welfare professors felt a need to advocate for free speech and to denigrate the phrase "politically correct" as an anti-intellectual, censorious response to a real problem. Professor Lipman, who taught the Introduction to the Profession course attended by all first-year students, was especially prone to mocking the "P.C. Police" (although like all social welfare professors, he spoke only seriously and respectfully of any disempowered groups). On the first day of class, he urged students to demonstrate "charity" by not taking offense at others' statements and "maturity" by being able to have their assumptions challenged, rather than shutting down debate with a "P.C. reflex." He himself poked gentle fun at "P.C. reflexes": the name plaque on his office door read, not "Professor Lipman," but "Professor Lipperson."

It is evident that the social welfare professor's identity is characterized by a series of elements in tension: it is authoritative yet sensitive in habitus; it is politically correct in practice yet intellectually committed to free speech. Another tension exists between its WASP character and its advocacy of cultural sensitivity. Social welfare professors regularly made statements about the necessity of recognizing cultural and class differences. They made gestures of solidarity with third-world people, as when Professor Alverson wore garments with "ethnic" patterns, and they acknowledged their privileged status, as when Professor Dunn periodically began sentences, "As a white male . . ." Yet the habitus of the social welfare professors I observed was steadfastly WASP and middle class in flavor. Professors employed WASP grammar and vocabulary, dressed in a middle-class manner, and, most centrally, continued to position the disempowered client pool as "other," that is, as people whose behaviors were difficult to understand unless one engaged in careful cultural interpretation and translation into terms comprehensible from a middle-class WASP perspective. This attitude proved alienating for many of the students of color I interviewed—something that would probably surprise and dismay the professors at Haviland Hall.

## Peers

Professors are widely acknowledged to serve as role models, and they sent important socializing messages in that capacity. But professional students do not model their behavior and habitus only on those displayed by their professors. The students I observed also served as role models for one another; they gauged their behavior and performance against each other's, looking to their peers, as they themselves put it, as "mirrors" or "yardsticks" against which to measure themselves.

A pair of phenomena revealed the influence students had over one another. The first was the striking convergence in dress that occurred in the first days students spent at professional school. For example, before classes began at the Law School, the 1Ls (first-year students) who came to Boalt Hall for orientation meetings, to buy books, or just to familiarize themselves with the confusing layout of the facilities were dressed in a fairly diverse manner. Some were casually dressed in T-shirts and denim cut-offs, some were conservatively attired in dress slacks with a button-down shirt or blouse, and some seemed to have taken their cue from television portrayals of lawyers and wore stylish and expensive-looking outfits.[8] But within a week, students' outfits had become much more uniform, settling into a casual preppiness. Similarly, at the School of Social Welfare, students arrived wearing everything from a suit and tie to neon-bright magenta hair but quickly converged to a restrained urban funkiness.

The other phenomenon that revealed that peers were socializing one another was the tendency for students to arrive at the first meeting of a class with the reputation of the professor firmly in mind. When I seated myself in Professor Hennings's Foundations of Social Work Practice class five minutes before the first session was to begin, the professor had yet to arrive, but the pair of students beside me were already discussing their anxiety about her propensity for intimidating students. Similarly, before the first meeting of Professor Santana's Property class, conversations made it clear that students were inclined to distrust him because they had heard that he was "too political." These preconceptions of the professors originated in conversations with upper-level students and then quickly circulated around the first-year classes. That these interstudent communications had socializing import and did not merely convey factual data was evident in Professor Santana's retaining a dubious reputation even though he expressed more sympathy for the 1Ls than did any other professor I observed, gave more pragmatic advice than the other professors, and expressed an orientation toward furthering social justice that ought to have resonated with many students, whose similar orientations were being uncomfortably challenged by other professors. Students might well have emulated Professor Santana had they not been swiftly socialized by other law students to see him as an inappropriate role model. The influence of peer socialization was strong, and it sometimes worked against students' best interests.

## Student Habitus

**At the School of Law:** If I were to draw up a list of adjectives describing the ideal habitus for the law students I observed—the demeanor that was characteristic of the students considered successful by their peers—I would include "upbeat," "self-confident," "competitive," "status conscious," "argumentative," "tough," "articulate," "apolitical," and "bantering." Students never drew up such a list, because habitus usually exists beneath the level of conscious awareness, but all were influenced by it. Some law students arrived with this habitus; some acquired it; some tried to emulate it through self-conscious role playing and some could or would not do so—but even the most dissonant of students, unable to articulate the nature of their difficulties, were able to identify as successful students those who exhibited this habitus. For example, Julia, who was experiencing identity dissonance, said:

> A lot of these people are very focused, and they know exactly what they're going to say. . . . I think they say, "She's not as smart as we are," because of the way I express myself. It's so easy for them, and they're so into the competition; . . . they just tear your argument apart, and they're smiling, it's a big joke. And so they'll come up with all these techniques for showing why your argument is bad, when they totally agree with you in the end.

Julia expressed irritation with the "model students," but she also saw them as smart students who excelled at lawyerly debate—the sort of people who would be likely to succeed in their legal careers.

The demeanor of law students was similar to that of their professors, although less formal. The law students I observed did not wear sports jackets to class or spout Latin phrases, but, as was the case with their professors, the successful students' habitus was congruent with white heterosexual male upper-middle-class culture. This was interesting because, unlike the faculty, half the law students were female and, compared to the faculty, the group included more people of color.[9] The long dominance of the legal profession by WASP men of privileged class backgrounds had different persisting effects upon faculty and students: men with such backgrounds continued to be disproportionately represented among the faculty; among the students, men with such backgrounds were disproportionately successful.

Initially, I was unsure why I received an impression of white maleness when observing law students, and I thought perhaps it was a comparative impression which I came to only because I was simultaneously observing at the School of Social Welfare, with its female-dominated and more racially diverse student population. It was only after I began to take notes on the gender balance in class participation that I realized that white men volunteered to speak in the Law School classroom at significantly higher rates than other students did. This was made dramatically clear one day in the fourth week of classes, when Professor Santana forced his rather reluctant class to discuss gender, and women volunteered to talk at a higher rate than men did, giving the entire class session an atypical feel. Because upper-middle-class white males usually dominated class discussions, their habitus had come to seem normative.

In almost every class meeting, white men made a disproportionately large percentage of the comments.[10] Moreover, they were more memorable to the professors I observed: both Professor Hoffert and Professor Tate knew the names of their white male students better than they did those of other students. In one class meeting, for example, Professor Hoffert kept comparing an existing contract rule with two alternate possibilities, which he named after the students who proposed them: one was called "Mr. Froebel's rule" and the other "her rule." Mr. Froebel was a foreign student whose European pedigree and expensive-looking attire seemed to impress Professor Hoffert; he respectfully addressed this student, unlike others, by last name. The other student, Yesenia, was Latina, and while the rule she proposed was memorable to Professor Hoffert, she herself was not; he forgot her name soon after calling it from his seating chart. My field notes indicate that at this early point in the semester, *all* the students whose names Professor Hoffert had memorized were white men.

When I say that the normative law-student habitus was congruent with WASP heterosexual male upper-middle-class culture, I am referring to more than the place of white male law students at the center of academic life. I mean that other students—women, people of color, gay men and lesbians, students with less lofty class origins, and so on—tended to have a habitus that was unusually congruent with white heterosexual male upper-middle-class culture. New law students of various flavors entered with a tendency toward a WASP masculine habitus due to self-selection: students may enter law school with misconceptions about the profession, but we know enough about the role of attorney in our culture that certain people are attracted and others repelled by it. Academically competitive people with strong English skills who enjoy logic and debate, who would like to have power and money, and who can imagine themselves wearing a suit apply to law school at much higher rates than do people who don't feel comfortable speaking standard English, or shy and sensitive people who can't abide arguing, or communards with multiple piercings and tattoos. And in a feedback cycle of mutual role modeling, the masculine, white style is reinforced at law school.

Recall that when students first arrived at Boalt, their dress was moderately diverse, but that it soon homogenized. The style toward which students converged in their attire was one that was worn most commonly in the early days by white males: a casual, preppy, J. Crew look.[11] A typical outfit might include a pair of chinos and a simple shirt. Button-down and polo shirts were popular, as were plain T-shirts (T-shirts with logos or slogans were apparently considered déclassé and were avoided). One thing which struck me was that the color palette was quite masculine: blue was by far the predominate color for shirts, followed by other stately colors such as olive and grey. Women scorned ruffles and took to wearing little makeup. The look students converged toward was country-clubbish in a masculine way. The men looked like neatly dressed "regular guys;" the women gave off a more androgynous impression.

If the ideal-typical law student displayed a preference for khaki slacks, he displayed a distinct aversion toward "whining." Part of this antiwhining bias was propelled by the competitive desire to display toughness. In a practice that one male interviewee described in obviously masculine terms as "weenie-wagging," students would engage in competitive storytelling, discussing who had gone without sleep for the greatest number of hours while studying, who had stood up stoically to the greatest amount of abuse from a sadistic boss, who had carried the most ridiculously heavy pile of books to the most outlandish location, or even who had skied most recklessly during a vacation. Law students with the valorized disposition didn't whine about what they had to endure; they bragged about their ability to "suck it up."

The normative law-student disdain for whining was also directed against "oversensitive women and minorities," who were deemed to have an unattractive tendency toward carping about P.C. grievances. For example, when some women of color aired their feeling of always facing double discrimination during the discussion Professor Santana initiated on gender, many other students' hackles were raised. Some rolled their eyes and sighed, and a few hissed audibly. One white male student complained, "It seems like there are people who have their feelers out at all times looking to find something to be offended at and attack." A number of students who were women or people of color tried to prove that they were not whiners during the discussion by saying that there was no problem of discrimination they were aware of, or that the problem was historical rather than ongoing, or at least that if the law was biased, it wasn't the fault of anyone in the class.

In my field notes, I described the students after a year of law education as giving me the impression of "difference without diversity" (although this should be taken as an overgeneralization rather than a literal description). Whatever their background, students gravitated toward a white middle-class apolitical heterosexual demeanor, just as they came to believe in the ideology of the law as neutral, a level playing field. Underscoring this tendency for me was the fact that few lesbian, gay, bisexual, or transgendered law students came out of the closet. The one student I observed who stated during a class discussion that he was gay was Fred, an average-looking white man in khakis and a button-down shirt, who came out during Professor Santana's class's gender discussion to make the following declamation:

> When I hear people throwing around slogans like "white male hegemony" or "the masculinity of law," I just shut down. I value rationalism, and I don't see it as somehow "masculine." I don't want a "feminine law," I want women to enter the rational world of law. Also, most of the white men in this class aren't part of some mythical group with no problems. Plenty of us face our own problems because of sexual orientation or class or some other factor. I say this as a gay man myself. I want society to change a little bit, but not so fundamentally that we reject our basic institutions.

Except for Fred, who came out in a way that affirmed his normative habitus, the gay students I encountered kept their sexual orientation fairly quiet so that they could embody the ideal as closely as possible. I wrote in my interview notes: "If people at Boalt could closet their race and gender as easily as they could their sexuality, the student body might resume its 1950s white male look." Just as they became more competitive, more tough, and more preppie, I observed law students in some way becoming more WASP-like, upper middle class, straight, and male as they looked to their successful peers as role models.

**At the School of Social Welfare:** The normative social welfare student habitus was sensitive, competent, caring, and earnest. Unlike the Law

School, where the influence of the minority of students who were white, male, and upper middle class was disproportionately large, the normative social welfare student seemed to be white, female, and middle class, because the average social welfare student *was* white, female, and middle class. The characteristic social welfare student demeanor was quite feminine. Most notably, it was markedly more feminine than that of the social welfare professors.

The typical social work student was empathetic and emotive. Students demonstrated their empathy in part by listening intently when another spoke, leaning in and making eye contact, and probing the other's feelings. As the year wore on and students' attitudes reinforced one another, I gained the impression that I was attending a support group or therapy session, because the students came so frequently to ask one another, "How did that make you feel?" In contrast to the law students, social welfare students provided one another with lots of support and affirmation; in fact they seemed to signal their appropriate professional habitus to one another through asking for and giving emotional support.

If law students valued toughness, social welfare students valued sensitivity. Students indicated their highly developed sensitivity by showing that they noticed subtle behavior such as a peer's falsely cheerful hello or her silent bristling at another's comment in class. Students demonstrated their self-awareness by raising with their peers "issues" which they realized they "had" themselves; classmates then had an opportunity to demonstrate their own sensitivity and problem-solving skills. Hence it is evident that sensitivity was linked to competence, another core value for social welfare students.[12]

Social welfare students did not want to be quivering piles of empathy; they wanted to be highly effective empathetic individuals. They demonstrated their effectiveness and self-confidence by assuming an attitude of expertise. This expertise might arise from theoretical knowledge, previous professional experience, or personal experience. For example, one day in the third week of Professor Alverson's class, students began to discuss the reduction in class size for kindergarten through second-grade classes in California. This discussion was off topic (the class was supposed to focus on selecting agencies and writing a résumé), but at that point in the semester, students were still feeling eager to demonstrate their competence to consolidate their professional reputations, and this topic provided a good opportunity to do so.[13] Two white men took the theoretical tack, debating the significance of the relationship between reduced class size and improved performance on standardized tests. A working-class white woman expressed her frustration at policymakers' tendency to debate rather than act, when in her professional experience, any action benefits a client more than no action. And an African American woman spoke from personal experience, relating the saga of her efforts to register her children for classes after the class-size reduction had put the entire school system into flux.

As this example suggests, men and women tended to take different approaches to demonstrating competence, with the men tending to be more abstract and theoretical, and the women more personal and concrete. But the men at the School of Social Welfare did not have a typical masculine habitus; most of them were fairly feminine in their manner, leaning in to listen sensitively, speaking softly, and providing support to their peers. In fact, during the first weeks I spent observing at Haviland Hall, I received the false impression that most of the male students were gay, because straight men do not usually have such feminine comportment. As my false impression indicates, male students arrived with a sensitive, feminine habitus, and this was a matter of self-selection. Hypermasculine, aggressive, and unempathetic individuals do not tend to apply to MSW programs.

The normative student habitus at the social welfare program was also white, in that it assumed the stance of polite interest in and sensitivity toward people of color usually displayed by liberal white people toward cultural others. Social welfare students demonstrated a refined racial etiquette, inquiring about one another's cultural differences, but the cultural disposition displayed by the students was most confluent with that of liberal middle-class white people. For example, this was evident in the food people ate: there was a remarkably hegemonic diet of health foods such as sandwiches of thick, hand-sliced whole wheat bread filled with tomatoes, sprouts, and cheese, or fresh yogurt smoothies, or hummus and a baggie of carrot sticks. These were the kinds of foods that were once eaten only by white hippies in Berkeley, but they were eaten by all the students at Haviland Hall. I never observed any students expressing their ethnicities by eating Southern fried chicken or bright red cha siu pork ribs (although healthy bean burritos were acceptable). Health-food standards usually considered white trumped unhealthy ethnic food preferences.

The social welfare student habitus was by no means as white as was the normative habitus of the law students—students of color made no effort to closet their ethnic culture in the way that law students did. Instead, coming from a minority culture was viewed as a professional asset. In fact, one of the whitest aspects of many students' worldview was the assumption that being a person of color was an unadulterated asset in the social work profession. Seeking to gain some of that presumed ethnic cachet, white social work students often did not identify as such: they emphasized other aspects of their identity.[14] When I asked their ethnicity, they identified as Jewish (or even "Semitic"), as Catholic, and as having Portuguese heritage. When I asked them to describe themselves to me at the start of interviews, white students identified themselves as part of a stigmatized group: as adopted, as recovering from a back injury, as an incest survivor, as a first-generation college student, as living in a committed same-sex relationship. I do not wish to disrespect such backgrounds in any way, but I do want to point out that there was a tendency for white social work students to emphasize these aspects of themselves while not acknowledging their white privilege.

If law students gravitated toward a WASP, country-club style of dress, social welfare students inclined toward making fashion statements of urbane ethnic sensitivity. For example, when I made a visual survey of the students in Professor Dunn's class one day during the sixth week of classes, nearly half were wearing garments or ornaments with ethnic significance, including a blouse with a print of Japanese origami cranes, a T-shirt illustrating traditional Hawai'ian culture, an Indian-print vest, a Native American pendant, a skirt with a Kente-cloth print, an Indonesian batik dress, and a T-shirt celebrating La Raza. On that same, unusually hot day, students also made an urban fashion statement by wearing black clothing; more than one-quarter of the students were wearing black garments, while none of the law students in the classes I attended at the Law School that day wore black.

As with other aspects of peer role modeling, the tendency to ethnicize and to want to appear in some way "other" functioned in a feedback loop. For example, when new social work students arrived on campus, many LGBTI individuals were wary about coming out, apparently operating under the naive impression that professionalism is always associated with heteronormativity. During the second meeting of Professor Lipman's class, when students were required to interview their neighbors as to their reasons for choosing to attend an MSW program, the two white male students sitting directly in front of me danced around the issue of their sexuality without daring to come out. The first man said, "Well, it was either this or the priesthood, and the priesthood was out." The second jokingly explained, "It was that nurturing, close mother and distant father constellation." This tendency to veil references to a homosexual orientation was quickly extinguished, and more and more students came out during the first month of school. Then, as students served as reinforcing role models to one another, students became more radical, speaking of the need for services to the queer community and criticizing the curriculum for being heterosexist. As is evident, students were influenced by one another's habitus, so that a normative professional student demeanor soon coalesced at each professional school.

## Student Behavior in the Classroom

**At the School of Law:** Boalt students' attitude toward one another in the classroom was highly competitive. Students entered with a tendency toward an adversarial attitude, and the importance of first-year grades for future success fostered competitiveness, but it seemed to me that the competitive spirit increased rapidly in the first weeks of class through a process of spiraling peer reinforcement. In the first few days of classes, students expressed an awkward, polite friendliness toward one another, as strangers in middle-class society generally do. When a peer was cold-called for Socratic questioning, classmates often offered encouraging smiles.[15] After only one week, when a student stumbled under Socratic questioning, several others shook their heads and muttered the answer, demonstrating their greater understanding rather than empathy. This soon became a normative response. Some students also took to nodding their heads when the professor spoke to indicate to everyone that they followed him. (That a fair amount of the attentive gazes and bobbing heads that faced the professor signified not students' understanding but their desire to display intelligence was made clear to me upon several occasions when professors called upon nodding students who flushed and sputtered but were unable to answer. Professor Hoffert snidely pointed out to one student, "You were nodding your head at the moment I called on you, were you not?" The student could only nod miserably.) As students reinforced one another's competitiveness, this increasingly influenced their habitus, becoming part of students' behavior patterns outside the classroom. To illustrate: I observed a group of students discussing the Constitution in the hallway; their conversation soon gave way to a race to see who could first recite the Preamble to the Constitution accurately.

Along with a competitive spirit, students quickly socialized each other not to see peers as reliable sources of support or empathy. I observed this process in action during the third week of the semester in Professor Santana's class when issues of social justice were raised. One of the most challenging aspects of a legal education—one which led to a great deal of identity dissonance —was that many law students chose a career in law because they felt attracted to the goal of ensuring social justice by promoting legal change, and discovered only during their Law School training that theirs was considered an unprofessional attitude held only by dreamers and radicals. (The ideology which was considered professional to espouse was to define fairness in formal and procedural terms, and to express concern that faith in the legal system not be undermined by ignoring precedent in the shortsighted desire to achieve a particular outcome.)[16]

During this session of Professor Santana's class, I twice observed students who felt that their social justice commitments were being challenged turn to their neighbors for support, only to be rebuffed. Before class began, two men sitting in front of me were discussing a controversial case that had been the topic of their previous Torts class. One said in a tone of disgust, "Well, now I finally have confirmation for the idea that lawyers are scumbags—they don't have to adhere to any ethical standards." It was apparent from his attitude that he was seeking affirmation and support for his outrage, but instead he was coolly rebuffed by his neighbor, who said, "That entire ethics area is a gray area." In the second instance, Professor Santana brought up an epigraph from the casebook which "posited" that people's human rights are more important than their property rights. A goateed man to my left murmured to his neighbor, "It's a great paragraph, isn't it?" The neighbor replied in a dubious voice, "It *sounds* nice." In both these instances, students seeking to have their commitment to social justice affirmed were rebuffed by peers wishing to assert a more professional neutrality.[17] This was probably a painful experience for the students reaching out for support, and likely to bring home to them in a memorable way that people in the legal realm valued self-interest over empathy. (It also made clear that people in the legal realm included the people seated beside them, although perhaps not yet they themselves—an anxiety-provoking thought.) After another two weeks of classes, students' behavior had become even less supportive, and, when Professor Santana led his discussion of gender, students rolled their eyes, emitted hostile snickers, and even popped gum to display their disrespect for others' comments.

The infamous gender discussion in which Professor Santana forced his students to participate also illustrates another point. This discussion was not tied in any direct way to the subject matter of the legal cases under study, nor was it part of a theme of addressing student identities and differences. It came, as I wrote in my field notes, "out of left field," as a digression from the orderly progress of case study. It confirmed the warnings 1Ls were given by upperclasspeople: that Professor Santana was dangerously "political." The danger here, as students made evident to one another in their comments, was not itself political—students did not fear being converted into raving radicals. The fear was that precious class time would be wasted on irrelevant nonlegal discussion. One student, who worried that Professor Santana spent too much time encouraging the class to "vent," stated to me, "I don't think that we are having to learn the rules of property the way we would in almost any other Property class." That the fright of the Boalt students was typical of law students is borne out by legal author Duncan Kennedy: "In most law schools, it turns out that the tougher, less policy-oriented teachers are the more popular. The softies seem to get less matter across, they let things wander, and one begins to worry that their niceness is at the expense of a metaphysical quality called 'rigor,' thought to be essential to success on bar exams and in the grown-up world of practice" (2004: 5).

The law students I observed were preoccupied with an anxiety about exams and grades that was contagious and grew like a gathering cloud, until I wrote in my field notes:

> Today I found myself worrying, as if some difficult examination were looming, and I ought to be buckling down and getting to work. Then I realized that my anxiety was purely sympathetic: law-student anxiety is in the air and I caught it. It's as if the law students were emitting a fear pheromone.

The 1L students were filled with a nervous desire to be prepared for examinations and learned from second- and third-year students that "politics" would endanger their success. As a result, when Professor Santana forced the class to discuss gender, the response was polarized. The majority of the students resented the discussion and felt that their time had been wasted by what one student openly labeled "bullshit" (in the hallway after class—not to the professor's face). For a minority, however, this discussion of feeling excluded or disempowered was, as Elana put it, "the most real class discussion we've had so far." This minority of students, composed disproportionately of those experiencing identity dissonance, found themselves cast by their peers as preoccupied with "policy" and as distracting the class from learning.[18] Thus we can see how identity dissonance was not necessarily a matter only of private suffering but could become a matter of peer conflict.

If many students resented it when professors "got political," almost all students felt greatly appreciative when professors gave them clear formulations of legal rules to learn. After Professor Hoffert spent a class meeting drawing up a diagram that consolidated all the class had studied so far into a flow chart of legal formulae, some students began applauding, and the rest quickly joined in, reinforcing for one another that this was what they admired and desired.

Instances where law professors spent the entire class on "political" discussion or on constructing legal formulae served as found experiments that yielded much interesting observational data, but they were highly atypical. During most classes, there were occasional excursions into policy discussions and occasional moments when the professor stated legal rules, but most of the time was devoted to studying individual legal cases. In these typical classes, law students continued to emit socializing messages as they took notes.

The students at Boalt Hall spent numerous hours every day in class engaged in note taking. This was their job, and, as the first semester passed, students came to look more and more professional at it. Some students took to using impressive-looking pens, such as fountain pens. Others began to photocopy pages from their casebooks, highlighting these and placing them with the corresponding notes in three-ring binders. But the most notable change in note taking was the replacement of paper notebooks with laptop computers. Laptop computer use proliferated wildly in the first two months of classes. ("It's great!" enthused Justin to an interested Professor Tate, when Justin started using his new state-of-the-art laptop during the second week of class. "I can type faster than I can write.")[19] At this historical moment at the turn of the millennium, law students at Boalt did not yet arrive on the first day of class with laptop in hand, leaving those with pen and notebook looking, like the Reese Witherspoon character in *Legally Blond*, hopelessly unprofessional. But once a few students began clicking importantly away on their keyboards, laptop fever spread quickly.

Note taking is an individual act, but it has a public and performative aspect. When students were taking notes, they looked down, scratching and clicking furiously. When they were not taking notes, they looked up and began to fidget, rustling papers and swiveling their chairs. In the older classrooms, such as Professors Hoffert's and Santana's, the chairs sometimes squeaked when students swiveled them, making the students' distraction piercingly audible. The visible and audible cues made it easy for students to tell when their peers were taking notes and when they were not, and as a result, it was rare for a classroom to be randomly split between students who were taking notes and students who were not. Students generally spent their time taking notes, but when a couple of students stopped and began to rustle and squeak, they acted as a catalyst for a wave of fidgeting and non–note taking that swept the classroom—rather like when a couple of people open their umbrellas and trigger a mass umbrella raising.

Note taking followed a clear and simple pattern: when the professor spoke about a case, students took notes, but when other students spoke, they stopped. This pattern emerged after just one week of classes. When the professor began speaking again, the students stopped swiveling and squeaking and resumed note taking. Thus, students socialized one another to respect professors' authority and to disrespect one another's, with a few exceptions. Certain students who spoke in a very authoritative manner commanded note-taking respect; Mr. Froebel was an example. The other exception to the rule of professor=noteworthy but peer≠noteworthy was that students stopped taking notes when a professor digressed. For example, when Professor Santana raised the issue of personal ethics in the context of restrictive covenants, note taking ceased, only to resume furiously when he began to list ways to defeat a covenant.[20]

The practice of taking notes on laptop computers can illustrate interesting patterns in the herdlike tendency of professional students to follow trends. One interesting fact: while one might assume that students at more prestigious schools, their confidence bolstered by the status of their institutions, would be less likely to conform to trends, the opposite is true. For example, in February 2004 I asked Professor Santana and an acquaintance at Harvard Law School to survey student computer use in their first-year Property Law classes. At Boalt Hall, fifty-two out of ninety students were using laptops, and a handful using PDAs, to take notes. Three students reported that they had tried using a laptop but had stopped because they were more comfortable taking notes by hand. At Harvard, however, all but two of eighty students were using laptops. My Harvard informant told me that failure to use a computer to take notes was seen as unprofessional and simply unacceptable, and that few students would dare damage their reputations by scribbling down their notes.[21]

Another assumption one might make incorrectly is that the two Harvard 1Ls who were not using computers were forced into this position by their underprivileged background. In fact, they were both white males. What their taking notes by hand indicated was apparently not lack of money or social capital, but nonconformist resistance born of comfort and confidence in their new role. Supporting this conclusion is an observation made by a law professor I spoke to at New York Law School: the students with the latest, sleekest computers were African American men, who used them, in her estimation, to shore up their professional look. It is clear that students taking notes in class are doing a lot more than learning new facts—they are also sending and receiving socializing messages about what behavior is professional, who looks professional, and who can get away with ignoring these messages.

In addition to influencing one another via note taking, law students at Boalt sent socializing messages to one another through conspicuous studying practices. Law students studied in public places. They sat in the sun on courtyard benches, highlighting their casebooks. They lounged on the benches of *terminalia superba* that lined the hallways, reviewing their notes. They spent an ostentatiously large number of hours in the library. When I arrived early to social welfare classrooms, I would be alone, but I never came early to a law classroom without finding it already occupied by students surrounded by circles of books, studying—and this pattern began early, in the first week of classes. The law students approached studying as a competitive sport—they didn't just want to work hard at it, they wanted their competitors to *know* how hard they were working at it. As one student put it to me, "It was all part of this sizing-up [process]." And in participating in this competition, students socialized one another to consider putting in long working hours a mark of prowess.

**At the School of Social Welfare:** In contrast to Boalt Hall, where the main themes that emerged with respect to peer effects in the classroom were competition and a pointed disinterest in philosophical issues of ethics or policy issues of justice, what emerged at Haviland Hall were student displays of sensitivity and the enforcement of moral standards. I have already discussed how, as part of their habitus, social welfare students displayed empathy while listening, and this was quite evident in the classroom: students listened intently, made eye contact with speakers, and treated one another with respect. At the Law School, as time went on students became less sensitive to one another, but at the School of Social Welfare, students became more sensitive. For example, in Professor Alverson's class Tanya became so lost while trying to make a point that she said, "So . . . what am I saying?" Instead of shooting their hands up competitively to demonstrate their greater knowledge, the other students smiled while making earnest eye contact with her, to give her moral support. Solicitude extended so far that when several students in a row made comments critical of a particular article, another student stepped in to defend the author from attack.

However, social welfare students could be quite unaffirming when it came to what they viewed as moral transgressions. Unlike the law students, who spanned the ideological spectrum from right to left, clustering vaguely around a staid centrism, the social work students were an ideologically homogenous batch. In 1995, when Professor Lipman had formally surveyed the first-year MSW students, 0 percent of the students identified as "right wing," 23.6 percent as "moderate," 47.2 percent as "liberal," and 29.2 percent as "left wing." My observations indicate that these statistics have continued to hold true. Being part of an ideologically homogenous group that chose a career which they tended to view in moral terms made students react with shock upon those rare occasions when a peer violated their norms.

Most of the violations of social work student norms occurred in the first weeks, when resocialization was at its peak. For example, in the third week of Professor Alverson's class, during a discussion of clients who try to "work the system," two men of color made comments that violated the student norm of showing respect to diverse clients. Ugo, who was Nigerian, complained about the need to "restrain the jaws" of teenaged female clients "who say, 'I can do whatever I want and I can say whatever I want.'" Into the uncomfortable silence that followed this remark, Luis, who was Cuban, dropped a comment about "sneaky" Hmong and Laotian clients who "manipulated the system" to get privileges.

Ugo's and Luis's peers were clearly disturbed by their comments, but they did not respond with either direct challenges or hisses, as affronted law students would. Neither did they make affirming statements about how they understood why men of Ugo's and Luis's background might make such comments. Instead, they responded by resorting to the classic practice of shunning: they turned stiffly away from Ugo and Luis and refrained from giving feedback on their comments. They would not make eye contact with the two men for several minutes, and their response to comments made later in class by Luis was chilly rather than smiling.

Shunning is effective when employed by a cohesive community whose members desire one another's goodwill. A law student might be fairly oblivious to being shunned, but at the School of Social Welfare it was an effective peer socializer.[22] It was evoked rarely—triggered not when there was a dissensus about an issue, but only when a student violated the moral consensus of most of her peers.

Students forged their moral consensus by expressing shock and disapproval at actions taken by impersonal agencies. Social work students apparently felt willing to give much freer reign to expressions of disapproval directed up at the socially powerful than down at clients or across at peers. For example, when students heard of a social welfare agency that reported a Cambodian man as a child abuser because he had engaged in the traditional healing practice of "coining" a daughter who was ill, leading the father to commit suicide in jail, the students expressed their shock and dismay freely, gasping, shaking their heads, crying, "Oh no," and covering their mouths for several minutes. In less dramatic cases, such as hearing of an agency which would not admit women whose partners battered them, students expressed group disapproval by squinting their eyes and curling their lips. And just as law students stopped taking notes en masse, MSW students frowned or gasped together, reinforcing for one another their moral norms.

The social welfare students' norms appeared to be more stringent than those of their professors. For example, Lisa raised the issue in Professor Alverson's class of a parent's demanding to know who reported him to Lisa's agency for child abuse. She asked for feedback on the idea of saying that she was not given that information. The class was critical of the idea, rejecting it strongly on moral grounds as an unacceptable and disrespectful lie, while the professor's response was mild and practical: it is easier simply to tell the parent that case workers are not permitted to disclose that information, and then to be sure that the case file is kept out of his hands.[23] Sometimes the students came across to me as so moralistic as to appear prudish in comparison to their professors. Members of Professor Alverson's class were convinced that childhood masturbation was abnormal and a sure sign of child abuse. Professor Alverson tried to convince them that masturbation was normal at any age, even in infancy, but her attempts did not seem successful, to judge by the expressions of disbelief worn by members of her class.

In addition to being more morally critical than their professors, social welfare students were also less academically inclined than their professors were. Schools of social welfare have been pulled in two directions: by their universities toward being more theoretical and academically rigorous, and by their accrediting agencies toward being more practice oriented. While the social welfare professors served as role models for the attempt to balance these two sets of values, social welfare students sent negative socializing messages to one another regarding the value of cold theory and academic rigor.

First-year law students were warned by veteran students that Professor Santana was insufficiently rigorous and overly political. First-year social welfare students were also warned about a professor before they met her—upperclasspeople warned them that Professor Hennings was excessively rigorous and insufficiently sensitive. When I sat down in Professor Hennings's class before she arrived for the first class meeting, students were discussing their trepidation regarding her reputation for intimidating students. As they shook their heads over this together, students reinforced in one another the idea that the ideal professor was likeable—competent, of course, but approachable.

Professor Lipman was more formal and conservative in his habitus than were his peers, which made students find him less approachable yet increased their impression of his competence. What tipped the balance in his favor and kept students from finding him frightening and unappealing was that he did not demand of them the academic rigor Professor Hennings did. While in addition to the required books he listed many suggested readings on his syllabus, by the fourth week of classes he had still not assembled them into a supplemental course reader. While law students would probably have deplored such behavior on the part of a professor, the social welfare students desired it. In fact, when Professor Lipman asked the class to vote on whether he should forget about having a supplemental reader made up and "just trust everybody" to read recommended articles on their own, the students voted *unanimously* in favor of the idea. Hands shot up, and more hands followed, until the entire first-year class had raised its hands to demonstrate to one another their preference for academic flexibility over academic rigor.

When the first-year MSW students entered school, they were generally more fluent in the language of feeling than in the language of theory. In an early discussion of a theoretical article in Professor Dunn's class, I noted that students' comments were twice as likely to reflect the students' personal feelings and responses to the article than a theoretical critique. As the year went by, most social welfare students picked up a lot of academic vocabulary and theoretical facility, but many (virtually all of these female) continued to voice an antiacademic bias. For example, Ramona stated to her peers during a Gerontology class break that she considered it "nitpicky" for a professor to care if she listed sources she did not use in the bibliography of a paper, and Jenny complained that her Foundations class was "floating around in theory" and not "drawing enough from real life."

Many social welfare students made it clear to one another that they valued practical advice over theoretical information. When it came to balancing personal lives with school and practice responsibilities, however, students were less sure where they stood. What they seemed to reinforce most in one another was the understanding that balancing personal and professional responsibilities was difficult. Unlike the law students, who competitively displayed toughness and stamina through conspicuous studying, and who boasted of how limited their personal lives had become, social welfare students agonized to one another over how to meet both personal and professional responsibilities. For example, toward the end of the semester, Audrey worried before two classmates about how to handle both her increasing workload and her fiancé:

Audrey:    So when Rich started going on about the movies we could see
           this weekend, I faced him and said very clearly that I was going
           to be very busy for the next three weeks.
Laura:     And?
Audrey:    And he just went on to another topic. So then I asked him, "Did
           you hear what I said?" And he said, "I guess I just don't want to
           hear that." So I told him how that made me feel angry, and how
           it made me feel guilty, too, but we didn't resolve anything.
Tae:       Well, sometimes when you tell someone that their feelings
           make you mad, they get defensive and just shut down. Of
           course you do feel mad, because you can't really cut back any
           more, and Rich isn't being understanding, but you might be
           able to put it another way.
Laura:     What you need to do is to let him know about your outside
           responsibilities in a way that doesn't make him feel like you're
           abandoning him.

In this exchange, the students demonstrate to one another the skills they value most—empathy, problem-solving ability, and practical knowledge. They socialize one another to treat both personal relationships and academic requirements as responsibilities to be managed.

Social welfare students also socialized one another through note taking, just as the law students did, although they sent different messages. While the law students spent most of their class time taking notes briskly, the social welfare students took relatively few notes. For example, during one meeting of Professor Ruth's Gerontology Practicum, most of the students took less than one page of notes, and two students took no notes whatsoever. Furthermore, students in Professor Lipman's class fidgeted, rustled, and squeaked in a pattern that was directly opposite that of the law students: they were attentive to discussions of social justice and inattentive to the professor's explanations of academic theory. For example, students fidgeted disinterestedly while Professor Lipman gave a theoretical lecture on the effectiveness of reactive versus proactive government policies, but they returned to an attitude of concentration and resumed note taking when he began to discuss the problem of date rape. But MSW students rarely took notes furiously in the way law students did. One of the rare times I observed them doing so was when Professor Alverson detailed their abuse-reporting duties: a list of responsibilities to endangered clients was one of the few things the students seemed to want to memorize exactly.

## Peer Influence outside the Classroom

**At the School of Law:** The general tone of the casual interactions I observed between students at the Law School was oddly bifurcated. On the one hand, law students exhibited what I termed in my field notes "an ethos of networking": students shook hands heartily upon being introduced to one another and assumed an attitude of polite cheerfulness toward one another so strong that it seemed to me forced. On the other hand, the student propensity toward debate combined with their diverse ideological affiliations to lead to a lot of conflict. In the period during which I carried out my observations, the dismantling of affirmative action policies was a lightning rod for many arguments.

An interesting characteristic of the affirmative action debates I observed was that students strove, as one of them put it, to "keep it intellectual rather than personal." But despite the eschewing of politics in the classroom and the uncivil debate I heard in the halls, newspaper reports showed that Boalt students had at times taken their polarized racial politics very seriously and personally. In 1995, someone put letters in the mailboxes of all the members of Law Students of African Descent stating that they were taking the places of deserving potential (white) law students. And in 1997, fifty-four students were arrested during a sit-in at the Boalt Hall registrar's office intended to protest the sharp drop in the admission of underrepresented minorities that year (Gray and van der Vegt, 1997).[24]

In the tension between, on the one hand, the normative avoidance of politics in the classroom and forced congeniality of interactions in the halls, and, on the other hand, the pattern of periodic dramatic political activity on the part of some students, a theme emerged which is characteristic of much of law-student behavior: one of repression and release. Law students tried so hard to avoid politics as a distraction, as something that could spin out of control and consume classroom time or fracture peer relationships along ideological fault lines, that when some did allow their political feelings free reign, they burst forth violently.

Few of the law students in my study sample gave expression to political passion, but most exhibited the pattern of repression and release in their leisure choices. Students kept their energy focused on academics most of the time. In interviews, they reported cutting back rather severely on their socializing, their domestic chores, their exercising—all other aspects of their lives. When students did allow themselves to indulge in leisure activities, they used the vocabulary of "cutting loose." They caroused and consumed a lot of alcohol, socializing one another to "work hard, play hard." On Fridays, a group of students regularly organized what was mockingly called the Bar Review, noting the name and address of a selected bar on the chalkboards of the large lecture halls so that students could combine some serious drinking with a networking opportunity.

Most law students did not allow themselves to cut loose too often because they feared it would distract them from their studies. What they did regularly to reward themselves for maintaining their studious concentration was consume luxuries. A Calvinist streak generally made students rationalize this consumption by buying only "necessary" luxuries. They did not want to appear gauche in their (anticipated) nouveau riche state, and they stayed away from ruby cufflinks or cocktail rings, but they did use their (often newly expanded) credit to purchase tasteful leather attachés, the latest laptop computers, salon hairstyles, and, above all, food.

For law students, lunch did not signify simply the requirement of eating a midday meal. In fact, when deadlines or examinations approached, students did not consider lunch a requirement at all and skipped it. Getting lunch allowed them to efficiently combine an opportunity to reward themselves for ongoing hard work with an opportunity for networking. When students felt they could afford to take an hour or two away from studying, they often went out to lunch in small groups, exploring the cultural resources of Berkeley and sampling its cuisine. At times when they felt more academic pressure, they met as study groups in the Belli Commons, enjoying lattés and pizzaioli without cutting into their preparation time. And when the pressure was really on, they skipped lunch and then let others know that they had, turning a nutritional loss into a competitive win.

Competition was an ongoing theme in all aspects of law-student life, and interactions outside the classroom were no exception. Students employed masculine conversation rules when talking together, dueling to get the next word in, engaging in verbal jousting, and in general seeking to score points. For example, I listened to two 3Ls compete in such a discussion to see who handled a larger caseload with greater ease ("The workload wasn't out of line with the number of hours I put in here"), who felt more comfortable socializing with partners ("I didn't find them to be stiff-shirted—they were friendly and accessible to me"), and who was given the more amusingly luxurious perks ("They got us a block of seats for a Yankees game and sent us all with bag lunches from Zabar's so we wouldn't have to eat stadium hot dogs"). Incoming students standing nearby listened with expressions of bemused admiration on their faces, absorbing the socializing import of the 3Ls' chest puffing.

When the law students participated in extracurricular activities together, they continued to socialize one another into a spirit of hardworking competitiveness. Boalt students took their extracurriculars seriously; at a meeting of Law Students of African Descent, members followed Roberts' Rules of Order, with a man in khakis and a blue button-down shirt presiding and two other members taking notes on laptops. The *Ecology Law Review* set minimum hour commitments like a law firm establishing minimum billable hours. Even the bar-review pub crawlers organized and announced their outings with cool efficiency.

In the end, despite the hearty handshakes and toothy grins, law students didn't seem to be having much fun. Over and over again they told me in interviews that they were putting their noses to the grindstone now so that they could reap the rewards later—but if they imagined that legal practice would be more relaxing, they were in for a rude awakening. By the time they graduated, however, years of influence by professors and peers would likely have caused them to become accustomed to hard work, long hours, and smiles unaccompanied by moral support. Meanwhile, most students professed to be enjoying themselves, because to do otherwise would make them look "weak." But students occasionally let loose less sanguine assessments of the Law School experience. One morning, walking through the central courtyard, I saw on one of the benches a large, chalked graffito reading, "This is HELL."

**At the School of Social Welfare:** If the behavior law students modeled for one another was characterized by numerous tensions—between the repression and expression of ideological diversity, between the compulsion to study and the desire for a respite from work, and between the ethos of competition and networking—the behavior social welfare students modeled for one another was much more homogeneous. They did not have to repress dissensus because there was so little of it in the first place. While the U.C. Berkeley School of Social Welfare had a reputation as a hotbed of strident, hyperpoliticized students, this was not what I observed.

One manner in which the students' consensus was revealed to me was in their response to the dismantling of affirmative action: unanimous disagreement with the policy. They expressed dismay at the falling percentage of Berkeley undergraduates from underrepresented minorities. But when I asked students during interviews whether they were aware that there had been a drop in the number of students of color admitted to their own school, most of those I asked gave surprised denials. I believe that the lack of controversy in discussions of affirmative action at Haviland Hall caused students to believe that nothing controversial could have happened there.

This tendency to be unaware of their own lack of awareness due to their shared liberal ideology occurred regularly in the area of race. The social welfare students displayed a highly developed racial etiquette. Students of all colors spoke of racism as a pervasive problem they must fight, white students deferred to students of color on issues pertaining to race and ethnicity, students regularly declared the need to tailor social welfare programs to reach out to all people, and students affirmed the need for social workers to have "cultural competence." Both white students and students of color expected to be "called on it" if they made a culturally insensitive statement.

But most of the white students did not seem to be aware that the demand for "cultural competence" made many students of color feel alienated, cast as outsiders by their own peers. There were two problems that led to these feelings of alienation: first, the term "cultural competence" was used only in reference to people of color, implying that it was normal for people to be familiar with white culture and ignorant of the cultures of people of color; and second, students of color were expected by their peers to act as representatives of their people, and to serve as cultural docents. As Pia put it:

> [Students of color] feel that they have to come into the classroom wearing two hats—teacher and student—because they feel like they're there to learn from the instructors, but then sometimes other students in the class . . . will say something expecting them to act as the teacher and say to them, . . . "I'm going to clarify this, I will tell you how it really is," and they have to serve as a teacher and kind of clear up some misconceptions.

Students from particularly underrepresented groups, such as Paula, who was a Pueblo Indian, complained that they were called upon so often "to represent" that they felt more like anthropological study subjects than students. But white students spoke only positively about how enriching the contributions of students of color were and seemed unaware of how their behavior sent alienating messages to their peers.[25]

Social welfare students' behavior did not always accord with their ideological commitments. Still, their ideological consensus was real, and it was consolidated and augmented through mutual reinforcement. One of the components of the students' consensus was that feelings must be disclosed, validated, and supported. If the law students lived a life of repression, the social welfare students lived a life of expression. As I have mentioned, I often felt when sitting with a group of social welfare students that I was attending a group counseling session, as everyone "owned" their feelings and "acknowledged" others'. The social welfare students never gave one another the forced smiles demanded by the networking ethos. Instead, I got the impression of the overwhelming earnestness of the therapeutic ethos.

Part of the social work students' therapeutic ethos was an emphasis on health and balance. Unlike their Law School counterparts, these students claimed that professional obligations should not keep them from eating right, trying to get a good night's rest, giving attention to their partners and families, or exercising. A good example that contrasts the two student mindsets is their attitude toward lunch. I have described how the law students tended to treat food as a luxurious reward to compensate them for their usual ascetic focus on work. For the social welfare students, however, food was treated like medicine: it had to be good for you. Social work students made a display of their adherence to the therapeutic ethos by eating lunch in class.[26]

When students began snacking in class during the second class meetings, there was a trend toward healthy snacks and environmentally sound reusable containers, but it was not yet hegemonic. In Professor Dunn's class, students snacked on a banana, pretzels in a sandwich bag, a bagel, a bag of Sun Chips, a chocolate-chip cookie, and a bag of Doritos. That students were already beginning to feel embarrassed to eat unhealthy food in front of their peers was evident in the behavior of the student eating the Doritos, who kept the bag concealed beneath the table and hid the chips behind her hand when bringing them to her mouth, while the other students munched openly. Two weeks later in the same class, students were flagrantly eating lunches in addition to snacks, and the health-and-environment-consciousness norm was firmly entrenched. One student drank a huge green wheatgrass smoothie that looked like a Big Gulp of puréed lawn. One Asian woman ate from a Tupperware container of pasta salad, and a second was eating a tomato, lettuce, and cheese sandwich on thick-sliced whole grain bread. Snacks included various fruits and crackers in reusable containers. Students sat surrounded by their displays of healthy foods much in the way law students sat surrounded by piles of books.

In their interactions outside class, social welfare students continued to operate according to the therapeutic ethos. They always tried to show that they were treating one another as ends in themselves rather than as a means to some end, and that they were available to help one another with support and problem solving. Their socializing pattern little resembled the abstain-and-indulge pattern followed by the law students; they socialized with one another regularly in pairs and small groups. Not only did they not organize pub crawls, they abjured such activity as unhealthy and leading to alcoholism. They displayed healthy, caring, environmentally conscious lifestyles to one another in their interactions because this enhanced their professional reputations, just as disdainfully ignoring one's well-being to focus on work enhanced law students' professional reputations.

In engaging in personal interactions, the social welfare students I observed employed feminine discussion rules. They did not interrupt one another; in fact, if two students started talking at the same time, a sort of "after you, my dear Alphonse" comic routine was likely to ensue. Rather than engaging in chest-puffing self-aggrandizement, they displayed modesty about their accomplishments and gave credit to others for their support. For example, after she was complimented for an oral report she gave, Chloe stated, "I was impressed by every single one of the reports that I heard, and if I hadn't gotten such good comments from Stephanie, my presentation would have been less strong than most people's." The social welfare students also rarely debated and instead tried to come to an understanding of one another's position. They socialized one another to view conversations as being not about winning, but about relationship building.

We have seen that students served as role models for one another and were an important source of socializing messages. Professional students entering an unfamiliar environment were on unsteady footing and looked to one another for cues to appropriate behavior. For this reason, their behavior struck me as unusually herdlike: students looked to see where their peers were moving and moved that way as well, so that propensities or trends were amplified. An androgynous look swept over women students at the Law School; a craze for health food and Tupperware took hold of the social welfare students. And in this process of mutual reinforcement and amplification, students not only picked up elements of a professional habitus, they exaggerated them. Law students abjured politics to a much greater degree than did their professors, and social welfare students were more moralistic and touchy-feely than were their professors. This tendency toward group hegemony had an alienating effect on students who did not participate in it in some way. That is, while it led some students to move in the direction of greater identity consonance, it aggravated identity dissonance in others.

# 5 Lessons Learned

*The Socializing Influence of Pedagogy*

If you were a newly arrived professional student, you would probably observe your surroundings, your professors, and your peers carefully as you tried to make sense of your new world. But you would almost certainly focus more intently on your schoolwork. After all, while students were not told that their professional success depended upon their successful internalization of professional identity, they were constantly told that they must "master" torts and contracts and constitutional law, or needs assessments, intervention plans, and case-management skills. What is important to note is that pedagogy conveys much more than the formal substance matter of the classes: the nature of the professional role is also conveyed, if indirectly. This chapter examines teaching at professional schools, not to consider what pedagogic methods are most effective, but from the perspective of their influence on professional socialization.[1]

## Pedagogic Methods

**At the School of Law:** The Law School professors I observed all employed what legal educators term the Socratic method of case analysis.[2] If Socrates himself were to visit a Law School classroom, he would hardly recognize the legal pedagogic method that bears his name. The progression from thesis to antithesis to synthesis is absent in legal pedagogy, as is the spirit of an open-ended pursuit of truth. Professors used their "Socratic method" to get their students to learn legal rules without telling them what those rules were. A professor would ask a student a series of questions about a legal case, through which the student was expected to derive legal rules by thinking on his feet. Professors claimed that the Socratic method would teach students how to "think like a lawyer," a skill which was never defined but highly esteemed. The learning of "black-letter law"—the governing legal rules—was said to be incidental and of secondary importance.

The Socratic classroom was an uncomfortable place for the novice law student. The lecture halls were amphitheatrical, arranged around a small stage upon which the professor stood at a lectern, with the students in numbered, assigned seats at rising arcs of tables. This allowed the Law School lecture hall to function as what Michel Foucault terms a "panopticon" (1979), fixing each student within the range of the professor's disciplinary gaze. In each classroom I observed, the professor employed a seating chart to call upon students by name. The three main professors in my sample all referred to students by their first names, but other Boalt professors used last names, which made the classroom seem an even more formal and serious place.[3]

The Law School lecture halls served to entrench hierarchical relations. Each student's seat was placed so she faced the professor but could see only the backs of the heads of most of her peers. Students quickly learned that their interactions with peers were considered irrelevant to professional success, since professors required that all comments be directed at them. In structuring what they referred to as class "discussions," professors would call upon a series of students, who would make their comments to the professor rather than to one another. Students could engage one another intellectually only through third-person statements to the professor (e.g., "I agree in part with Brandon's argument, but it can't apply in all situations"). Hence, students were given the message that peer interactions were unimportant, while hierarchical relations were highly consequential.

Sometimes professors would solicit volunteers for Socratic questioning, but more often they would "cold call" students without warning.[4] This meant that although the typical first-year Law School class included about a hundred students, most of whom could not be called upon on a given day, no student could ever feel safe from exposure, pinned in his assigned seat as he was. Professors would often call upon a student who was looking down, highlighting a casebook, or trying to look busy yet inconspicuous—that is, whoever looked like she was trying to avoid being called upon. Nor did enduring one cold call provide immunity from the possibility of future questioning. Professor Hoffert in particular was fond of inflicting repeated cold calls upon the same student.

Although, according to the ideology of the legal profession, the Socratic method is aimed at teaching students to reason quickly and logically, in practice its effect is quite different. The series of questions asked by Boalt professors often seemed aimed primarily at tripping up the unwary—catching a student in a contradiction or "sloppy" thinking.   Interestingly, two of the three professors I regularly observed (who engaged in this sort of prosecutorial questioning no less than the third) claimed that their pedagogic behavior was more humane than some archetypical Socratic ideal; for example, Professor Santana told students he would employ a "modified Socratic method, that is, a Socratic method with an unenforceable promise to be nice." He continued, "I have no intent to humiliate, but I *will* push you." These disclaimers served to delegitimate the fear that prosecutorial Socratic questioning evoked in students (since, after all, this professor was trying to be *nice*).

Although the questions a professor asked were almost always open-ended, fairly often he had in mind a specific answer. These "what color am I thinking of" questions were frustrating for the class, leaving the student who had been called upon feeling intellectually inadequate as he tossed out a series of incorrect answers, and the rest of the class irritated at him for appearing so dimwitted. Yet at least with this type of question the professor would state when an answer was correct. An even more common pedagogical tactic was for a professor to question a number of students about a case, allowing each to develop a different theory to explain its outcome. As a class drew on while an ever-growing plethora of contradictory theories staggered into being, students would grow ever more confused and frustrated. When the professor finally summarized and clarified the rule, it was as if he had pulled a rabbit out of a hat, magically resolving the students' confusion. This tactic lent the law professors a patina of brilliance and authority, especially when students felt that justice demanded a certain case outcome and threw out whatever strained theory came to mind that might reach that end. After one emotional discussion of a case involving the seizure of traditional lands from a Native American tribe, I wrote in my field notes: "The students seem to be flailing around endlessly about the rights of Native Americans; Santana then responds articulately, making their less well-rationalized responses, which are grounded in emotional or moral impulses, sound mushy and poorly considered."

In general, Socratic questioning reminded me of a hazing ritual. A student, when cold called, would often give a start or flush, evidence of a flash of adrenaline that indicated she experienced the call as a threat. She then had to endure an inquisition before a large audience.[5] As a participant observer, I felt sympathetic anxiety for a student who was floundering, and relief and respect if the floundering student salvaged the situation and came up with a response that received the professor's approval; I could see by their expressions that other students often experienced similar sympathetic feelings. Suffering together through a hazing ritual is a source of solidarity, whether in a fraternity, the army, or a law-school classroom. Although the law students I observed were not drawn together by direct classroom interactions, they bonded by surviving Socratic hazing.

Although Socratic hazing has the positive effect of producing solidarity and a sense of pride in those who endure it well, it also produces negative effects. First, it produces fear and anxiety among all initiates. For those who fail a Socratic test, unable to come up with a satisfactory answer to the professor's questions, there is humiliation and a sense of intellectual inadequacy. I observed that students whose performances flopped in the amphitheater withdrew for some time from paying attention to the ongoing progress of the class. According to one of my interview subjects, this was because students who fail adequately to respond "rehash everything that they said, and everyone thinks that they're so stupid for saying this." Such rehashing behavior, in which students replay their performances and consider what alternative responses might have salvaged the situation, detracted from students' learning experiences both inside and outside the classroom.

I observed that law professors made light of the fear they inspired, prefacing their questions with comments such as "Let me pick on you," or moving on from a floundering student by saying, "I'll name another victim." This light, mocking tone was intended to diffuse tension, and in fact such comments always inspired a wave of laughter, which served to release anxiety. However, such light mockery also delegitimated students' fear; the message to students was that they ought to toughen up and stop taking things so seriously. It also had a sadistic edge: it was directed at students who were at their most vulnerable. I believe that this contributed to the fact that, as the semester progressed, students came to lose sympathy for those who became flustered or froze under questioning. Identifying with the oppressor, as it were, students lost patience with those who floundered; some shot their hands up to volunteer a more adequate performance, while others contented themselves with sighing impatiently or fidgeting. This decrease in empathy, an element of emotional habitus, makes it clear that the Socratic method, while not the most efficient teaching technique, functions well as a socializing procedure.

**At the School of Social Welfare:** Students entering the School of Social Welfare did not encounter a unitary pedagogic method, in marked contrast to the situation at the Law School. Instead, a professor's pedagogic methods depended upon the type of course and the professor's preferences. This use of multiple methods sent the general message to students that the profession of social work lacked hegemony—that it was flexible (looking at the multiple methods positively) or that it lacked consensus (looking at them negatively). Because of this lack of consensus, social work has been deemed a "weak" profession by sociologists (see Turner and Turner, 1990). But my observations revealed the social welfare classroom to be a place where socializing influences functioned strongly.

Professor Lipman's Introduction to the Profession was an interesting case, because the lecture-based pedagogic method employed was atypical compared to that of most social work classes, yet it was experienced by all the first-year students in the cohorts I observed, being the sole course the entire class was required to attend simultaneously. Professor Lipman's class was somewhat similar to the Law School classrooms, in that a hundred students sat in fixed rows facing him, although the rows were straight rather than amphitheatrical, and he did not stand on a stage. The pedagogic format Professor Lipman employed was typical of college courses rather than of law school: he lectured while students took notes, and he periodically invited students to respond to some point, staging a limited discussion. This arrangement was clearly hierarchical, although it lacked the hazing elements of a Law School course: all participation was voluntary, and rather than peppering a student with challenging questions, Professor Lipman treated positively and respectfully whatever contribution a student made. Also in contrast to Socratic pedagogic practice, student interactions were encouraged, both informally (students were given a ten-minute break during class to stretch and chat) and formally (in classroom debate).

Professor Lipman made a rather extensive effort to foster debate, which was atypical among the social welfare classes and not terribly successful. The other social welfare professors I observed all employed a discussion paradigm rather than a debate paradigm. Professor Lipman saw debate as academically rigorous and avoidance of debate as a weak "P.C. reflex," and he sought to train students in principled debating techniques. On the first day of class he distributed a handout outlining Dahmer's Discussion Code and proceeded to go over its principles.[6] That he offered the handout suggests that Professor Lipman did not expect his students to be familiar with debating practice. (Consider, for example, that he did not give handouts on how to take notes, access the Internet, or demonstrate sensitivity to the feelings of peers, each of which he expected students to do.) Despite the handout and his advocacy, however, Professor Lipman's efforts to foster debate among his students were not very successful. I do not believe, as Professor Lipman seemed to, that this was because students feared to make controversial statements because they would face an attack by the "P.C. Police."[7]

Instead, I believe that students were being trained to foster another habitus in the rest of their classes that was antithetical to the debate paradigm.

In the other social welfare classes I observed for any time (a total of seven), professors employed a discussion paradigm of pedagogy, seeking to emphasize consensus rather than conflict. A central skill taught in each of these classes was affirmation: the ability to respond to other people in a way that would make them feel heard and accepted. For example, Professor Dunn modeled affirmation skills by leaning forward to listen, nodding or murmuring "mmm-hmm," and responding to each student's input with positive words, such as, "Thank you for adding that. Great. I appreciate it." Students received no handout titled "The Principles of Affirmative Discussion" because there was no need for one: although differing pedagogic formats were employed in different classes, in all the classes I observed except Professor Lipman's, the principles of affirmative discussion were employed.

According to the unwritten principles of affirmative discussion, when an individual hears a point of view with which she does not agree, she ought to seek a reason to affirm the other's point of view anyway (often by grounding it in different life experiences), or, if her search is unsuccessful, she ought still to say something supportive. A common professorial response under such circumstances was to say, "Thank you for sharing." It would be a violation of affirmative discussion principles for one discussion participant to negate another's input by saying, "You're wrong." For example, in Professor Ruth's Gerontology Practicum, when a student asserted something with which the professor disagreed, she modeled an affirmative style of disagreement by beginning her rebuttal, "I hear what you're saying, but in almost all cases I have been involved with . . ." In short, the principles of affirmative discussion are discordant with debating principles (which aim to disaffirm), and it was in affirmative discussion principles that most social welfare professors I observed trained their students. That students modeled affirmative discussion techniques is evident in this statement by Janice, one of my interviewees: "I think most of the professors are very encouraging and think of what we have to say; even if it's wrong, they try to turn it their way, and actually watching them do that is really good for me because I see how they use the situation and kind of turn it around and say, Well, this is a good way to look at this, and it's kind of nice to learn to use with my clients."

The classroom run according to affirmative discussion principles seemed an empathetic place. No social welfare professor would ever cut off a floundering student by saying, "I'll name another victim." On the contrary, professors expressed to students that they were conscious of the potential for their exercises of authority to hurt students' feelings, and they attempted to diminish this potential. For example, when Professor Dunn told a student, "I won't call on you every time your hand is raised, to give others a chance to participate," he went on, "if you're okay with that," and waited for her nod of acceptance, which he acknowledged with a nod of his own. It is important to note, however, that neither this open acknowledgment of the potential of their power to hurt nor the seeking of confirmation that the professor's actions had not hurt a student's feelings meant that the social welfare professors lacked authority.

As a matter of fact, the consensus-seeking authority of the social welfare professors I observed was more effective than the law professors' imposition of power. Law students fearing humiliation might obey the orders of their professors with alacrity while thinking rebellious thoughts. But when a social work professor asked, "Are we ready to move on?" or said, "Whenever you're ready," to a small group that continued their discussion after the others had finished, he received both external obedience and internal compliance. Social work professors asserted an authority that was often greater than their words objectively suggested.

Besides the use of affirmative discussion techniques, a commonality among all the social welfare classes I observed, other than Professor Lipman's, was that they were held in the seminar rooms of Haviland Hall. These classrooms contained either several movable conference tables and chairs, or thirty or so of the sort of chairs with small, attached arm tables commonly found in high schools. These were typically arranged so that students could sit in a circle, with the professor's authority quietly marked by her position at one end of the tables, or at her own table, or a central position by the blackboard. When class included small group exercises, the students rearranged the furniture into suitably sized groupings. If the Law School classrooms taught fixity with their immovable chairs, the social welfare classrooms taught flux.[8]

The circular shape of the social welfare classroom arrangements created omnidirectional power relations, shaping the circle not as an absence of hierarchical power but rather as the full presence of horizontal power relations. In other words, whereas at Boalt each student was constantly responsible to the disciplining gaze of the professor, at Haviland each student was constantly responsible to the disciplinary gaze of every other student, as well as of the professor. If the Law School classrooms were Foucauldian panopticons, the social welfare classrooms were omniopticons, resulting in a more effective perfusion of the classroom by discipline than the Law

School's amphitheaters could produce. Yet this effect was denied by social welfare professors, who presented their circular classroom arrangements as liberating and egalitarian. When Professor Alverson termed as "controlling and hierarchical and generally unfriendly" the rows she found the chairs in her classroom arranged in, she implied that as the students moved the chairs into a semicircle, they removed control and hierarchy from the classroom. By denying that surveillance and power operate in their classrooms, the social welfare professors delegitimated their students' sense of being observed, evaluated, and controlled.

Authority in the social welfare classroom was not reduced but diffused, and hence its sources multiplied, as every student became a potential source of discipline for his peers. A central way in which students were made to feel responsible to and for one another was through the pedagogic technique of assigning group exercises. Professors teaching the Foundations of Social Work Practice classes all employed group exercises to teach practice skills. For example, Professor Dunn organized a role-playing group exercise in which students playing social workers were to attempt to mediate between representatives of the homeless and representatives of business, police, and local governmental agencies who want to "clean up the streets."[9] First, students met in small groups to agree upon their positions as ostensible business leaders, civic leaders, and so forth. Then, Professor Dunn arranged the chairs and tables into three concentric circles for the role-played mediation. Students who volunteered to speak as the representatives of their small groups sat in the center circle.

As the exercise progressed, while the group representatives did all the talking, they were subjected to surveillance by the circles of students surrounding them. Students from each group kept their eyes upon those of their respective representatives; they indicated with nods when they felt that their points were being conveyed correctly by their representatives, and with frowns or tiny head shakes if they felt a point was going astray. After the representative from the homeless group made an impassioned speech to the other representatives, members of her group showed their approval by smiling and symbolically clapping with silent fingertips. And when the representative of the police made points that the homeless group felt were insensitive, they rustled their papers and huffed. In the social welfare classroom, every person in the room functioned as an evaluator, with the professor's authority differing not in kind, but only in degree.

Social work students were made to feel responsible for one another as members of quasi–support groups in their Practicum classes. Professors of the two Practicum classes I observed periodically invited students to raise incidents or issues from their internship placements that were causing them concern. In some cases, professors expected students to provide one another with moral support. For example, in Professor Ruth's Gerontology Practicum there was a long discussion of "first-day jitters" in which students expressed the anxieties they felt while the rest of the class gave affirmative responses to encourage them. In other cases, professors expected students to provide concrete advice to one another.

The following classroom exchange provides an example of the dynamic that arose when students were asked to offer one another guidance:

> Rachel:   I'm worried that I could sort of allow myself to be codependent with a client of mine. She's a seventeen-year-old single mother. I'm feeling worried about how I took her to the Medi-Cal office because I knew she wouldn't do it herself, because she has transportation issues that she wasn't dealing with, so I picked her up and took her there myself and made her fill out the papers. I can feel that I'm trying to take care of her because I like her.

[Members of the class laugh lightly, say "Uh-oh," and mockingly shake their heads. Two students raise their hands to comment, and Professor Alverson calls on them in turn.]

> Luz:   You don't have to feel like it's necessarily so bad, because a seventeen-year-old is different from, like, a thirty-year-old, and a seventeen-year-old, you know, needs more support.
>
> Jocelyn:   Yes, a seventeen-year-old is probably not mature. But if you keep taking care of her in this way, my experience is that when you leave, the client falls apart. So do what you feel you have to, but you need to make her take some responsibility so she learns the skills she needs.
>
> Prof. Alverson:   Thank you for your suggestions. What *I'd* like to suggest is that there is an alternative to either making excuses for the client or coming down hard on her. Find out what her motivation is, and why she's resisting, so she can learn to be accountable. She may not know her own motivation

> and need help connecting the dots. . . . Meanwhile, it's
> appropriate for you to give her the sort of concrete
> assistance she and her child need.

In expecting students to guide and advise one another, Professor Alverson gave them partial responsibility for one another's instruction. Yet by steering these group-advice sessions and providing what amounted to the final word, she retained her authority. Although she phrased her comments as merely one set of suggestions among others, it was evident that she and her students treated her comments as more equal than others. This typical classroom exchange reveals a dynamic wherein responsibility is diffused among professor and students, surveillance is shared by professors and students, and ultimate authority is retained by a professor while hierarchy is concealed.

If looked at side by side, legal pedagogy looks more authoritative, rigorous, and harsh, while social welfare pedagogy appears less authoritative, softer, and gentler. A law professor might believe that a social work professor was weak and ineffective. In fact, however, as we have seen, social work professors wield more authority in the classroom than they proclaim for themselves. Moreover, the understated authority of the social welfare professors is in fact more powerful and influential than that of the law professors, at least from a socialization perspective. An analogy can be made to the distinction between the regimes of torture and discipline in Foucault's *Discipline and Punish* (1979). As Foucault explains, although torture is more fearsome, discipline is more powerful; the former produces external compliance, and the latter, internal changes. Although both the legal and social work classrooms are in fact disciplinary arenas, legal pedagogy is closer to its crude origins in the system of punishment, while social welfare pedagogy is more evolved, positioned further along on the disciplinary continuum. As a more advanced disciplinary regime, the School of Social Welfare can make claims of humanitarianism, liberation from cruelty, full participation, and individualized attention while it alters its students more effectively and with less resistance than can a more punitive regime. Every time a social welfare professor asks if the class is ready to move on or forges a consensus on an issue of practice, she shapes the identities of all her students in some way, however small; when a law professor is subjecting a student to Socratic inquisition, the other students are to some degree free to ignore him or even to resist him in the privacy of their own thoughts. To the extent that such resistance is possible, identity dissonance can be prolonged for greater lengths of time.

# Professors as Humorists and Mentors

In addition to instructing students in the subject matter of their chosen professions, the professors I observed saw themselves as having other roles to play in students' lives (even if they did not understand these to include serving as role models of professional habitus). This fact emerged during the process of what sociologists term "entering the field," as I solicited professors who would be willing to allow me to observe in their classrooms. During preliminary discussions with them, I explained that I intended to observe the effects of professional education upon students. All the professors had something to say on the topic, and some commented at length about their role as educators and their desire to do more than impart substantive knowledge. They spoke, *inter alia*, of wanting to provide moral leadership (Professor Lipman), wanting to demystify the rituals of professional indoctrination (Professor Santana), and wanting to provide support to students from underprivileged backgrounds (Professor Alverson). The professors all acknowledged that attending professional school was a stressful experience and tried to take some steps to relieve that stress for their students. At the Law School, the preferred method of relieving stress was to lighten the tense mood in the classroom with a good laugh. At the School of Social Welfare, professors instead focused on making students feel more secure by giving them advice. Acting as humorists and mentors, professors sent important socializing messages to their students.

## *The Use of Humor*

**At the School of Law:** As I have mentioned, the Law School professors liked to establish a light, bantering tone in their classrooms. Law students facing Socratic inquiry were a serious and anxious bunch, and by inducing them to laugh, professors sought to lighten things up a little. It appeared to me that law professors viewed humor as a form of public service, a way to distribute pleasure instead of pain. Professors were obligingly liberal in dispensing humorous remarks.

I was struck by the markedly cruel flavor of the humor employed. It was largely gallows humor, making light of fear, pain, and injustice. Gallows humor, as the name implies, is usually employed to lighten the fear of people *in extremis*, and its use indicated the degree of stress that the law students were suffering. Since gallows humor is intended to release tension regarding anxiety-provoking phenomena, we can deduce the nature of students' anxieties by focusing on the subject matter of the jokes they were told.

One topic for law professors' jokes was the Socratic method itself. For example, fifteen minutes into the first day of class, Professor Hoffert introduced the topic of consideration by stating the legal rule.[10] He then said, as an aside, "I'm cheating now by giving you the formula instead of trying to Socratic it out of you." The class burst into laughter. If you think of what words usually fill the blank in the phrase "____ it out of you," you can see that the Socratic method is presented as a matter of domination, assault, or torture, and this is in fact how many students whom I interviewed experienced it, especially in the first months. Most students would much rather have had their professors just tell them the legal rules, and the joke gets its punch by playing on the professors' usual unwillingness to do so.

Other jokes about Socratic inquiry played upon students' frustrations with the "what color am I thinking of" nature of much Socratic questioning. For example, after a student answered a question posed to him by Professor Santana, the professor stated, "Good answer, because it is the one I wanted, and if you didn't give it we'd have to go on and on." In another joke that played upon Socratic cruelty, a student in the same class responded to a line of questioning by Professor Santana by saying, "I know what you want me to say, but I don't want to walk into your trap." Professor Santana replied, with a mocking smile, "Why not? This has great pedagogical value." That got a huge laugh, arising out of students' concern that their feelings were given little weight in comparison to abstract intellectual values.

In constructing hypothetical situations for legal analysis, the law professors I observed often included a supposedly comic theme of cruelty toward students. Professor Tate began a series of questions by stating, "Let's say I throw my pen at Judy, intending to scare her." After twenty minutes the hypothetical had escalated to the point where Professor Tate was playfully pretending to throw bricks at people with the intent to hurt them. Again, laughter arose from students' apprehension regarding Socratic assault at the hands of their professors. Students particularly enjoyed situations like these where the professor playacted assaulting them, perhaps because the professors seemed to ham it up in their most slapstick mode when they made light of their own power in this way. Students were chortling and hooting when Professor Santana explored the law of trespass by invading their personal space, shouting at them, and clapping erasers together to sprinkle them with chalk dust. In other assaultive hypotheticals, the humor rode on the student's hypothetical retaliation, as when Professor Hoffert jestingly proposed a situation in which he threatened to kill a student, in hypothetical response to which she went out and bought an AK-47, after which he said, "Fooled ya!" and she sued him to recover the cost of the gun.

Other jokes at the Law School played upon students' fears that they themselves would become cruel once they were fully socialized. Some humor presented cruelty as necessary in a lawyer, as when Professor Hoffert provided students with a legal claim that they could employ to throw their opponent "into a healthy state of terror." Other jests jokingly presented cruelty as inherent in the structure of the law, as when Professor Hoffert said, "Now we'll get to a case where the result is at last unfair—as it should be!" Still other jokes mocked disempowered individuals. Such politically incorrect jokes were commonplace; examples include Professor Tate's question about a five-year-old involved in a case—"You don't think the little bastard was just lying?"—and Professor Hoffert's proposal to improve a homeless man's lot in life by giving him a bottle of single-malt scotch. Such jokes got their impact at least in part from making light of students' anxiety that they would lose their concern for social justice.

In no class was sadistic humor more prevalent than in the Torts class I observed. Since all tort cases involve injury and redress, they have the strong potential to kindle students' sense of sympathy and justice. Yet there is a tradition in law schools of torts professors making light of plaintiffs' suffering, and Professor Tate provided a paradigmatic example of this phenomenon. His "humorous" hypotheticals went far beyond throwing pens at students; in just one class they included a husband mistakenly giving his wife arsenic to spoon into her tea, students latching a locker-room door so that the only way for a fat peer in the shower to exit would be to walk through a gym filled with three thousand basketball spectators, a furrier sealing an assistant in a refrigerated stockroom and not realizing it until being served a frozen dessert, and a baby being accidentally locked in a bank vault. Professor Tate sometimes indulged in sadistic humor for no obvious pedagogic reason, as when he brought in a newspaper clipping about a bank robber who put into his pants a packet of bills which contained a concealed explosive dye packet. The packet exploded, burning the bank robber's genitals. Professor Tate's comment was, "Now that's what I call hot pursuit!" The constant barrage of sadistic humor in Professor Tate's class conveyed the message to students that a callous attitude was an appropriate part of a lawyerly habitus and a good coping mechanism for students. Certainly a student with a sensitive, uncalloused nature (such as was typical for social welfare students) would experience Professor Tate's class as a constant assault on her sensibilities. In fact, during the first couple of weeks of classes, some students occasionally gasped in shock in Torts class. As students became desensitized, however, this came to an end. Students either joined in the laughter or looked on with an expression of irritation rather than of pain and shock.

If Professor Tate's favorite subject for humor was pain and suffering, Professor Hoffert was inclined to jest about the wealth of lawyers. When presenting the case of a client who was having difficulty making a legally enforceable gift of cash, he bantered, "As a lawyer, you will gladly and easily relieve the client of his money." When introducing complexities into a legal regime that at first seemed simple, he was fond of remarking, "If that were all that was involved, no one would pay lawyers lots of money." He even made a money joke at my expense, when he constructed a hypothetical in which a student loaned me, the "poor sociologist," a thousand dollars. The laughter that rippled around the room at these jests revealed that students were anxious about the positions they would soon occupy near the top of the economic class system.

The humor employed by the professors at Boalt Hall played generally on the theme of power. Professors made light of their power over students, and of the power students would hold over others as lawyers and as members of the ruling class. The coping mechanism they held out to their apprehensive students was desensitization to the pain students and others felt. The message professors seemed to send was for students to grow a callus over their bleeding hearts and learn not to take things so seriously.

**At the School of Social Welfare:** The last thing professors at the School of Social Welfare wanted was for their students to become callused and unempathetic. As a result, while their counterparts at the Law School were tossing off one outrageous quip after another, the social welfare professors maintained a serious, earnest tone in their classrooms. Moreover, the professors of social welfare proselytized against the use of humor as a defense mechanism.

Social welfare professors cautioned that, while laughter was a wonderful thing, it should always be used in an affirming rather than an injurious manner. Jokes were therefore to be approached very carefully, because so often their humor was at another's expense. The professors, in fact, were so cautious about jokes that they almost never made them.[11] It was only social workers visiting to talk about their agencies who told war stories in which clients' actions were mocked, or who cracked jokes about their clients' incapacities ("He was one brick short of a load"). The professors modeled disapproval of such incidents. The day after a practitioner at an adoption agency came to speak to members of her Practicum and quipped, "I'm in adoptions because I don't want to deal with the scum of the earth," Professor Alverson took time to lecture students regarding the impropriety of disrespectful humor.

If a well-socialized law student were to have had to listen to Professor Alverson's lecture on the dangers of humor, he might have rolled his eyes, perhaps trotting out the hackneyed charge that feminists have no sense of humor. Certainly no place better demonstrates the tendency of jokes to be cruel and insensitive than does the Law School; nevertheless, there is a grain of truth in the charge of relentless sobriety. Professors at Haviland Hall sometimes made comments that would sound like jokes almost anywhere else, but they and their students did not crack a smile. For example, one day Professor Lipman extolled the virtues of the Internet. After he had explained to students that they would be required to do a fair amount of their research online, he solemnly warned his students to "beware Internet addiction." At first I thought he was making a straight-faced joke about how social welfare Web sites were so useful and interesting that students would want to spend a lot of time exploring them, but he went on to mention symptoms students should recognize. He was serious—earnestly, gravely serious.

The humorous remarks that I did hear in social welfare classrooms came from the students' mouths. Instead of being directed downward at the disempowered, the students' quips were aimed upward at the powerful. For example, in Professor Dunn's class, where exercises centered on the issue of homelessness for several weeks, students tossed off several witticisms in defense of their hypothetical client population. Speaking with exaggerated patience to a student acting as a representative of local government, a student acting as an advocate for the homeless defined the problem as her clients understood it: "We need a *home*—that's why we're called the *homeless*." And when, during a class discussion of a shelter that accepted only clients suffering no problems with being addicted or battered, Professor Dunn asked a student, "What population *does* this agency serve?" the student snidely replied, "The perfect homeless." While humor in the Law School classroom was uncomfortably evocative of kicking the dog, the social welfare student quips were more in the nature of protests against such insensitivity.

### *Professional (Practice) Advice*

**At the School of Law:** If the Law School professors were free with their humor, while the School of Social Welfare professors forbore to indulge, the situation was reversed with respect to distributing advice. The law professors I observed conceived of themselves as mentors only toward the few students who worked as their research assistants or who met with them regularly in their offices.[12] The bulk of law students comprised an audience to be enlightened, entertained, and evaluated but held at a professional distance. To give too much explicit advice was deemed "hand-holding," a term implying both coddling and unseemly intimacy. If law professors stood in any way *in loco parentis*, it was as distant, authoritarian, paternal figures—like the military father who requires his children to address him as "sir."

During the first days of classes, each of the law professors I observed offered their fledgling students a minimum of advice on how to operate in legal academia. Professor Hoffert repeatedly exhorted students to speak in a louder voice, like a drama coach teaching students to project. Professor Santana urged students to volunteer to speak, rather than waiting fatalistically for a Socratic cold call. And Professor Tate gave students a demonstration of how to analyze a legal case by "briefing" it. This was little advice indeed for students plunged into a disorienting new milieu, but at least it was something.

In fact, the advice law professors offered students on performance in the classroom was quite generous in comparison to the advice professors offered regarding actual legal practice. Professor Hoffert gave the rather preposterous suggestion to his students that they immediately publish "novel solutions to intractable legal problems" and thus become famous before they even graduated. Professor Santana gave students a smattering of more practical suggestions: he told them to say, "May it please the court," before speaking to a judge; he suggested they use a style of argument that would come across as positive rather than negative; he listed some stock arguments; and he explained the importance of framing the "question presented" by a case in a favorable light. But to expect law students to learn to practice based upon the little advice they were given would be rather like expecting circus apprentices to learn to juggle merely by giving them some verbal pointers and suggesting that they try to become stars.

Notably missing from the smattering of pragmatic advice offered by the law professors was any suggestion about how to deal with clients. Whereas, as we shall see, social welfare professors discussed at length issues of communication and rapport involved in relating to clients, law professors trained their students only how to speak, not how to listen. Clients were abstractions in the law classroom—the faceless individuals who served the purpose of giving legal cases their titles.

The law professors also told their students few cautionary tales. Professor Tate presented as an object lesson a case in which a plaintiff with a "good set of facts" lost because of poor lawyering. The "moral" of the story was, according to Professor Tate: "The lawyer just plain blew it. He didn't think about it carefully enough." This statement of the moral of the tale provided little concrete advice to students, while framing lawyering in purely cognitive terms (ignoring as usual the role played by professional identity). The only other cautionary advice I recorded was Professor Hoffert's repeated caveat that students should disbelieve judges' statements that they do not consider fairness when determining whether there was sufficient consideration tendered in a case to create an enforceable contract. Professor Hoffert's assertion was that the law was fairer than it claimed to be (rather than vice versa).

Taken together, the bits of advice distributed by law professors to their students covered little of the new territory students had to master. As parental figures, law professors practiced tough love, tossing their students into the deep waters of the law and expecting that they would quickly learn to swim. They tried to offset the anxiety this sink-or-swim strategy provoked with humor, but not with hand-holding. This strategy sent a socializing message to students that an ethic of care was unlawyerly.

**At the School of Social Welfare:** If law professors reminded me of distant, military father figures, social welfare professors gave me the impression of what it might be like to have a pastor or rabbi for a parent: they were busy professionals but also extremely earnest. They wanted to be good role models and mentors. They liked to identify problems and give both pragmatic and moral advice on how to solve them. They empathized with confusion and anxiety but cautioned sternly against transgression. They were always concerned.

The social welfare professors I observed gave their students a lot of advice. They advised them on professional socialization, on the workings of the social welfare profession, and on professional practice. The advice they gave on professional socialization was scanty in comparison to the other types of advice they distributed, but it interested me a great deal, since it involved the topic of my book. Professor Lipman gave students advice on professional socialization on two occasions. Early on in his class, he told students that he was involved in a longitudinal study of social welfare students and warned them that they might lose their sense of purpose:

I'm sure you can still vaguely remember what you had in mind when you came here. That'll be completely gone in a few weeks, so you might as well take notes on it now. What Bradley and I are finding in our research is that students are less clear on what they want to do in the field than they were when they came in . . . and I think that's not a good thing.

This is a portrayal of the professional socialization process in negative terms, as leading to a loss of direction rather than redirecting naïve aspirations into more professional and effective channels.

Professor Lipman's negative view of professional socialization was also evident in the other bit of advice he gave on the topic. He explained that the helping professions such as social work and teaching provided underprivileged people with a route to middle-class status, but that in this process of having their class status raised, underprivileged individuals became interested in serving middle-class client populations, so that their community of origin did not benefit from their professionalization. Professor Lipman urged his students to serve poor populations and resist the "idea that you can only be a professional if you are tied to serving the middle class." He seemed concerned that students entered the social welfare program intending to serve underprivileged populations but would lose this sense of purpose and leave as comfortable counselors of the middle class.[13] On the one hand, his warning might have served to inoculate some students against undergoing such an alteration in their path. On the other hand, Professor Lipman himself had a notably upper-middle-class manner, and being committed to urging students to engage in direct services to the poor is not the same thing as engaging directly in serving the poor. In other words, Professor Lipman proselytized that students follow one path but modeled another, and students may have been influenced more by his habitus than by his exhortations.

Professor Alverson offered a piece of direct advice on professional identity to her students, and it was much more optimistic in tone than was Professor Lipman's advice on professional socialization:

There are all sorts of ways to be a professional. People learn to use their particular personal style to build a professional style on it, to make their personalities work for them. You will all learn to do it as well, and it will come to seem natural to you and to others.

It is interesting how this advice both elucidates and obscures the process of professional socialization. Professor Alverson explicitly informed her students what it feels like to internalize a role as identity: what at first seems unnatural and awkward comes to feel natural and smooth. This advice might have helped students gain insight into the process they were undergoing. But in her rosy portrayal of becoming a professional, professional socialization proceeds smoothly for everyone, and professional identity is consonant with a wide range of personal identities. This portrayal was inaccurate and did not prepare students to cope with identity dissonance.

The professors of social work I observed did not give a great deal of advice on professional socialization (although even one piece of such advice was 100 percent more than was offered by the professors of law). The professors at Haviland offered much more advice on the profession and practice of social work. A good deal of this advice related to professional power. The professors' comments revealed a deep ambivalence regarding the assertion of professional power; for example, Professor Dunn advised his students that they must be "assertive" and "control" all conversations with clients, but that they must not dominate, interrupt, or disempower their clients. This required of students a certain androgynous relation to conversational power: they should employ neither feminine deferential speech patterns nor masculine dominating speech patterns but should somehow control client interactions without dominating clients.

The social welfare professors both claimed and disclaimed professional power in their advice. They disclaimed power in part to prepare their students for instances of professional failure, as when Professor Dunn warned his students to watch out for the "miracle-worker fantasy."[14] More often, they disclaimed power for ideological reasons: they sought to promote the ideology of client empowerment. Professor Dunn claimed that while it might appear that funding organizations had great power, social workers moderate power, and clients little power, in fact the relationship was reversed. (He based this claim on a redefinition of power that shifted it from socioeconomic power to the power to alter a client's pattern of behavior.)[15] Professor Lipman claimed that social work was recognized as a profession solely to benefit clients, not social workers. He stated that the reason social work was granted professional status was so that a licensing requirement would be imposed, "not to grant status, but for consumer protection,"

Yet at the same time they disclaimed power as social workers, professors of social welfare warned students that they would wield power as social workers—power that was subject to abuse. Professor Alverson warned her students on several occasions that various parties might try to abuse the students' power to sanction parents or remove children from a home: angry neighbors might make false claims, or children might try to use the students to control their parents. Professor Lipman warned more generally that all social workers "need people to need us," and that this might lead social workers to create dependency and use people to gratify an urge to power.

I believe that the message professors sent with their mixed claims and denials of power was that to enter a "helping profession" was to enter a conflicted field. Helpers should be gentle and subordinate, while professionals should be authoritative and dominant; apprentices in a helping profession must somehow learn to be both. This was a much more complicated task than was required of law students, who had the straightforward mission of becoming powerful.

Professor Lipman seemed to believe that one of the themes all MSW students should be exposed to in an Introduction to the Profession class was that conflict and tension lie at the heart of the profession of social work. He described social work as characterized by a "conundrum" (social work sees poverty as a structural problem but intervenes on an individual level), by a "tension" ("being yourself" implies working with people like yourself, while "being a professional" requires working with different people), and by a "basic schizophrenia" (society licenses social workers to control dangerous clients, but social workers want social change to empower clients). Professor Lipman did not suggest that students might resolve these tensions, but he did convey that he acknowledged the difficulties they presented and empathized with students who found them frustrating.

A tension which no professor ever mentioned but which was pervasive in the advice they gave was the tension between the rational and the emotional imperatives of the profession of social work. Students were always advised to feel empathy for all clients, no matter how stigmatized they were as drug addicts, homeless people, child abusers, and so on: "We need to learn to experience these people as real human beings," said Professor Alverson. Students were also warned against becoming callous in an inappropriate self-protective strategy of "insulating" themselves. At the same time, students were warned against becoming overinvolved. When a student reported that she went home and cried about her clients, Professor Alverson counseled her: "That will lead to burn-out. You have to learn to protect yourself and avoid codependency." So not caring enough was deemed callous and unprofessional, but caring too much was deemed codependent and equally unprofessional.

That social welfare students were urged to learn to experience the appropriately moderate degree of empathy was one manifestation of a larger phenomenon: instrumental intimacy. While relationships between friends are "primary relationships," ends in themselves, relationships with clients are "secondary relationships," promoted as a means to an end. As Professor Dunn described them, relationships with clients should be characterized by limited involvement. Social workers should be empathetic and should engage in the limited sharing of emotions "in the interests of the client," but never to satisfy the social worker's own needs.

Furthermore, while the limited instrumental sharing of emotions was deemed professional, Professor Alverson advised that allowing "personal" feelings to impact professional decisions was unacceptable. For example, caseworkers should only remove a child from a home to prevent imminent harm from abuse or neglect; if students felt pained by not acting when a child was being treated poorly, although he was not in imminent danger, Professor Alverson cautioned, "You need to work these feelings out—not insert them into the decision to remove the child or not." Professors regularly made it clear that professional decisions were to be made rationally, and that while feelings and personal experience were valuable, rationality must be the ultimate guide in professional analysis. For example, while social welfare professors usually listened attentively to student expressions of their personal experiences and emotions, they tended to become less receptive to these in discussions of professional evaluation and decision making. For example, when Professor Dunn asked students how to tell if an agency was effective and received only responses based on personal experiences and feelings, his manner became somewhat abrupt, and he emphatically urged students to employ "the rational test": to ask if the agency accomplishes its stated goals.

As in the case of power, in the matter of balancing the rational with the emotional, the conflicted nature of a feminine profession was conveyed to students. Femininity is associated with emotionality in our culture, and professionalism with rationality. Social work students were shown that they should be sensitive and empathetic but in control of rather than ruled by their emotions, and, furthermore, that professionalism requires that their actions display the primacy of rationality. This was a complicated calculus of rationality and emotionality for students to become familiar with and internalize.

Not all the advice that social welfare professors gave their students was conflicted, however. Students were the beneficiaries of numerous tidbits of concrete advice about professional performance. At various times in various settings, students were counseled in how to dress professionally, how to combine organizational skills with direct service skills, and how to avoid coming across as "prissy."[16] They were told to ignore people who claimed you cannot help someone if you have not experienced what they have experienced, and they were warned not to skip lunch. They were given area-specific practice advice in their Practicum courses. They were even warned about the hazards of dealing with lawyers.[17] If students at Boalt Hall were metaphorically left by their professors to sink or swim, students at Haviland Hall were given swimming lessons, lifeguards, and water wings. The flurry of warnings and advice might have been overwhelming at times, but social welfare students could feel that someone cared about them and wanted them to be prepared for professional practice.

Professional schools are often thought of as places where students meet mentors who will shape their professional careers. It is interesting to note that when considered in this light, at least, the School of Social Welfare conforms to expectations more than does the School of Law. But professional schools are not considered to be sites primarily for mentorship; they are more centrally thought of as places for training and evaluation—that is, as disciplinary regimes. It is in this light that we consider them next.

## Schoolwork: Assignments, Apprentice Professional Performances, and Examinations

That professional schools are disciplinary regimes is evinced by student training that is largely unsupervised and self-directed: it is accomplished through homework assignments in which students must exert self-discipline as they try on their own to extract substantive knowledge and information pertaining to professional roles. Students must also endure the examination and ranking processes that are characteristic of disciplinary regimes. Finally, professional students must demonstrate that they can apply their knowledge in professional practice through supervised professional performance opportunities. These three requirements—homework, examinations, and apprentice professional performance—constitute the work that professional students must undertake during their training. Each of them provides further opportunities for professional socialization.

### *Homework Assignments*

**At the School of Law:** For each of their courses, the law students at Boalt were required to purchase a casebook; typically these were heavy tomes, about 1,500 pages in length, with unornamented hardback covers and unillustrated interiors. Their serious appearance conveyed a message about the seriousness of the legal profession. For every class, students were expected to have prepared to discuss a certain number of cases. The reading load was quite heavy, and if a student failed to read each page carefully, he risked the humiliation of failing to respond successfully when cold called for Socratic questioning. Professors expected students to come up with the exact wording of relevant passages from the assigned cases, and students had to study the cases carefully to be able to do so. Whereas, under the principles of affirmative discussion, social welfare students were given as much time as they desired to gather their thoughts or to refer to their notes before speaking, law students were given very little time to respond to a professor's question. For example, when asked to state the court's holding in a particular case, Jason gave an answer that paraphrased the holding. When Professor Tate asked Jason to provide the exact wording, he began flipping frantically through the casebook for the relevant passage. Although Jason had clearly prepared for class, Professor Tate allowed him only two seconds of page flipping before he called on another student. This level of time pressure meant that less than thorough preparation was little better than none.

Given the consequences of insufficient preparation, many law students quickly reordered their priorities to prepare fully for class before attending to anything else (including relationships, laundry, and sleep). As a result, one month into their law schooling, the students I observed were already engaging in before-class discussion of their exhaustion and fear of being caught nodding off in class.

The great bulk of Law School homework (and a great bulk it was indeed) consisted of the activity termed "briefing cases." Case briefing is a concrete, formulaic process, and students beset with the anxiety that attends Socratic performance seized upon this formulaic approach like a life raft. Law students were not taught legal rules and procedures in a straightforward way—they were supposed to ferret these out by studying cases—but they *were* taught the skill of case briefing in a straightforward manner. Professor Tate even gave his students a handout on case briefing.[18]

To brief a case, students were supposed to describe a series of characteristics of the case: the question presented, the facts, the procedural history, the decision, the holdings, and the reasoning. It was a mechanical process, but it required a good deal of close reading and thinking. For example, as Professor Tate stated: "The first thing we want are the facts—but what are those facts? They are the facts which are relevant to the legal issues which the case presents." The first thing a student called upon for Socratic questioning was likely to be asked was to recite the facts of a given case, and a student who repeated all the facts he had read would be peppered with questions about relevance. Hence, students had to read a case, then puzzle out the question presented, procedural history, holdings, and so forth.

Case briefs were written up in a ritualistic way; students followed a convention which they knew their own professors had followed as law students, once again absorbing messages about tradition and consensus in the legal profession. Students even learned to use a traditional note-taking shorthand—for example, K for contract, $\pi$ for plaintiff, and $\Delta$ for defendant—making their notes oddly reminiscent of scientific formulae. In fact, one of the central effects of case briefing was that it trained students to conceive of jurisprudence as a science. Having distilled the assigned cases into formulaic briefs, students applied the laws of logic to attempt to reconcile their holdings and derive the legal rules that they were taught lay behind the gaps and contradictions which the cases at first presented.

In fact, the idea that jurisprudence is a science and that simple rules lie behind the chaos, gaps, and contradictions that appear in case law has been disclaimed by legal academics since the birth of legal realism in the 1930s. Legal academics now acknowledge that the law is made by people and hence is incomplete, inconsistent, and vulnerable to bias. No professor I encountered introduced case briefing as the scientific method of jurisprudence; instead, they presented it as a convenient technique for class preparation. Nevertheless, the notion that legal rules can be derived by the established methodology continues to imply that there is a seamless legal truth to be discovered.

The requirement of case briefing did have two important effects, both arising from its training students to approach all cases with an attitude of detached scientific scrutiny. The first of these effects was that case briefing required students to pay close attention to cases that were, most of the time, astonishingly dull. Duncan Kennedy calls these "cold cases" and describes them as "technical, boring, difficult, obscure legal case[s]." He says of a cold case:

> It can be on any subject, so long as it is of no political or moral or emotional significance. Just to understand what happened and what's being said about it, you have to learn a lot of new terms, a little potted legal history, and lots of rules, none of which is carefully explained by the casebook or the teacher. It is difficult to figure out why the case [was assigned] in the first place, difficult to figure out whether one has grasped it, and difficult to anticipate what the teacher will ask and what one should respond. (2004: 6)

The case-briefing method gave students a way to manage this dull and yet anxiety-provoking cold caseload. Being required to brief a large load of boring cases taught students how to embrace the dull rather than recoil from it, which prepared them for legal practice.

The second effect of the requirement of case briefing, which I believe is even more important than the first, was that it short-circuited student critique of case outcomes in what Duncan Kennedy terms "hot cases" (2004: 12): that minority of cases in which the judgment goes against a plaintiff who engages readers' emotional or political sympathies. There is no heading in a case brief for critiques; instead, the student is taught by the case method that the rules of law and logic must require that outcome, and by the requirement of case briefing that his job is unemotionally to determine why that outcome was necessary. Hot cases provided important occasions for resocialization, as both dissonance and habitus modifications are likely to be evoked in a student's having to engage in rationalizing an outcome that initially outraged her.

Aside from reading and briefing cases, law students had few other assignments. They were required to take the Introduction to Legal Research, Writing, and Advocacy course, which involved writing assignments in the fall and moot court in the spring, but this course series was a second-class citizen when compared to the core curriculum: it was worth only two credits in the fall and one in the spring (compared, for example, to Torts' five credits or Contracts' six); it was taught by a combination of recent alumni and upper-level students; and it was graded on a pass-fail basis. Students were accordingly disinclined to take it too seriously. They learned that pragmatic rather than abstract knowledge had little relevance to their success at the Law School. [19]

**At the School of Social Welfare:** Just as the pedagogy was more varied at Haviland Hall than at Boalt, so was the homework. There was no unified approach to homework equivalent to case briefing. Instead, all social welfare professors assigned readings for students to approach in whatever manner they preferred, and most assigned writing assignments. Both reading and writing assignments were highly varied: students had to read books, quantitative research articles, popular press articles, and Internet sources; papers might be long or short, and based on class readings or individual research. This variety trained students to expect less certainty or professional consolidation, and to be more flexible and self-directed.

Aside from the Practicum classes, one thing social welfare courses shared with law courses was the heavy reading load assigned. But unlike law students, social welfare students were not expected to read everything on the syllabus. On the first day of the semester, in the Introduction to the Profession class that all first-year social welfare students attended, Professor Lipman explicitly told students this. He prefaced this advice with an exhortation for students to prepare well for class: "If you don't do the readings, and then you stand up to say something in class, you may say something stupid, and it will be evident to me that you didn't do the readings." Following this exhortation, Professor Lipman told the students that "you need to learn to scan the readings—you'll find that many social workers tend not to write well and repeat themselves a lot—so you should just get what's important, or you won't make it to December."[20] In many social welfare courses, the syllabi listed for each week a substantial number of required readings and an even larger number of recommended readings. For example, Professor Dunn assigned 47 book chapters or articles as required reading and 103 book chapters or articles as recommended reading in his Foundations of Social Work Practice class.[21] Few students could possibly read everything listed on all their syllabi.

One message conveyed when the professors of social work presented their students with an unwieldy mass of materials yet did not expect them to read all of it was the assumption that students were able to manage their own workloads and set their own limits. This assumption conveyed more respect for both student autonomy and real life than was shown by Law School professors to their students. Social Welfare students were expected to balance their course work, social work agency placements, and personal lives. On a less positive note, the assignment of more than could be completed left students with constant guilt about work undone. Students felt overburdened and anxious about whether they were concentrating on the right portion of the readings; as one student put it, "I know I should focus on the articles that could help me with my future work, but how do I know what that will be?" As students learned to prioritize readings and live with ongoing anxiety about work undone, they were also being prepared to deal with the overlarge caseloads that many social workers must manage.

One reason MSW students were assigned such a large and varied body of readings is that the theory of social welfare is not consolidated into a formal and abstract system of knowledge the way legal theory is.[22] This lack creates uncertainly for students, because there exists no equivalent for them of the bar-review guides that outline all the information a law student must master to be certified as professionally competent. Instead, professors assigned students a smattering of readings from varied specialties, therapeutic approaches, and theoretical schools to expose them to the various extant literatures. But even if she read every reading suggested, a social welfare student could never attain the feeling of mastery, certainty, and closure about her academic preparation for professional practice that a law student could.

In doing the readings and preparing for class, social work students did not rely on any single method comparable to case briefing. Most students I observed relied on highlighting and taking notes in the margins of their books to engage in a running analysis of the text they were reading. Rather than focusing on recapitulation, social welfare students approached the reading materials critically, since they were expected to speak critically of them in class. Students critiqued the readings from three general standpoints: they looked for analytical failures, such as the misinterpretation of data or logical flaws; they looked for ethical or political problems, such as racial bias; and they looked to their own experiences to see if they supported the author's assertions. Of these three avenues of criticism, critiques based on personal experience were made most frequently but generally earned only mild respect from professors, while critiques of analytical logic won the greatest respect but were made least frequently (and, I observed, disproportionately by white men).

In addition to their reading assignments, social welfare students were given writing assignments by virtually all professors. Unlike law students, who regularly wrote case briefs only for their private use, social welfare students regularly wrote for other eyes and received feedback on their "logical organization, clarity of expression, and depth of thought" (as the Foundations of Practice syllabus put it). The MSW students were assigned a variety of types of papers: research term papers (in the Introduction to the Profession class), weekly short papers applying the readings to real or hypothetical social work situations (in the Foundations of Practice class), and actual contracts and reports related to their clinical placements (in the Practicum courses). As a result, the social welfare students acquired a much more concrete sense than did law students of what writing skills would be required of them in professional practice.[23] This gave them a sense of practical competence that the first-year law students lacked.

## *Apprentice Professional Performances*

Professional schools are supposed to prepare students for professional practice. While this supposition was always resoundingly clear at the School of Social Welfare, one might lose sight of it at the Law School. The curriculum and pedagogy at the School of Social Welfare were practically oriented: students received training in concrete skills and useful information. At the Law School, the education was abstract and academic: students learned to "think like a lawyer." (At neither school did students receive any significant overt training in professional identity, however.)

**At the School of Law:** Many things were required of the law students I observed, but clinical experience was not one of them. Prospective law students are not expected to have had any legal experience; I even overheard one professor speculating to another that experience as a paralegal was "not only irrelevant but detrimental" for law students. Most law students graduate without ever being involved at school in an actual legal case.[24] Boalt Hall did offer several clinical courses while I was there, notably the two regularly offered in collaboration with the Berkeley Community Law Center and the Environmental Law Community Clinic, but the opinion of most students was that only that minority of their peers expecting to pursue a career in public-interest law needed to take a clinical course. Clinical work was devalued in comparison to the core curriculum: students had to work 16 hours per week at a clinic to earn four credits, while students earned the same number of credits for attending Property class only 4.25 hours per week.[25] First-year students were prohibited from taking clinical courses at all, sending the message that clinical experience was considered unnecessary and distracting from the important business of abstract academic work.

Although there was no clinical requirement, Boalt students were required to take some practice-simulating courses. The 1L curriculum was comprised of the core courses of Civil Procedure, Contracts, Criminal Law, Torts, Constitutional Law, and Property, and, in addition, the Legal Research, Writing, and Advocacy course in the fall and the Gordon Johnson Moot Court Program in the spring. I have already noted the devalued nature of the practice-related courses in legal writing and litigation practice that were appended to the core curriculum: they had no impact on a student's grade-point average and were conducted by upper-level students and recent alumni.

The Legal Research, Writing, and Advocacy course was supposed to prepare students for their moot court requirement, and moot court was supposed to give them a taste of legal practice. The simulated advocacy experience of moot court provided only minimal preparation for legal practice, however. The cases were unrealistic, constructed by upper-level students to have provocative subject matter yet to be straightforward, simple to research, and balanced, so that neither party had an advantage. Moot court participants had to follow few actual practice conventions, such as the intricacies of formal pleading, rules of evidence, or rules of procedure. Students learned what brief paper looks like, and how to introduce themselves to the judges—"May it please the court, my name is John Sherman, and I am counsel for the defendant"—but this is precious little preparation for the business of lawyering.

To be admitted to practice, law students must master a large body of abstract knowledge and pass the bar exam. They must incorporate appropriate professional identities to meet these requirements. Oddly enough, however, they do not need to have any understanding of what lawyers actually *do*. Boalt students could graduate without learning how a lawyer got clients; how a lawyer interviewed a client; what legal practice was like in different settings such as law firms, corporations, and government agencies; or how to handle relationships with superiors. They are vaguely led to expect that they will pick up these practical matters on the job.

**At the School of Social Welfare:** Unlike their law-student counterparts, students of social work were expected to graduate fully prepared to take on a substantial caseload and handle clients professionally. This expectation was made clear even before matriculation: unlike law students, who were not encouraged to seek out legal experience before applying to the Law School, applicants to the social welfare program were expected to have demonstrated an interest in providing care to populations in need, and the majority of matriculants had engaged in paid work in social service organizations. While the field of social welfare might be theoretically unconsolidated, and while social welfare students might therefore worry whether they were arming themselves with the correct theoretical knowledge for future practice, all students awarded the MSW graduated with extensive clinical experience and practical preparation.

In each of the social welfare classes I observed, situations encountered in professors' and students' actual practice were regularly raised, and hypothetical practice examples were regularly presented. Abstract knowledge was rarely imparted without relating it to practical applications.[26] For example, in comparing the "diagnostic perspective" with the "functional school," Professor Dunn stated that the former theory "assumes a stand-alone professional relationship between social worker and client—a one-to-one transaction," while according to the latter theory, "the client is interacting, not with you, but with your agency, and you are just a functionary." He then elicited student experiences regarding the provision of client services within agencies and concluded after discussing these that the truth lay between the two theoretical positions: what existed was "a relationship between social worker and client in a particular context," and while students should therefore not think of themselves as mere functionaries, they should always bear in mind that they were "never truly alone in the room with the client." Discussions of student experiences functioned as empirical tests of the value of any theory or authority.

One of the core course requirements for social welfare students was the Practicum, which was specifically geared to preparing students for clinical practice. Unlike the legal writing and moot court requirements, the Practicum courses were extensive, concrete, and closely related to students' actual practice in their required clinical placements. The social welfare students I studied tended to consider the Practicum to be the most relevant of their course requirements: a complete inversion of the situation at the Law School. This was because the reference point for relevance was different for the two groups of students: social welfare students were oriented toward "real world" practice, while law students were oriented toward academic achievement at the Law School.[27]

In the Practicum courses, all aspects of social work practice were addressed, including selecting agencies to which to apply; interviewing for a job interview; analyzing typical organizational structures; drafting learning agreements; interacting with clients, peers, and supervisors; and funding. Therapeutic interactions were addressed in great pragmatic detail. For example, in her Gerontology Practicum, Professor Ruth devoted almost an hour to the issue of how to get clients to disclose fully the problems they were facing. She advised that "effective social work requires the disclosure of dark, anxious secrets and embarrassing facts, often during a time of crisis," and that the key to obtaining such disclosure was "to develop trust." She went on to enumerate multiple techniques for developing the requisite level of trust, including how students could display interest in the client, how they could demonstrate competence, how they could convey that they were "seek[ing] the authentic person," how to project "the belief that people have the capacity to solve their own problems with resources and encouragement," how "not to make explicit the power differential" in social work relations, and how to project the necessary "unconditional regard" for clients with unpalatable racist or sexist attitudes. While it is true that lawyering, too, involves "the disclosure of dark, anxious secrets and embarrassing facts, often during a time of crisis," law students were not instructed in techniques for ensuring full disclosure because this sort of practical knowledge was considered trivial—a matter of craft which new lawyers could pick up in an offhand manner once they began to practice. But at the School of Social Welfare, the professional practice of care, rather than abstract intellectual maneuvering, was considered central.

The MSW program required social welfare students to engage in clinical practice in a social service agency during both the first and second years of the program, ensuring that all students graduated with significant professional practice experience. Professor Alverson promised her students that they would "learn much more from practice than from reading theory, because new ideas enter the field way before articles appear on them." Students' apprenticeships in their clinical placements provided them with supervised practice and structured learning opportunities; they were expected to master an enumerated list of "competencies" and drew up learning agreements with their fieldwork supervisors that specified how they would be given the opportunity to become skilled in each competency. Graduates of the School of Social Welfare were therefore much more competent to practice than were graduates of the Law School, who mastered theory rather than praxis. What is ironic about this situation is that the MSW graduates received less respect than did the neophyte lawyers because, according to Abbott, "[e]xpert action without any formalization is perceived by clients as craft knowledge, lacking in the special legitimacy that is supplied by the connection of abstractions with general values" (1988: 103).

## Examinations, Evaluations, and Grades

**At the School of Law:** Grades were extremely important to the law students I observed. They were important on an objective level, because students' grades and ranking determined the status of the jobs they could secure upon graduation. They were also important on a subjective level, because the students who attended Boalt were generally competitive and grade-conscious people whose sense of self-worth had been shaped strongly by their academic success in high school and college. These were students who had always gotten As, and who demanded continuing high performance of themselves. These high self-expectations set most students up for a Law School experience ridden with anxiety and disappointment.

In most 1L classes at Boalt, as at other national law schools, grades were determined solely by performance on a final exam.[28] Students worked for hundreds of hours on a course, but only the last three hours—the final examination period—really counted. Furthermore, folk knowledge holds that first-year grades determine career success; as a 3L at another school stated, "From the beginning, everybody tells you that when it comes time to job hunt, your first-year grades are the most important" (Morocco, 1990: 66). This put an enormous amount of pressure on 1Ls to perform well on exams, which left most of them apprehensive before their finals and dissatisfied afterward, as the following interview exchange indicates:

CYC:    How confident do you feel about exams?

Julia:  What is really strange is that I always had been really comfortable with tests, and I don't know if—when I went to UCLA, I always did really well; even if I thought I didn't do well, I always did really well. This semester, when an exam was coming up, I was a mess, and I would be sitting there, and my mind would be blank. And I said, "Oh my God, this is so important because my whole grade for the whole semester, my whole life, depends on this grade. Oh my God, what am I going to do?" And I would fall apart a little bit, and it would just be really nerve-wracking.

CYC:    So, were you satisfied with your first-semester grades?

Julia:  No, I wasn't. Actually, I wasn't satisfied—when I looked at the grades, I had two Ps [*passes*] and two Hs [*honors*].

CYC:    That's good. It's better than average.

Julia:  It's okay. I could have done better, I think. When I looked at the grades, I really felt as if I could have done better. It wasn't that the material was too hard. I think I didn't prepare in the right way, and I was so stressed during the test that I couldn't think. Things came out of my head and I wrote them down, but I didn't reflect on them at all. Or I'd look up, and I'd have ten minutes left or something, and I'd just be frantic. But at the time, when I finished exams, I thought I got all sub-Ps [*failing grades*]. I was convinced that I was going to get all these letters, and they were going to say, "I'm sorry, you're going to have to leave the school, you did so poorly." So when I looked at the grades, I was surprised, but I know that I can do better.

The anxiety produced by having so much riding on final exams so impaired Julia's performance that she feared she had failed her exams. The relief that she felt upon discovering that she had in fact performed adequately was short-lived, however, quickly transformed into a feeling that she had failed in a less dramatic manner by falling short of her own high standards.

Most of the law students I observed and interviewed were dissatisfied with their grades. This occurred for the simple reason that Boalt regulations required that examinations be graded on a forced curve: 10 percent of students received high honors (HH), 30 percent received honors (H), and the remaining 60 percent received a passing (P) or failing (sub-P) grade. Since few sub-Ps were distributed, most students in any given class received a P. Yet most incoming students expected to receive H and HH grades; although they were warned by upper-level students that this was unlikely, they projected from their academic success in college a similar success at law school. Listen to what Sita had to say in her first semester:

> Well, people are saying that you usually don't get more than one high honors, and you should expect at least to get one P, but I'm still really hoping to get high honors in everything. Maybe because we haven't really gotten any grades on any assignments yet, so it's hard to really know where I stand. But I'm definitely hoping and trying—I'm putting in that much effort. So I'm not like, Well, I'll get a P anyway, so it doesn't matter. I feel like if I try there's definitely a possibility.

Having expectations which they did not acknowledge to be unrealistically high, many students were dissatisfied with the objectively good grades they received, as Julia was with her two Hs and two Ps.

That getting good grades was central to many law students' sense of self-esteem combined with the forced scarcity of high grades to create a good deal of competition among students. Even if an entire class studied cooperatively so that each became highly knowledgeable, the majority still would not receive honors grades. From a perspective of rational self-interest (and this perspective was popular at the Law School), it did not behoove a student to raise the bar by contributing to a generally increased level of knowledge. Yet students who studied in isolation were often unaware of the gaps and errors in their understandings of the subject matter of a course. In seeking to balance the benefits of cooperation and competitive noncooperation, students regularly formed small study groups with the purpose of collectively organizing the cases presented in class into a systematic outline of the legal principles covered in the course. These outlines were jealously guarded to preserve the advantage of those in the study group.

That student collaborations in study groups represented group efforts to secure an advantage over others in the class rather than a spirit of cooperative learning was made clear by an incident related to me by Colin, a 2L. Colin told me that in his 1L year he had been a member of a study group of five people, including Joanna. Near the end of the second semester, as finals approached, Joanna took pity on an anxious and depressed friend and shared the study group's outline with her. According to Colin, there was a big uproar in the group when they found out about the friend's freeloading. Colin described Joanna's action as an "ethical breach;" essentially, he viewed the study group's outline as a secret document that Joanna had traitorously disclosed. The end of succoring a distressed classmate did not justify the unethical means, in Colin's estimation.[29]

The law students whom I observed studied hard, spending many hours preparing for classes, and many more studying for finals. Sometimes they collaborated, and more often they competed, but the goal of doing well on the all-important examinations remained constant. What was ironic about the situation is that those hours of study in no way guaranteed that students would do well, because students were unsure what the grading criteria were. Moreover, because the final exam usually constituted the last interaction between a student and a professor, students did not get an opportunity to be debriefed on the final. They could retrieve their exam papers, but generally they would find only a few cryptic marks on the papers (professors with one or two hundred exams to grade in a week did not have the time to make detailed comments, even if they had the inclination). In short, the law students were often unsure where they went wrong.

Among most of the students with whom I interacted, the response to grades that did not satisfy them was to dedicate themselves to more hours of class preparation and study. But often the impediment to getting honor-level grades was not a lack of substantive knowledge, but the absence of an appropriate habitus. In other words, the demonstration of an appropriate professional identity was one of the central grading criteria. This was not articulated to students because professors did not articulate it to themselves; instead, they gave the highest grades to the exam papers that were most "clear and concise, logical, and persuasive." What apparently constituted clarity, however, was a verbal style much like the professors' (a hyperarticulate upper-class WASP style). An assertive, masculine verbal style was deemed most persuasive. For example, most examinations were largely comprised of "issue spotters," hypothetical situations for which students had to determine the legal issues raised, and which contained a variety of cross-cutting facts. A student would be graded much more favorably if she wrote, for example, that "the court should hold for the plaintiff, because of legal arguments A, B, C, D, and E; the opposing counsel would make arguments F, G, and H but would be unsuccessful," than if she wrote that "the answer could be that the plaintiff should win because of A. But perhaps the defendant should win because of F, which we learned was important. The

plaintiff could argue B, C, D, and E; but the defendant would say G and H."
In short, the student's style of presentation could be determinative.

Because students did not receive significant feedback to explain their
final exam grades, they, like Julia, continued to focus on studying rules of law
rather than on altering their habitus. As a result, the students I interviewed
who entered the Law School with personal identities that were generally
already consonant with a lawyerly professional identity reported both higher
grades and greater grade satisfaction. While my data on differential grade
performance are based on the fairly small interview sample of thirty-five
law students, data gathered by other researchers support my finding. For
example, Ann Bartow's gender-focused study of students at the University of
Pennsylvania Law School found that in the first year, men were almost three
times as likely to be given grades which placed them in the top 10 percent
of their class. Men's grade advantage shrank over the course of their law-
school careers. They were "only" twice as likely to be in the top 10 percent
as women in the second and third years (Guinier, Fine, and Balin 1994: 38).
This was probably because women's comparatively high rates of identity dissonance decrease somewhat as socialization progresses.

The significant disparity in final exam performance within my subject
pool accords with the documented tendency of white male law students to
outperform the other members of their classes (Bernstein, 1996; Connecticut Bar Association, 1995; Guinier, Fine, and Balin, 1994). This advantage
in grades translates into a lasting advantage in class ranking, the status of the
jobs secured upon graduation, and long-term salaries, all said to be merit
based and determined objectively by intellectual performance, but in fact
based in large part upon consonance between personal identities and the
lawyerly role.

**At the School of Social Welfare:** Objectively speaking, there was
much less grade pressure at the School of Social Welfare than at the Law
School. Professor Lipman set the tone for all the first-year students on the
first day of classes: "I've never really understood grading in a professional
context, but the university requires it. You will find I don't like grading. I
don't grade on a curve, so if all of you do well, you will all get As." None of
the social welfare professors I encountered graded on a curve, and most
were quite liberal in distributing A grades. Also, since all professors gave
multiple graded assignments, students' hopes for good final grades never
rode on a single exam. Students were given a variety of graded assignments,
including short papers, group projects, long research papers, tests, and

demonstrations of clinical ability. The variety ensured that students who felt anxious about their performance on one type of assignment, perhaps examinations, could demonstrate their competence on another type of assignment, such as written papers.

While the objective grade pressure was markedly less at the School of Social Welfare than at the Law School, subjectively speaking, the pressure to get good grades remained strong. Students wanted to prove their competence to professors and to themselves; moreover, while they lacked the academic monomania of their Law School counterparts, social work students were all college graduates with commendable academic records who enjoyed having their intelligence affirmed. For example, Miryam told me that she was dissatisfied with her first-semester grades. When I probed to determine how poorly she had fared, Miryam confessed, "I had one grade that was not an A and so I was disappointed." Like the law students, social welfare students were prone to having unreasonably high expectations of how well they would do.

Demonstrating the influence of their internal pressure to perform, social welfare students regularly spoke of "pulling all-nighters" to write a paper or study for an exam, and they expressed a great deal of anxiety about grades to one another. For example, one day in the Commons Room I observed Ellen express to a group of her peers her fear that she would fail an exam. Another student attempted to reassure her by pointing out that "no one cares about your MSW grades"—neither employers nor PhD programs—"and everyone gets As and Bs anyway." Ellen refused to be reassured and reiterated that despite staying up all night to study, she feared that she would fail.[30] Despite students at the School of Social Welfare hearing a cheerful prognosis regarding the import and valence of grades, subjective grade anxiety remained moderately high.

Moreover, anxiety about grade performance was continuous, because assignments were due throughout the academic year. While law students' fretting about grades was intensely concentrated at the end of each semester, social work students' apprehension about grades was less intense but more constant. Both pools of professional students complained regularly of exhaustion and stress. (The social welfare students seemed to have fewer inhibitions than did the law students about disclosing just how frazzled they felt. Their greater inclination toward sharing meant that complaints equal in number to those of the law students represented a lesser degree of anxiety.)

The absolute level of anxiety among students was somewhat lower at Haviland Hall than at Boalt because academic performance was less central to the social welfare students in general than it was to the law students. At the core of most social welfare students' self-concepts lay an ethic of care.[31] Academic performance for social welfare students was a means to the end of competent performance in their chosen helping profession, whereas for most law students, academic performance was an end in itself.

Another factor that attenuated performance anxiety at the School of Social Welfare was that students were encouraged to cooperate rather than to compete. There was no forced curve pitting students against one another; instead, group exercises and assignments socialized students toward a habit of collaborative learning. The result was that students regularly studied together. Unlike the closed study groups like Colin's at the Law School, which guarded their outlines with paranoid jealousy, social welfare students' study groups were of mutable, open composition. For example, I observed a group of three students preparing for a midterm together at a table in the Commons Room. Other students drifted over to them to chat and commiserate, and the group freely shared their knowledge, condensed onto a set of index cards, with students who asked them questions.

Anxiety about grading was also less because students got regular feedback on their performances—especially on their papers and their apprentice professional work in their fieldwork placements. The criteria for good performance were thus elaborated for the social work students early in their schooling careers in a way that they were never made clear to law students. Students received regular critiques of their writing styles from their professors; these critiques pointed out not only substantive errors, but also problems of style and approach—in other words, of habitus. Evaluations of students' clinical performances were, as Professor Alverson said, "quite rational": students were given a handbook which listed the competencies they were required to demonstrate; opportunities for practicing these competencies were provided in the learning agreements students drafted with their agencies; and students' demonstrations of these competencies were evaluated on 1 February and 1 April of their first year in the program, and on 1 November and 1 April of their second year.

The social welfare students I observed were often initially distressed by the regular critiques they had to face. The knee-jerk reaction of most people being criticized is to resist, and many social welfare students felt that they ought to reject the critiques on moral grounds. These students, almost all of them women, had a highly empathetic and nonrational habitus. When told to rely more on the rational in their writing and practice, these students chafed with identity dissonance. Yet the regular instruction they received on how to conduct themselves provided them with guidance on how to revise their personal identities to achieve identity consonance. Not all students were receptive to this guidance, but over the course of the year, a good number of students found that their writing and clinical performance garnered more professorial approval as their identities were transformed (although the students were unaware of the nature of the transformation and believed only that they were learning more theory and better techniques). We can conclude that the examination and evaluation experiences that the social welfare students encountered were more effective socializers than were the finals the law students faced.

In the course of doing their work—their readings, exercises, clinical work, and examinations—students participated in their own socialization under the disciplining supervision of their professors (if often far from their literal gaze). Each time the law students briefed a case and maintained the same clinically detached attitude of attention whether the case was hot or cold, or whenever social welfare students worked to master a competency in their clinical placements, their identities shifted in small ways. The cumulative effects of these small alterations could be slight or dramatic.

# 6　The Identity Crisis

## Consonance and Dissonance Experienced

In the previous chapters, we have seen the various mechanisms through which socialization influences the identities of professional students. Each particular element or moment of socialization may be small, but just as small grains of sand blowing in the wind can shape mountains, small phenomena such as the layout of a classroom, a supportive peer comment, or a sadistic professorial joke can influence identity. Some students arrive at professional school with the contours of their identities already shaped in a manner appropriately streamlined, so that the grains of socialization slip smoothly around them. (These are the identity-consonant students.) Other students, however, have identities that are not conveniently preshaped, and the socializing grains scrape them stingingly, each having its small molding effect. Positively dissonant students wish to be reshaped and do what they can to open themselves to socialization's sculpting, painful though it may be. But negatively dissonant students do not wish to be reshaped, and they experience socialization as a sandstorm with ugly erosive effects that they attempt to minimize.

## The Subjective Experiences of Identity Consonance and Dissonance

### The Experience of Identity Consonance

Several narratives of identity-consonant students—those of Brian, Miki, and Peter—appeared in the introductory chapter to this book. Recall that all three students were enjoying professional school. They felt that they were working fairly hard without being overworked, and each

117

continued to enjoy leisure activities. All were doing well academically, both in the classroom and in terms of their grades. They attributed their success meritocratically to their good preparation. This is the great privilege of identity consonance: the way it invisibly eases a person's efforts, allowing him to take credit for his success. In describing the function of privilege, Michael Kimmel uses the metaphor of running with rather than against the wind:

> You do not feel how it pushes you along; you only feel the effortlessness of your movements. You feel like you could go on forever. Only when you turn around and face that wind do you realize its strength. Being white, or male, or heterosexual in the United States is like running with the wind at your back. It feels like just plain running, and we rarely, if ever, get a chance to see how we are sustained, supported, and even propelled by that wind (2003: 1).

Identity consonance can be seen as the mechanism through which social privilege functions at professional schools—the wind at the back of the star students.

While each identity-dissonant student's experience was unique, the identity-consonant students tended to be alike in their satisfaction. In fact, their interviews make rather dull reading. Al, a Latino social welfare student, provided an unusually engaging demonstration of identity consonance in response to my question of whether he thought he would be a good social worker:

> I think I will. I think I've learned a lot in the internships; I've learned a lot of stuff they're teaching us here. But then again, I think I could always have been a good social worker from the beginning. The whole idea, the whole notion of social work and the whole beliefs of social work—I think I've already had them before because of my status in the society. We were on the lower rungs; I knew how to respect people from the beginning. I didn't need anyone to teach me that, I knew that already. I knew how to work with different people. I grew up with different people. But it's prepared me in certain ways. I think it's just basically taught me the rules of the game, and that's about it. I already knew how to play; I just didn't know the rules that were there. I have been playing street ball, and now I'm finally learning to play with the referee and the regulations. That's about it.

Al's basketball analogy is an excellent one: the identity-consonant student arrives with the core skills and talents in place, ready to become a professional by mastering the technical rules.

The identity-consonant students all swiftly became integrated into their programs and gave the process of becoming acculturated little thought. As Kirsten, a law student, put it dryly, "I'm appalled by how easily I fit in." Consonant students do not pay much attention to their personal identities at professional school; they are in agreement, whatever their personal characteristics, that these are an asset in their chosen profession. A consonant social welfare student, Gregory, termed his homosexuality "a resource for empathy," saying, "I do call upon my feelings of being an outsider a lot." His peer Dante said that social service agencies "are very interested in hiring African American males such as myself, as they should be, to serve African American male client bases." And Elliott, a straight white social welfare student in the management track who noted that he tended to dominate class discussions, acknowledged that this is "a stereotype for males, but that won't stop me from participating when I want to."

Of course, not every identity-consonant student led a problem-free existence; in fact, almost all students had some complaint about their lives as professional students. I categorized students as dissonant only if they had difficulty internalizing a professional identity, not just because they had a gripe.[1] Leah, for example, was a white social welfare student who was politically very liberal and was critical of the social welfare program for making insufficient efforts to "combat racism, sexism, and homophobia"; nevertheless, she was comfortable, confident, and identity consonant. Her peer Monica was consonant despite the opposite perspective: while confident and comfortable, she felt Berkeley students were too liberal on issues of race and sexuality. Gary, a white law student who had been a graduate student in philosophy, was "deeply disappointed by the small-mindedness of many law students, with their pedestrian refusal to look beyond particular rules of law toward the higher-level philosophical issues being raised"; he too was confident and consonant, if disgruntled. Many of my interviewees, like Leah, Monica, and Gary, were consonant despite being dissatisfied with some aspect of their professional programs.

Some of the students I interviewed were experiencing significant but irrelevant identity dissonance: they were identity consonant with respect to professional identity, but identity dissonant along the axis of some other personal identity. Eric, a law student, provides a striking example of this. Eric had a habitus that was consonant with a lawyerly identity but not consonant with an African American identity; a self-described "neoconservative" who opposed affirmative action, Eric spoke, moved, and dressed like an affluent white man—which is what he claimed to be during the course of our interview.[2] Yet Eric had the phenotype of a light-skinned African American (although apparently his parents and siblings did not). He asserted that his appearance was due to a "genetic mutation," and that he was "one of those people you hear about who inherits a recessive gene, and it stops recessing and comes out." (While all his ancestors were said to be white, his grandmother was adopted, and Eric speculated that she had some African American ancestry of which no one had been aware.)

Eric had strong and conflicting feelings about his race and about racial classification generally. He said he had a "fear of ethnicity," which he found to be "alienating" and "dangerous." He felt prejudged by African Americans because he didn't "know some of the things that go with that hobby of ethnicity." Yet at other times he felt pride in having accomplished so much despite not being "Hitler's wet dream." In short, Eric was experiencing identity dissonance along the axis of race. Nevertheless, his habitus was consonant with a lawyerly identity, and he was doing quite well at law school.

## The Effects of Identity Consonance

Since identity consonance does not need to be managed, the consonant students I interviewed were free to focus on their academic pursuits and generally found my questions about their identities irrelevant. As Allen, a social welfare student, put it:

> I don't feel like I've changed too much by virtue of being here. I sort of feel like I came here to learn some new things, to get some practical knowledge, to get a degree (which is necessary), to make some contacts, but I didn't come here to [have] the whole set of circumstances explained to me, and I didn't come here to find myself. I didn't come here to lose myself, either.

For the consonant students, the weltanschauung of the profession agreed with their own, and it rarely even occurred to them that this might not be so for other students. Rather than finding or losing their self-identities, the consonant students unconsciously benefited from this synchronicity of habitus, as not only were they able to concentrate on their studies, but also they had the vocabulary, cultural assumptions, and habits of mind that made their course work seem exemplary to their professors. Proof of this lay in the fact that *every one* of the consonant students I interviewed reported very good academic performance. Furthermore (as I show in the next chapter), of the students I observed, all whom professors treated as star students displayed identity consonance.

I do not wish to imply that the identity-consonant students I interviewed were not working hard for their good grades. In fact, many were working long hours on their academic assignments and were limiting activities they had taken for granted before matriculating. Listen to the list of activities that Gregory, a social welfare student, was eliminating from his life:

> I cut out some of the suggested reading. I've cut out any hope of outside employment, other than my fieldwork for school. (I had sort of been counting on holding a part-time job, and I've cut that out.) I've cut out exercise, which is bad, but I've cut that out. I've cut out a lot of TV—I really haven't watched much TV at all. I've cut out renting videos and going to movies . . . I don't clean worth shit anymore . . . My apartment is just trashed, and I'm going to leave it trashed until spring break, which is a couple of weeks away. I've cut out laundry—I just buy more clothes. Thankfully, I have a lot of underwear that I've accumulated throughout the years . . . I haven't read a real book in a long time.

Many consonant students, like Gregory, were making a lot of personal sacrifices in order to achieve professional success. They had the satisfaction of feeling that this was worthwhile, because they were receiving the success to which they felt their sacrifices entitled them.

## Positive Identity Dissonance

### The Subjective Experience of Positive Dissonance

Identity-dissonant students lack the smooth correspondence which identity-consonant students enjoy between the conscious and nonconscious components of their personal identities and those of the proffered professional role. The characteristic that distinguishes positively dissonant students from those negatively dissonant is that they embrace the displacement of their conflicting personal identities by nascent professional identities. I found that this openness to being changed was demonstrated almost exclusively by women—only one of my male interviewees, Adam, an African American law student, was experiencing positive dissonance. In all, just under one-quarter of the students I interviewed experienced positive dissonance between their fledgling professional identities and other identities such as racial, class, or gender identities.

Most of the positively dissonant students felt that they were achieving a life's dream by attending professional school, as did Vera, who said she had wanted to be a lawyer "as long as I can remember." Unlike the consonant students, who described themselves as "just going to school," the positively dissonant students said they were "finding themselves." As Janice, a Filipina social work student, put it:

> I think I am finding myself. Because the issues always come up with how you look at the world, how you treat other people, what is your plan in terms of helping people. Are you going to retreat and go off in your own little world, or are you going to continue on? And now I know how to answer those questions, and I can feel good about who I am.

In finding themselves, most of the positively dissonant students did not feel that they were changing so much as that their true selves were being revealed; they were, as Christine said, becoming "self-actualized."[3] An illustration of this sensation of becoming a more authentic self is the following quote from my interview with Grace, a Chinese social welfare student:

> I came into the program with conservative views, and to be honest a big part of that was . . . I feel like I've grown a lot in the past several months. A lot of it wasn't my views; it was what I grew up learning in church, and my cultural background has a very conservative view of a lot of things. I think I've shed a lot of that, in terms of not saying, "This is the way," because of [growing in the program].

Grace felt religiously called to enter the social welfare program, and although she was shedding a lot of her conservative religious views, she retained a strong sense of following her calling. There was a clear association between holding the belief in having a calling, being a woman of color, and positive dissonance among the students I studied. Tarrah, an African American law student, said her "steps here were ordered" by God; Chinese social welfare student Christine felt that "this was what was intended" for her;

Jackie, an African American woman, said social work was her "destiny"; and African American social welfare student Shandra told me:

> What I feel deep down inside is just that it's part of the big master plan of what He's got for me to do. Because my life could have turned out different but it's turned out this way . . . I'm being prepared for something and I can't say what it is, but I know it's part of God's plan, and it's a wonderful feeling . . . I'm helping people because God wants me to help people, because I've been helped and I have to give something back . . . I'm turning into this better person and it's not because of me.

Students such as Grace, Christine, Jackie, and Shandra opened themselves up to the socializing forces of professional school willingly because they felt it was God's will.

Although the positively dissonant professional students viewed the changes they were experiencing as growth or self-revelation, they were having to release important self-identities which they held at the time they entered their programs. Some students were giving up cognitive/ideological identities, such as Grace and Janice, both of whom were originally strongly defined by their conservative ideologies but were becoming more liberal. Others, such as Joy, a Korean American law student, were changing their emotional identities; Joy was trying to become more rational so her emotions wouldn't "sway" her and her reasoning would become more "predictable."

Still other students, in adopting professional identities, were displacing core elements of their habitus, such as Christine, who was moving away from her "traditional Chinese" racial and gendered habitus as she grew professionally. Another student who was undergoing a process of deracialization was Vera, who had grown up in an all-black community and attended a traditionally black college, but who was now avoiding getting involved with African American social circles. She distanced herself from racial politics at Boalt ("I wasn't looking for any problems, you know. Frankly, I'm on a mission—I have my own personal goals."), and she tried not to get emotionally involved in classroom discussions about racial discrimination. ("One of the persons mentioned the *Brown v. Board of Education* case, and for a second, I felt a little weight, but then I said, 'Oh well, it's not my issue.'") Letting go of racial solidarity seemed to be painful for Vera, but she felt it would lead to professional success.

Some of the identities which positively dissonant students willingly gave up are less socially valued than their replacements; for example, Charmaine, who was introduced in Chapter 1, gave up an identity as a client of social workers to become a social work professional, as did Miryam, a Jewish social welfare student. When a student gives up a socially stigmatized identity for a socially valorized one, we might imagine that the process is easier than displacing an identity that we view as essential, such as a racial identity. In fact, all the positively dissonant students I interviewed found the process traumatic (although they embraced and promoted it nonetheless).

## The Reported Effects of Positive Dissonance

Positive dissonance was traumatic for the students I interviewed who experienced it because they needed to justify their changing self-understandings to themselves and to others. The family and friends of identity-dissonant students were often alienated by the changes in the students and complained about them, often bitterly. Vera, for example, was willing to engage in whatever self-revision was called for to develop a successful professional identity, but she had to pay a price to do so. People from Vera's hometown had harsh things to say to her about the changes she was making in her racial comportment. She said unhappily, "It's like crabs in a basket: whenever one of them tries to get out, the others try to find a way to pull it back down." Yet Vera felt that she was making her escape from that basket and endured the pinch of positive dissonance.

Changes in identity can have a particularly painful impact upon relationships with spouses and partners. Christine's fiancé broke off their engagement as she became less "traditional Chinese" during her first year in the MSW program:

> He told me that I was not the woman he had wanted to marry any longer, and that being in the program had "ruined me." And my mother has been extremely upset with me because she already thought of him as a son-in-law. It saddens me very much that they can't see how good it has been for me to be in the program, because I have grown so much. And I hate to think that I could have been in a relationship for so long with a man who didn't want me to become empowered, and that my mother would take his side. So I just try not to think about it, and to focus on being here and learning and growing.

Like Christine, many of the positively dissonant women were having relationship difficulties. Jackie was having marital problems because her husband was upset with her for "sort of losing interest in my wifely duties," and she was upset with him for not respecting the amount of work she was doing—raising four children and attending a professional program. Miryam's lesbian partner of ten years was also complaining about feeling neglected and about Miryam's becoming like "people who work in the field [of social work who have] a certain mannerism that she does not trust or like." Both Miryam and Jackie alternated between feeling guilty for disappointing their partners, and angry that their partners did not embrace the positive changes they were undergoing.

Most of the positively dissonant students I interviewed were feeling affiliational ambivalence. Many felt conflicting loyalties between their communities of origin and their new professional communities. Recall from the introductory chapter how Charmaine said that it was only with people from her old impoverished neighborhood that she felt "I'm able to be myself, truly be myself," but that she had nevertheless chosen not to disclose to these people that she was attending a social work program, feeling they would not understand and would judge her negatively. Harmony felt a similar ambivalence. On the one hand, she said of her community of origin, "It's just so much easier, when you're from the same culture, when your parents dealt drugs together and your parents were single parents, and whatever; you understand, you don't have to explain things." Yet on the other hand, Harmony felt alienated from people from her community of origin and believed their attitude toward her was, "We're proud of you, but you're different from us now." While positively dissonant students might feel good about "moving up," as Pia put it, they were troubled by fears of "losing touch" with the people and values that had been familiar to them.[4]

The business of having to manage their evolving identities was stressful for the professional students who were experiencing positive dissonance. Many reported experiencing anxiety and physical symptoms that were anxiety related. For example, Vera stated she was suffering from "heart palpitations," Susan was having disabling menstrual cramps, and Sharon reported having migraine headaches almost every day.

Unlike their identity-consonant peers, who were able to focus on their studies free from identity-related distractions, the positively dissonant students faced many distracting phenomena. While they embraced the process of change and sought to foster it, the process of self-editing was difficult. If they were altering their ideologies, they were struggling with moral questions; if they were altering their habitus, they were shifting such basic traits as their speech patterns, gestural repertoires, and empathic impulses (or lack thereof). In the process, they were alienating friends, families, and partners. In short, the students experiencing positive dissonance faced an identity crisis that their consonant peers did not, and this identity crisis distracted them from their studies.

As a result of facing a distracting identity crisis, most of the positively dissonant students I interviewed reported having academic difficulties. Many, such as Janice, Shandra, and Joy, rarely if ever volunteered to speak in class because they did not feel equipped to participate, although they knew this choice would negatively impact their grades. Other positively dissonant students managed to give their silence a positive cast, as is evident in this quote from my interview with Grace:

> A lot of people have very different points of view that I just never thought about, and it really helps to hear them, and that's a big part of why I like to just listen, because sometimes the thoughts are things that I've thought about, but other times it's like, Wow, I never thought about that, and I appreciate it a lot. It's not always to my advantage to just listen and not speak up, because I know a lot of professors grade on participation, and I know I've gotten docked a lot of points this last semester. But it doesn't really bother me, actually. I know it's important, but it's not a big thing to me anymore. I'd really rather sit back and watch people interact.

Grace had come to feel that her learning and growth as a person were more important than grades. Many of the positively dissonant students had this general orientation, which was adaptive for them, since most were underperforming. Only two of the positively dissonant students in my sample reported above-average grades. Most of the positively dissonant students had a habitus that did not conform to the professional role, and this proved an impediment to good academic performance.

The other major effect which positive dissonance had on the lives of the students I interviewed was that it placed greater time pressure upon them. Lacking the consonant habitus that made the grammar, logic, and assumptions of their professional academic work feel intuitive, students experiencing positive identity dissonance took longer to complete their assignments—in fact, some students felt it was impossible to complete all the work in the time given and lived in fear of being revealed as unprepared by professors. Jackie, for example, reported having been "caught out" by a professor for not completing her readings on the day before our interview.

Students who were experiencing positive identity dissonance also needed to devote a good deal of energy to managing their dissonance, which added to their already full plates. Between their slow-moving academic work and their distracting identity crises, many positively dissonant students were suffering from a nerve-wracking time bind. They felt forced to reduce their other activities, such as unstructured time with partners (Miryam), sleep (Jackie), and exercise (Christine), and many lived busy, highly scheduled lives with little time for themselves. Janice described her time rationing like this:

> I only get six hours of sleep a night: midnight to six. I cut sleep. I try to jam everything in; I cut down on going out—it's reduced to once a week or less. I think I'm fortunate that I live alone so I don't have social pressures. I'm very mindful of my time . . . I do my errands on weekdays instead of doing them on the weekends when everyone else is trying to get their groceries or their laundry done . . . I cook in bulk so I can freeze and reheat the leftovers. I don't chop things because that could take half an hour.

Janice's feeling of being so busy she has insufficient time to chop her vegetables may sound extreme, but it was a normal sort of sensation among my positively dissonant study subjects.[5] The time bind they experienced was more pervasive and severe than that faced by the consonant students. Furthermore, what they received in return for the sacrifices they made was not the academic success the consonant students enjoyed, but merely the avoidance of failure.

## Negative Identity Dissonance

### *The Subjective Experience of Negative Dissonance*

Positively identity-dissonant students encounter hardships due to their identity dissonance, but they accept these because they prefer the professional identities that are germinating within them to the conflicting personal identities that these are displacing. But the students who are negatively dissonant find the conflicting elements of the professional role they are supposed to internalize consciously distasteful or nonconsciously indigestible, and so they may attempt to escape the forces of professional socialization to avoid them. This attempt endangers their professional success, because one cannot be a successful professional without a well-integrated professional identity. Moreover, the attempt is futile. Unless a student drops out of professional school, he will be subject to socialization forces of the myriad subtle varieties explored in previous chapters and cannot avoid experiences that will accumulate in his habitus. For the students who do not drop out of professional school—and very few do—there are only two choices: attempt to manage dissonant identities, or edit their conflicting personal identities (consciously or nonconsciously) and embrace the change.

Whereas the positively dissonant students felt they were finding themselves at professional school, negatively dissonant students felt they were losing themselves. Stacey, a white law student, for example, was a college English major and athlete, an all-American cross-country runner who had won important meets. She had hoped to attend graduate school in English, but her father talked her out of it because "he said my job prospects would be nonexistent and it was unrealistic," so she applied to law school on his advice. She had an unsettled sense of self when I interviewed her midway though her second semester. Before law school, she worked out regularly for 2.5 hours per day, with additional practices for her track meets, but she felt she had to cut out most exercise at law school because it now appeared "frivolous." Yet she said contemptuously that "the students here are really out of shape—it's pathetic." Stacey was doing well enough with respect to grades, but she was by no means the star she had been as an athlete, and she was not enjoying herself.

> All the fun has drained out of my life, and my simple pleasures are gone. I guess I didn't appreciate what I had at the time. I'm just too serious here.

Having given up the athleticism that had defined her life, Stacey felt lost at law school, and it depressed her. What she had lost was her positive self-identity.

This sense of having lost oneself, of being lost at sea in professional school, was common among the negatively dissonant students. When I asked Tammy, a Korean American law student, to describe herself to me at the outset of our interview, she said:

> It's funny, but that's a hard question for me to answer right now. The reason that it's funny is because I wanted to go to law school because then I would know what I was doing with my life, and I'd really know who I was and where I was going . . . I'm not even sure why I'm here anymore. So it's hard for me to describe myself for you.

The sense of losing oneself expressed by Tammy and other students experiencing negative dissonance was disconcerting and unpleasant, quite unlike the empowering feeling of finding oneself which positively dissonant students savored. (It was for this reason that I gave the two terms their positive and negative valences.) And negative dissonance was by far the more common among the students I studied: fewer than one-quarter of the first-year students I interviewed were experiencing positive dissonance, while more than half were experiencing negative dissonance.

Like positive dissonance, negative dissonance could be experienced along any axis of personal identity (such as gender, race/ethnicity, or status as a person with a disability), and within any element of identity (subjective identity or nonconscious habitus). It was common for the students I interviewed to be experiencing dissonance along more than one axis or element at a time, and each instance of dissonance had to be managed.[6]

## The Experience of Ideological Negative Dissonance

Many of the professional students who spoke with me were experiencing negative cognitive/ideological dissonance. Because this type of dissonance is easily accessible to students for conscious analysis, they were often able to articulate it clearly.[7] Students with strong political ideologies provide an example. Law students with strong conservative ideologies did not necessarily experience identity dissonance. A lawyerly identity is compatible with *fiscal* conservatism, which meshes easily with the essentially libertarian lawyerly role. Michael, for example, who described himself as a "nonrabid conservative" who intended to be "financially secure," was identity consonant. Fiscal conservatism did not lead to identity dissonance at the School of Social Welfare either, if it was combined with social liberalism. (Recall that Peter, an identity-consonant student introduced in Chapter 1, combined the two.)

The students I interviewed who had strong *socially* conservative ideological identities, however, usually experienced negative dissonance at U.C. Berkeley. Often these were students with evangelical Christian identities who felt they had a personal relationship with God. At the School of Social Welfare, where the professional role was strongly linked to liberal political ideology, a number of students with strong Christian identities were experiencing ideological identity dissonance. For example, Janice, a Christian student who stated that she had "very conservative Republican views," had a vehement religious objection to abortion and was unhappy that she never heard class discussion "in terms of the rights of the child" but only in terms of "a woman's right to choose." She was having great difficulty resolving an internal tension between "the ideal of being unconditionally accepting"—an element of the social worker role that she had internalized—and her impulse to make negative moral judgments about her clients (and peers). Janice very much wanted to be able to bestow "unconditional positive regard" upon her clients, and she spoke with great pleasure of an occasion upon which her supervisor praised her for not showing "any discomfort or any kind of judgmentality" to clients. Yet she simultaneously felt she had a moral duty to protect the rights of unborn children. Her tentative solution to the problem of drug-addicted women bearing children with "diminished quality of life" was that women who have given birth to an addicted child should be sterilized. This draconian solution lay beyond the ideological borders of the social welfare professional role.

Fewer students with fundamentalist Christian views were attracted to the Law School than to the School of Social Welfare. Those few students who did hold religious rightist views experienced ideological identity dissonance. An example was Joy, a Korean American woman who often felt uncomfortable at the Law School, where homosexuality was "displayed" and pro-choice views were common. Joy often refrained from socializing with her peers because the activity proposed to her involved going to a bar or a party where drinks would be served, and she was morally committed to abstaining from alcohol. She was concerned about lawyerly amorality:

> People see [attorneys] as having no scruples, they have no values, they just turn their back on everybody, and they just do whatever they want. For me, that's not how I've been brought up, and my beliefs are completely against that—when something is weighing against my deep beliefs, I would not change them for whatever the amount they're paying me. And because of that, I think I will be a good lawyer.

What Joy had either not yet understood or had glossed over despite understanding it is that part of the professional ideology of the law is that everyone is entitled to representation. And while the codes of legal ethics allow an attorney to decline to accept a case, they require the attorney to pursue vigorously whatever course of action an accepted client desires that is not illegal. Joy's moral principles, which she asserted would make her a "good lawyer," conflicted with the ideological tenets of her chosen profession.

Some of the professional students I interviewed were also experiencing cognitive/ideological dissonance because of their leftist ideologies. This was often true at the Law School, where students attracted by the history of civil rights litigation ran headlong into the discovery that legal ideology is essentially conservative, because the legal system is based upon following precedent—that is, preserving the system, not changing it. Politically liberal, social-justice–oriented students were often shocked to find out how few of their professors and peers shared their ideology. Julia, a liberal white woman, had this experience:

> Well, before I entered law school, I was really excited about changing things, and being really involved in public-interest issues, and I had a lot of energy, and I was really excited to be in law school. Since I've been in law school, I've been kind of wondering what the point of law school is, and I feel like a lot of my energy has drained out of me. I'm really disappointed by the people around me and their goals.

When I asked her about law students' goals, she replied:

> I used to think that we were all here for the same reason, that we all wanted to go out and help people and do all these great things. And people would always say—when I would say we're after the same thing—they would say, "No we're not! So-and-so is here for the $80,000, and so-and-so wants to join his father's law firm." And I didn't believe them at first.

Jed, a white man with roots in the impoverished Ozarks, shared Julia's dissonance and dismay, stating that, at Boalt, "leftism means being a slightly-left-of-center Democrat" and that activism is equated with radicalism.

Although the ideology of the social work profession is much more liberal than is that of the legal profession, ideological negative dissonance arising from leftist political commitments was no less common at Haviland Hall than at Boalt. This was because the ideological midpoint of social welfare matriculants was further left than that of the professors and the professional role they demonstrated. For example, the first-year social welfare students tended to hold more queer-positive views than the readings and course work proffered, and lesbian, gay, and bisexual activists often demonstrated ideological identity dissonance. Philip, for instance, was a gay white man who responded to my question about whether he felt comfortable in the social welfare program by stating:

> I was when I first started the program. Then I had a really bad experience with a professor on gay and lesbian issues. Since that time I have not been very comfortable and I am very reluctant to speak out.

Lesbian, gay, bisexual, and transgendered activists had well-developed sexual-political ideologies and were able to articulate their identity dissonance perhaps more clearly than any other group I encountered. Here are some excerpts from a long disquisition by Miryam on the topic:

> As a lesbian I find [the social welfare program] is not a program that is very gay friendly in content.

> One of the things I was told was that [the admissions committee had] a question why . . . someone with interest in working in the gay and lesbian community would be interested in the Berkeley program, which has no courses that exclusively address the issues. That kind of set it up for me, especially since I was working predominately with heterosexual clients at the time.

> The terms that come to mind from what I hear in the program are, "This is not our target client population." When you're a lesbian and you are in a program and you're told that your community isn't a "target population," it's not good.

Miryam discoursed on the topic of her alienation due to her sexual politics for more than fifteen minutes. Jessie, another lesbian social welfare student, did so for close to a half-hour.

That ideological dissonance exists at the conscious level meant that students I interviewed were able not only to describe it cogently and at length, but also to reduce it to pithy statements. Susan cracked me up when she described her seemingly soulless, social justice–eschewing peers as "lawyers of the corn" (referencing the horror film *Children of the Corn*). And Miguel, a public-interest-oriented professional student, described the lack of empathy and the hypercompetitive spirit he felt emanating from his peers like this: "It's like on those Bugs Bunny cartoons, where you're stranded on an island, and the other person starts looking like a turkey."

## Managing Ideological Identity Dissonance

The sensation of negative ideological identity dissonance is an uncomfortable one. How can students live with feeling they have entered a profession whose values strike them as immoral? How do they deal with the socialization pressure to conform to an ideology they despise? How, in short, do individuals manage their ideological identity dissonance?

One might imagine that the management technique most students adopt when faced with ideological dissonance would be to confront and resist all the socialization pressures they could identify, but in fact few students whom I interviewed took this tack. Miguel was one of these; he said emphatically:

> One of my big goals this semester is to get a sort of a sense of purpose back. Regardless of how I do or what's happening, I want to do the things I want to do and I want to do it my way. I don't care what the official way is; it's my way or no way.

The Sinatraesque stance adopted by Miguel requires a very healthy ego. The few interviewees who adopted this posture of defiant resistance were all confident males.[8] They described their struggles in rather heroic terms, as Ed, a white law student, does here:

> Inculturation pressure doesn't bother me, because whenever everyone else is thinking one way, and that's what they're all shooting for, then they have the weight of the sort of established ideals of law school also behind them, you know, all pushing them in the same direction. Well, it's pushing me too, but if I'm strong I can stand against it as long as I do a critique of the process, which I do. I deconstruct the process almost every day.

The strategy of resistance was an uncommon one; the technique for managing ideological dissonance that proved to be the most common was the much less confrontational strategy of alienation, in which the student avoided engaging with the law-student experience and distanced himself from the school both physically and psychologically. As Nicole, a law student of mixed racial descent, explained:

> I'm not really, really engaged in the Law School, like the way I was as an undergrad. So because I'm kind of disengaged, I can be comfortable. It's kind of a safe distance kind of thing.

Susan, a white law student also managing her ideological dissonance through alienation, sought to keep her emotional tone light and uninvolved, despite disliking the program and her peers: "There's not much I can do about it, but I don't worry about things like that." And Julia, like many similarly situated students, spent as little time at Boalt Hall as possible:

Julia:    I feel like I still know what I want to do, eventually, but the whole process isn't what I thought it was, and I'm just excited to get out of school and get back to what I know I can do. . . since I've been here, I haven't been involved in things at school. As soon as classes are over, I just want to get off campus. I do my work and try to get involved in other things.

CYC:    So you feel you have to shield yourself from law school, rather than that it fosters you?

Julia:    Yes, and I think that's harmful. I should try to work at this in a different way, so instead of being threatened by the whole experience and the people there and the environment, that I am more accepting of it; rather than it hurting me, maybe it can help me. But I don't accept it, and I just shut it out and kind of fight it.

Remaining disengaged from professional school lessened the socialization pressure ideologically dissonant students experienced, but this came at the cost of a lack of integration into their professional programs that left them feeling isolated and lessened their chances of professional success, which, after all, required that they be properly socialized.

Whereas students employing a strategy of alienation from professional school felt numb or guilty about their relationship to the programs, students employing a related strategy of aloof superiority felt proud of their lack of integration. Philip, for example, referred to the social welfare professors as "idiots" who focused on semantics and jargon instead of on skills: "Instead of saying something in a paragraph or less, they take a seven-hundred-page textbook from hell to put this point across or make it even more confusing than it is." Philip's may sound similar to the statements of the students who employed a strategy of resistance, but what distinguishes the management techniques is that the resistors engaged in an active process of confrontation with their programs, while those employing a stance of aloof superiority withdrew from engagement no less than the alienated students did. However, they put a sort of sour-grapes spin on their disengagement rather than feeling guilty, like Julia, or trying to feel nothing at all, like Susan. Sam, a disengaged South Asian law student who considered himself a superior scholar and "quite clever," sought to rationalize his poor grades: "I have to feel that some of these professors are bad lecturers, and they're able to use the Socratic method to disguise that fact. Because if they had to speak for an hour, they would be incapable of coherently and lucidly explaining material." Who would want the sour grapes of being validated by such inferior professors?

Related to the strategies of alienation and of aloof superiority was the management technique of self-censorship. While consonant students and resistant dissonant students confronted professors and peers with whom they disagreed, others, including the alienated and aloof students, avoided confrontation by keeping quiet. As Erin, a liberal Asian Chicana law student, put it: "I want to be respected—otherwise I'll never become successful as an attorney. So I keep my negative thoughts to myself." Joy, a conservative, voiced a similar sentiment, saying she was "hesitant to speak up about what I believe, and what I feel is morally wrong, especially because [religious opposition to homosexuality and abortion] is seen as so extreme, and I don't want that reputation."

The self-censorship strategy was so widely used that it was noted even by professors. For example, on the third day of Professor Tate's Torts class, he informed the students that the course would discuss tort law "from a positive rather than a normative perspective"—in other words, class discussions would not address moral issues. Professor Tate invited students to respond to his proclamation, but no hands rose, and he said, "Surely some of you are alienated by this approach? Have things changed so much in recent years? No?" The class remained silent, although I know from my interviews that many students did object to the "amoral" flavor of the Torts class.

If many students coped with their cognitive/ideological dissonance by keeping silent before what they felt to be unreceptive audiences, many also sought out like-minded individuals with whom they felt free to speak their minds. Cecilia, for example, found solidarity with "like-minded souls" who were "the saving grace for sure" for her. Students were able to use this dissonance-management technique of solidarity to attenuate the socializing classroom messages they deemed ideologically distasteful. Philip, who described his class background as "very, very, very poor," hated what he viewed as the classist slant of much social welfare classroom discussion, but he said, "I think there are other people in the program that have grown up under similar circumstances that make it bearable, and we just sort of roll our eyes and whatever, and go, 'There she goes again!'" Other students found a particular friend to provide solidarity for them. Nicole sat next to her African American friend Shandra in all her classes.

> We write notes, like as if we were in high school. She really makes law school bearable for me, because we can talk about the teacher through notes . . . she's very, like, black, and sometimes I need that here. Because there aren't very many of us at all, and she's that way, so that I feel safe, I feel comfortable.

As Nicole's case demonstrates, students were able to combine the self-censorship and solidarity strategies, remaining quiet and passive in the classroom but privately resistant in the company of coconspirators.

In fact, most students experiencing negative ideological dissonance employed more than one management strategy. Students might combine more engaged strategies, such as resistance, solidarity, or both, with more detached strategies, such as alienation, aloofness, and self-censorship; or they might employ only detached strategies, but more than one of these. In attempting to cope with the discomfort of negative ideological dissonance, the students I studied acted creatively, adding and discarding management techniques over time. The difficulty remained that no technique was wholly effective, and that to the extent students were able to stave off socialization pressures, they damaged their chances for professional success.

## The Subjective Experience of Dissonance at the Level of Habitus

The most prevalent form of negative identity dissonance among the students I spoke with was that at the level of habitus. This was because the category covered a lot of territory—habitus dissonance can exist along any axis of identity, such as emotional orientation, ethnicity, sexual identity, or familial status. It was rarely accessible to conscious analysis by the person experiencing it, requiring me to probe students' feelings of discomfort, disjuncture, or incompetence.[9] (Because habitus is nonconscious, it cannot be understood through interview data alone; I address my observational data regarding habitus in the next chapter.)

Many of the students of color I interviewed were experiencing negative dissonance between their racial or ethnic habitus and the worldview that was deemed professional. Adam, one of the few African American men at the Law School, said, "I had the hardest time concentrating on my course work, none of which had anything to do with race, and it was really hard because race was always in my head." His course work seemed to address some other realm entirely from the one he was occupying, and its apparent irrelevance was distressing to him. While the course work seemed interesting and relevant to consonant students, many students of color shared Adam's experience of finding the readings and lectures dry, as well as tangential to the issues that confronted them.

Another habitus problem faced by students of color was that they often did not share the verbal style or cultural reference points employed by their professors. Vera described her feelings of inferiority in her Contracts class as

> related to my professor, with his style that's just so high. I feel like I'm coming for an hour of Shakespeare or an hour of culture, because he's very fine and very, sort of, English, and so that's an intimidating factor as well, because he has such a command of the English language, it's incredible. I can't—he has such a twist to the way he portrays things, and he can toss out Latin. . . .You want to tell it in a way that he feels, "Like, wow!" but I could never.

Paula, a Native American social welfare student, voiced her experience of not sharing her professors' habitus in this way:

> You know, they talk about "cultural competence," and they never assume that anyone will know anything about Native American cultures, but then they assume that when they talk about things from their culture that everybody's going to know what they're talking about. They talk about things like 1950s television shows and life in the suburbs. I guess I must be culturally incompetent, because I don't know about them. It's like they get to feel proud knowing what a dream catcher is, but I have to feel dumb because I didn't know who Ozzie and Harriet were.

Students of color also experienced habitus dissonance when they were uncomfortable interacting with their white peers. Tarrah, an African American law student, described the awkwardness she felt:

I feel really bad, because you know how they put you in these modules, or whatever. My module people were always sort of . . . first of all, I'm the only black person in my module. And we don't have too much in common, but they'll still invite me when they go out drinking, but I . . . first of all, I don't drink. And then it's like, well, sometimes I'm just like, Okay, I'm going to go, just to go. I don't want to be antisocial. And then I'm like, Well, why should I do it just to sort of appease them? 'Cause it's just going to be weird.

Tsong-Min, a foreign student from Mainland China with shaky English skills, felt even more socially awkward than Tarrah did and had attended not a single social event with his Law School peers. Because he was working long hours on his case briefs and outlines, he said, he had not really noticed his isolation until he developed marital problems and realized that "there is no one to talk to about my problem; I realize I have no friends."

Janice, the social welfare student who said she was "too rational," also described an inversion of the usual pattern of racial habitus dissonance. Although she was a Filipina, she was raised largely by her white stepmother, so when her classmates "would ask me, 'Is that what the [Filipino] culture is like?' I said, 'I don't know, because I was raised primarily with a white mother.'" This cultural incompetence presented a problem for Janice in her interactions with Asian clients and peers:

I am Asian, but I don't know anything about the issues that Asian communities are dealing with. People would come up to me and invite me to Asian groups and things of that nature, and I felt like, Well, I don't know, and how come you can't ask my friend who's white, can she go too? Or are you just picking me out because I look that way? So I had a hard time dealing with that . . . I'm a lot more self-conscious now of where I am now and how I'm perceived. Like when clients come up to me thinking that I might be able to represent them or at least have some language base, and I don't have it.

As Janice's experience suggests, MSW students of color had to strike a difficult balance to embody a professional identity successfully: they needed to display a nonethnic professional habitus and simultaneously were expected to provide specific ethnic services to clients of color. And while displaying the mannerisms of the dominant white culture enhanced professional success, it acted as a barrier to ethnic community solidarity.

Professional students needed to perform a similar balancing act between gender and professional habitus. Women at the Law School were particularly likely to describe feeling conscious of their gender every day, as did Bobbi, a white woman:

> There's a lot of sexual innuendoing and there's a lot of gender references [in class]. And I'm very aware of it; I don't know if it makes me uncomfortable, and yet I think even in fact there is a separation, as a student in the class, when gender is introduced, there is a separation. You become a man or a woman. And there are definitely more jokes at a woman's expense . . . I think there's this whole discussion that if you want to make it in the professional world as a woman, you have to become more like a man. I think in ways that's true . . . when I'm in a professional situation, I get a lot more serious, a lot colder, and I tend to be somewhat sarcastic and joking in general with people, and that goes away instantly and I'm very worried about what I have to say and how I'm being perceived.

The gendered issue that women raised most often in our interviews was that of having a cooperative versus a competitive habitus. As Annmarie put it:

> Law school in general [is] really fitted to. . . I don't want to say the male model. . . you know what I mean? It's adversarial, and it's all about showing the other person that they're wrong. That's what the whole legal system is all about, and maybe that might be part of it, but I think most women. . . I'm generalizing now . . . the normal way most women interact with each other is not about showing each other they're wrong. It's about making sure everyone's okay . . . that could have something to do about people—about men—already knowing how to deal with law school. I don't know.

The competitive spirit of their consonant peers was alienating to a fairly large percentage of Law School students.[10] Julia stated in exasperation:

> If a student will raise a point, the other students are only concerned about tearing them down so that they don't look weak. They could never concede a point. And they'll fight about ridiculous things. We'll go out for lunch, and they'll spend an hour fighting about how your hamburger should be made, like you should put the pickle first, then

the ketchup, then the onion, then the lettuce. And they'll argue about it for an hour, and no one will give any ground because it's weakness. It's just ridiculous.

The competitive Law School inclination that many female students found distasteful was the orientation that was sanctioned by their profession, which presented them with a problem that few of their male peers faced. At the School of Social Welfare, the competitive habitus also presented a problem only for the women I interviewed, although the nature of the problem was inverted. Those few women in the MSW program who had the sort of predilection that would do them credit in the competitive legal profession were perceived as ungentle and unempathetic at the School of Social Welfare. Rina, a Jewish woman from New York with a background in business planning, described herself as primarily rational, "cynical," and de-bate oriented, and her classmates as "squishy." She was feeling unhappy and confused that her peers avoided her, and she had not made many friends (although she was doing very well academically).

Some students ran into gender-habitus trouble because they did not conform to typical gender roles. Kyle, a gay social welfare student with a theater background, was, as he put it, "pretty queeny." He liked to play with the way he dressed and had long, bleached-blond hair. He confessed that

> sometimes I feel a little uncomfortable in that I'm more of an artist type than my peers, and generally in the classes I think that I may have more creativity and more different ideas and stand out a little bit as being a little bit different. And while it's great to be an individual, sometimes you can feel a little uncomfortable.

Susan, a law student, had the opposite problem. She claimed to be "aller-gic to frills," and she arrived at our interview makeup free, wearing denim shorts, a navy sweater, brown Birkenstocks, and circular, wire-rimmed glasses. Susan said that "nothing on earth could make me wear foundation" and objected "on moral grounds" to the expectation that female lawyers should wear skirts, pantyhose, and makeup. She was worried about future confrontations with cocounsel and judges over her appearance.

I found it ironic that for men to have a "feminine" inclination toward empathy in the social welfare program or for women to have a "masculine" tendency to be competitive at the Law School enhanced students' profes-sional success, but that if these same students defied the norms of gendered appearance, they suffered. Why professionalism should be associated with gender-stereotyped appearance I cannot say, but I did find it to be so.

Students from impoverished backgrounds also suffered from negative dissonance at the level of habitus. Miryam described her class-based comportment problem in terms of etiquette:

> There is a handful of us in the program who were clients first. But I think often I am unaware of [what I'm doing wrong]. It's more my insecurities than anything else, because I very often feel like I don't know the etiquette. So I am learning the etiquette that it seems like the people who come from a different class background with a different path already know.

Jed also felt he had more to learn about social graces and tastes before he would seem like a "convincing" lawyer—although he felt his lifestyle had already changed enough to make him worry about alienating his family. He humorously described what it would be like if his parents were to visit Boalt: "I'd take them to the café for a latte, and my dad would just roll his eyes and ask for 'a regular cuppa Joe'." Like the students of color, students with working-class or impoverished backgrounds had to grapple with the realization that habitus alterations that would enhance their professional success could lead them to become estranged from their communities of origin.

A few students suffered the opposite problem from those with impoverished backgrounds: they endured problems as a result of a *loss* of status. While for most students, attending professional school was status enhancing, for those who had previously held high-powered positions, being a student was a definite step down. Neal, a law student of South Asian descent who had been a well-paid environmental engineer, was ambivalent about his decision to attend law school and become a "low man on the totem pole." He sighed and said:

> I do miss being a professional in that I had a place. I had an office with a door and a huge window, and this was my spot. If I wanted to get work done, I could toss my door shut and put up a Do Not Disturb sign and call up my secretary and say, "Don't let anyone bother me." I can't do that here. I'm just a student, and that's kind of a shift. That makes me less comfortable.

Neal's habitus made him uncomfortable at the Law School, but it should be noted that he felt more prepared to engage in professional legal practice because of it. His problem was limited to life as a professional student.

Some professional students who were older than average reported habitus problems that were, like Neal's, limited to life as a student. Kammi, for example, who was thirty-five, felt that in her maturity she lacked the "perkiness" of her younger peers and couldn't become as energized and excited as they did during class discussions. But Kammi also felt she had an advantage over her perky peers, stating that "they may have more energy but I have more maturity, and I feel I have at least a little more depth than most of them." She asserted that with her greater work and life experience she would make an excellent social worker. Ana, a Latina social welfare student, echoed this sentiment when she stated that although she did not feel socially integrated with her young peers, she wasn't concerned. "I have children their age," she stated with equanimity.

A fair number of students who entered professional school straight out of college were uncomfortable because they felt young and inexperienced, and, in contrast to the older students, they were particularly uncomfortable about their youth when I asked them about whether they would be good lawyers or social workers. Social welfare students, who engaged in clinical work, could already see that their youthful mien posed a problem. Grace described running into habitus difficulties in her placement:

> I've had a lot of problems with [being young], even on the phone. I've had two instances where parents wouldn't let me speak to my clients because they thought I was one of their friends. I think the way that I speak, too, sounds young. I called late—it was the only time I could call—and they said, "I'm sorry, she can't talk to you, she's busted," or whatever, and I have to explain myself. I can make myself sound older, but I don't naturally talk like that.

A large part of the problem of appearing young, as Susan noted, was that "you don't seem authoritative." Probably the fact that women in our society are not accorded the same degree of authority as men explains why almost all the students I interviewed who were anxious about their youthful demeanor were female.

The small number of students I interviewed who had visible disabilities also suffered from habitus problems. Laura, for example, was a deaf social welfare student, a graduate of Gallaudet College who was used to operating in the deaf community and communicating with sign language. She communicated to me that being the only deaf person in her class was a real "culture shock" for her. She could not communicate directly with any of her professors and peers and had to rely on interpreters or written communication. And because American Sign Language rather than English was her first language, she tended to make grammatical errors in her writing and was worried that she "would not be seen as smart." Participating was difficult for her, both because her interpreter lagged behind the swift oral conversation and because students did not raise their hands to participate but jumped in verbally, which she was unable to do. On the one hand, Laura found the MSW program exhausting and extremely stressful; on the other hand, though, she expected to be an excellent social worker, able to help her client population of deaf teenagers much more effectively than hearing social workers could.

An interesting group of students with habitus dissonance was composed of women who were contemplating pregnancy, who seemed to suffer from a problem that other students with spouses and families did not share: family loomed much larger in the priorities of these women than did career. For Susan, who described herself as a "housewife wanna-be," and who was planning to get pregnant soon, attending law school was just a means to an end: if she and her husband both lived student lives, they could share child-care responsibilities and avoid the use of daycare, and when they graduated they would be able to provide their child with financial security. She said of her attitude:

> I know it's unusual. Most of the people here are completely focused on themselves and their success. They have a very narrow focus, and it's aimed at high status and high salaries, personal success—themselves. I don't care about an astronomical salary; I'd rather have time to spend with my kid.

Tammy was not planning to get pregnant until after law school, but she was similarly disconcerted by her peers' career focus:

> I don't think it's right, because I just feel very strongly that family should come first. My relationship with my husband and wanting to have children come first for me, before law. And I think that's the way it should be. I was really shocked to find out how self-centered people are here; I think it's really sad. I have a close male friend . . . and he's

been in a relationship for a long time, and we were talking about our relationships, and he said that his girlfriend was 10 percent of his life, and law school was the other 90 percent. I think that's wrong, and really sad.

The problem with Susan's and Tammy's habitus was that a notable valuing of family over career is considered unprofessional. (Students I interviewed who had entered professional school as parents did not share the devaluing of a career focus which Tammy and Susan exhibited.)[11]

Dissonance as a result of a clash between a student's emotional orientation and the emotional posture required by her chosen profession was common among the students I studied. Almost all the students suffering from negative emotional dissonance experienced themselves to be more emotionally oriented than is the norm for their profession. To discuss a client or case professionally, they had to repress an empathetic reaction that felt natural to them. As Tammy, who described herself as primarily emotional, put it, "The law is basically rational and cold, and that's how you're supposed to approach cases." She continued, "I guess I can't say that this is wrong, because you need to be logical, but I get lost in all the abstractions, and it drains the passion out, and sometimes it's hard to remember why I came here at all." Adam, an African American law student, also felt uncomfortable unemotionally debating technical legal points and ignoring the underlying human suffering: "The whole time you're detached, and you're arguing the legal elements, when here you have a mother and her daughter was just killed . . . there's just no human element as far as the teachings go."

Besides feeling disconnected from the clients and cases as a result of their emotional dissonance, students often felt disturbed by the lack of empathy demonstrated by their peers. Susan said that class discussion seemed

> just so emotionless and cold. And also the fact that they're like that, it gives the impression that a lot of people don't care about what's behind a case, and they're taking this very impersonally. Like in classes, if a case comes up, people will laugh at the absurd hypos [*hypotheticals*], and they don't see that this is wrong.

While Susan was disturbed by her peers' lack of empathy for clients, Stacey was disturbed by her peers' lack of empathy for one another. She saw her classmates as backstabblingly competitive and said she had been unable to make any close friends at Boalt because "the kind of people who go to law school are just basically self-centered."

Another problem faced by students experiencing negative emotional dissonance was that situations elicited emotional responses from them that were deemed unprofessional. Jessie had "gotten into trouble" at her prior social welfare organization "because things that clients told me were so painful that I cried," she said.

> I know I need to be strong for them, and so I understand why people say that crying is unprofessional. But I am just an emotional person, and it's because I care so much that I'm here in the first place. And I don't know how you just don't cry, which is what my supervisor told me to do. She said if I had issues I should see someone, but that I could not cry in front of the clients, which is . . . I guess I understand, but I'm not sure it's so wrong.

Feeling professional pressure to censor emotional reactions was not confined to female students. Kyle, a gay white male social welfare student, had an experience similar to Jessie's:

> I definitely have an emotional response, and while I may not act on it, it still comes out and I'm very aware of it; it's really prevalent. I have sort of a lot of access to my emotions, I think, and what social work asks me to do is to not have those emotions be prevalent and to not have them run freely . . . it's a problem right now that I'm trying to work through because sometimes I have a response that's instinctual, like some client told me that something really major had happened to them and I felt like crying because of it.

While almost all students experiencing negative emotional dissonance felt that they were more emotionally oriented than their professions deemed proper, a few female social welfare students felt that they had the opposite problem. Janice, a Christian who tended to view her clients in morally judgmental terms, reported that she was having trouble demonstrating sufficient empathy:

> A lot of what we're learning is to get rid of our inside garbage so it won't get in the way of connecting with clients. We're dealing with a lot of our countertransference issues and checking to see if we do

have biases against certain groups or income levels. To me, that's more emotion driven than rational . . . they're always talking about unconditional positive regard, and I think it takes a lot to actually get to that place, to accept all clients.

Janice said she had to repress her rational, judgmental reactions in the classroom, which was difficult for her. Rina, too, was used to reacting in a rational, organized, and efficient manner and felt uncomfortable trying to conform to "the general touchy-feely ethic" at Haviland Hall.

The quotations I have selected to illustrate various sorts of habitus dissonance capture only a small part of the range of problems with manner or worldview. Individuals often are unaware of their habitus precisely because that level of our identities is nonconscious. Who, besides actors, teenagers, and politicians, consciously consider how to move their arms when they walk, or how loud their voice is in ordinary conversation, or how to respond to a photograph of an old man with his buttocks exposed? This last example may seem bizarre and somewhat shocking, which is precisely the point: a person's reaction to such a photograph is likely to be spontaneous and directed by habitus. (An individual with a demeanor consonant with a social worker identity would likely respond with concern, outrage, or both; an individual with a mindset consonant with a lawyerly identity would likely respond with amused detachment.)

### Managing Habitus Dissonance

Whether it is along the axis of race, gender, class, age, sexuality, disability, or some other personal identity, habitus dissonance exists below the level of consciousness and was therefore problematic for my subjects to manage. It was difficult for those suffering it even to recognize what the problem was. Many found the professional school experience uncomfortable some or most of the time, but they were not able to articulate why, since the reasons existed in nonconscious assumptions and demeanor. Unable to address their habitus problem, they sought to respond in conscious, cognitive ways. Most frequently, since professional school seemed "hard" to them, they responded by studying hard. Less frequently, feeling that something nonacademic was wrong, they focused on conscious ideological differences and sought to manage them. Neither the cognitive nor the ideological responses reduced the experience of habitus dissonance; both were ineffective.

A mismatch between personal and professional habitus led to reduced academic performance, which is evinced by most of the students with habitus problems receiving at best average grades. There were a few exceptions, as in the case of Tim, a gay white male law student. Tim was getting a joint doctorate degree in the Jurisprudence and Social Policy program, in which he was excelling, and his performance on the Law School examinations was also excellent. He had an impressive vocabulary and knew a lot of theory. He nevertheless suffered from a disposition problem at Boalt, because he was, to put it succinctly, shy. As he confessed:

> This has been a very tough year. It exacerbated problems which I already had: I hate speaking in class. It's been relatively easy to remain silent in most of my graduate seminars. So it caused me a great deal of anxiety—the thought that I would have to speak and endure the Socratic method; that they call on you randomly just fills me with such dread. So that has been horrible . . . I usually flub it up because [*he stutters*], because I have trouble talking. I'm too busy hyperventilating.

Tim presented an unusual case because he was aware of what the appropriate self-presentation was but was unable to embody it. When permitted to perform privately and on paper, he excelled, but the requirement of live professional performance left him frozen with dread. The rest of my subjects with habitus problems suffered them during performances on examinations no less than during class.

Because, unlike Tim, most were not receiving the above-average grades they had been accustomed to, the most common (but ineffective) management strategy employed by my habitus-dissonant interviewees was to devote a great deal of time and energy to studying. Their grades were not affected, but their personal lives were: most were suffering from a time bind. Listen to how an international student, Tsong-Min, described his life:

> I have to study hard, very hard, because I have had trouble with grades. I study every night until one or two in the morning, and I must get up early enough to review cases before class. It is very arduous. I do not have time for anything else. I used to spend much more time with my daughter, and I would help with shopping and laundry. Now my wife must do everything. I cannot go out to see a movie, to go to a restaurant, to take my daughter to the park.

Because professors at Boalt and Haviland assigned a lot of work, even the identity-consonant students often put in many hours working, sacrificing sleep, domestic order, and personal lives to do so. For habitus-dissonant students, the time bind was exacerbated by their reliance on an ineffective strategy of overwork.

Another common strategy adopted by students who knew that they were not receiving professorial approbation, although they could not tell why, was to frame the problem ideologically, as one of discrimination. They could see as well as I that there was a marked tendency for upper-middle-class white men to receive a disproportionate percentage of the high grades and professorial approval, and since they could not understand why this was so, they attributed it to bias. Tsong-Min believed his classroom remarks were poorly received as a result of "discrimination against Asian students because of my accent"; Jessie believed her comments received a lukewarm reception because of homophobia; and Rina asserted her social welfare peers were not befriending her because of their anti-Semitism. I by no means want to downplay the instances of bias and discrimination that professional students do encounter. (For example, recall that in 1995 someone put letters in the mailboxes of all the members of Law Students of African Descent, stating that they were taking the places of deserving (white) potential law students.) Yet the problem of identity dissonance is much more widespread than are blatant acts of prejudice, and no matter how much energy the students I interviewed devoted to combating bias, it did not reduce their dissonance.

Another commonly employed strategy for managing habitus dissonance was denial. Being unable to determine the nature of their problem, students frequently resorted to the ostrich strategy. Very often, even though they were virtually twitching with stress, students who were demonstrating multiple levels of identity dissonance assured me that they were comfortable in their program, that they enjoyed their classes, and that they were sure they would do well in the profession. Denial revealed itself in conflicted statements, such as this description of a Contracts professor by Rosemary, who had stated at the outset of the interview, "I like my classes, and the people are really friendly":

> Oh, he's a great teacher. He calls on you; it's very random, and he drills
> you just like you hear about law school being. And you know he's a nice
> person and a good teacher, but I am not comfortable about it at all
> because I feel like I am so worried that he's going to call on me at any
> moment, and even though I may have briefed a case perfectly and I

understand it, there's just this panic feeling of hearing your name called out like that and then getting grilled with one question after another, and I feel I'm going to get flustered easily, and so it's just the whole apprehension of it—I don't think it's a good learning environment for me.

Besides revealing itself in conflicted statements like Rosemary's, denial surfaced when students made statements which strained credulity, protesting a tad too much that something which certainly sounded problematic was no problem at all. Here is an example from my interview with Philip, a social welfare student:

> Do I dress like a social worker . . . you know, this reminds me of the class I hated most last semester. We actually spent two lectures on how to dress like social workers, which I snoozed through. I have always been a jeans and T-shirt and jeans, any-type-of-casual-clothes type of person. I hate wearing suits; I don't like wearing suits; and I will never wear a suit unless I am absolutely forced to. So, even when I had to go provide trainings to a bunch of administrative bureaucrat types who were all in their three-piece suits when it was like a hundred degrees in Sacramento, I had my pair of jeans and an old T-shirt. I felt like people paid attention to me and what I had to say and didn't care much about what I looked like. Suits are bogus; they didn't care at all.

It seems unlikely that the same bureaucrats whose slavish devotion to suit wearing Philip disdained "didn't care at all" about his tattered attire. It seems much more likely that Philip was trying to deny to himself that his aversion to professional dress presented a problem.

Rather than blustering through their denial as Philip did, some students managed to cling to an illusion that they had no problem by avoiding actions which would make their dissonance evident. Joy, a Korean law student, was one of these. Calling herself a "devout Christian" in her opening description, Joy suffered not only from conscious, ideological dissonance as a result of her fundamentalist Christian ideology, but also from a related habitus-level dissonance. When making decisions about how to act, Joy's first response was to turn to her relationship with God to guide her—the "what would Jesus do" response. In her worldview, decision making based upon rational self-interest or economic cost-benefit analyses was "amoral," and she had a visceral aversion to it. Joy avoided displaying her habitus problem by remaining silent, which allowed her to continue to assert:

> So, even if my views seem different, I don't think that [my professors and peers] would actually look down on them, just because it is different. It might actually be quite average here . . . they're regular people. They can't be all that different.

On some level, Joy was aware that, in fact, her professors and peers *were* quite different—why else would she so steadfastly remain silent? But she was determined to deny that a problem existed.

Denial is not just a passive management technique; students must actively avoid admitting that a problem exists, and this avoidance is stressful and difficult. For this reason, students who were denying their habitus dissonance often needed to buttress their denial strategy with activities that prevented them from having to think too much about their lives. Because it was socially sanctioned and readily available, overwork was the favored enabler of the denial strategy. Another popular prop was alcohol consumption, especially among law students. As Erin put it:

> I do a lot of drinking. I do bar review with people from my module, and on the weekends I party pretty hard. It keeps me from dwelling on things.

Another fairly common technique for managing habitus dissonance was to maintain doggedly that whatever their problem was, they would overcome it in time. Using this strategy of determined optimism, students chose to label unpleasant incidents as growth experiences. Kammi, for example, had to struggle for some time to get a schedule of classes that she could negotiate with her mobility limitations. Nevertheless, she said, "That was kind of empowering, because through my awful experience that I had to go through they realized something, and they're going to make changes, hopefully." And Kyle, who did not fit into the social welfare milieu because of his "queeny" demeanor, and who disdained the "mainstream" demeanor of professors, supervisors, and peers, nevertheless stated that he was finding the program "pleasant." He asserted that being forced to be "serious" instead of creative and "fun" was "maximizing more of my brain," which would mean "that I can run my own program one day."

Students who employed the strategies of denial and determined optimism tried to convince themselves that they did not have a problem, while they were aware of some distress, if not of its origin. Other students seemed not to be consciously aware of the tensions identity dissonance created in their lives and tended to employ a dissonance-management strategy of alienation.[12] Students employing the strategy of alienation kept their physical and emotional distance from the socializing impact of professional school. As Tarrah put it: "Primarily I come to law school and I go back home, where I can be myself. This is not my life, in a sense." Similarly, deaf student Laura communicated to me: "I haven't made any close friends in the program. I keep my emotional world separate from school." By avoiding the socializing setting, students could avoid discomfort. In fact, authorities on identity politics often advocate that members of disadvantaged groups avoid injury to their identities and self-esteem by retreating as much as possible to a "safe space" such as a black student union or off-campus apartment with coethnic roommates (e.g., Tatum, 1997: 77–78). The problem with this strategy of keeping one's distance is that the very thing it fosters—the protection of a cherished personal identity through avoidance of painful professional socialization—endangers the student's professional success. Rina came closest to articulating this when she said:

> I wanted to get a master's degree, and the social work degree was the one I decided to get because that was the area I was interested in going into, but I don't see myself as becoming a social worker. I see myself as a program director or something. But I found that to come here day to day, you need to sort of accept the fact that you're a social worker right now . . . you have to be in the culture in order to get the most out of it.

The students I interviewed whose negative dissonance problem was the result of their emotional orientation often employed the strategies of denial and alienation. In addition, they devised (haphazardly, as always) two techniques unique to the management of emotional dissonance.

The first of these was the related strategy of repression. Repression is a classic method for managing emotions that an individual feels cannot be appropriately expressed. Sita, a Bengali law student, was one of the students who employed repression to deal with her emotional dissonance: "At first, when I'm dealing with [a case], I'll lean toward the emotional a little more, but I think I've kind of learned to put that aside and start being rational and logical." The problem, as Freud noted, is that repressed emotions tend to seek expression. Sita acknowledged that the emotions she repressed would "come back" later when she wanted to relax. Kyle suggested that the best that could be done was to defer the expression of overly empathic reactions for a time; he wanted to "be aware" of his emotional reaction but "not make it known," to "hold it until a later date or just a few moments later until I can express it." Like all dissonance-management techniques, repression was an imperfect solution.

The other strategy for managing dissonance that was unique to emotional dissonance was translation. I asked Cecilia:

> If you feel you have a strong emotional orientation but the world of law expresses itself rationally, what do you do with that emotional side? Do you suppress it? Or do you express it despite the fact that it's not the dominant mode?

Her response was to pick neither of the options I presented to her:

> I think I translate it. I think it drives my sense of right and wrong and what the outcome should look like, and then I use the rational to make the argument for how to get there. I don't think that I would use the rational, or that I did before use the rational, as much as I do now. Now, I feel like before it comes out of my mouth, it has to already be translated into rational argument.

Nicole also spontaneously used the concept of translation to explain her experience:

> If you say that a covenant in property law is discriminatory because x, y, and z, and you're impassioned about that and you're explaining how you feel, people in the class will actually kind of snicker, because I think showing your emotions and passions is really considered not valuable in the law . . . what I try to do is to take my gut feelings and my anger and translate it into "rational" and come out in class with the rational speech. It's going to have some passion behind it, because that's just me, but I do try to translate it into acceptable—you know, sort of white male acceptable speech—because that's what's going to be persuasive, unfortunately.

The problem with the translation strategy was that it required a lot of effort. Just as students taking a class taught in a foreign language have trouble participating because, by the time they have been able to compose a comment, the discussion has moved on, emotionally dissonant students expended a lot of effort translating their responses, causing them to lag behind in the fast-moving conversation.

Some students employed more complicated strategies to try to preserve their habitus yet absorb the messages of professional socialization. The most dramatic of these was to split their identities. Many students did this to some degree, having a different self-presentation for different situations—for example, being more argumentative when at the Law School than while speaking with old friends, or using a more polysyllabic vocabulary at Haviland Hall than at home. A couple of students split their identities to a remarkable degree. Jasmine, introduced in Chapter 1, was one of these. Recall how Jasmine's entire habitus differed depending upon whether she was at school or at home with her Filipino community in Los Angeles:

> In the legal culture . . . you have to adopt a different way of being, a different vocabulary and way to carry yourself . . . you have to in order to . . . that's how I got this far. And when I go home, if I act the way I do here, if I speak the legalese, they won't get it. So I have to go back to the different way and rechange the way I talk and everything.

Recall too that when moving between the two environments, Jasmine experienced an awkward period of transition:

> Sometimes it's weird where I'll go home and my cousins and my friends say, "What did you say? What?" When I go home it's always, "You're kind of whitewashed." And when I come here I have to get back my law style.

Sita, a Bengali American law student, also split her identity quite dramatically. She was a classically trained Indian dancer, and the summer before law school she had danced six hours per day. Once law school began, however, she cut that down to an hour or less and spent her time studying. She came to our interview dressed in jeans and a black turtleneck, wearing light makeup, looking and sounding like a typical law student. Yet over the weekend, when she went home to her Bengali community for a Hindu religious festival, she spoke Bengali and wore traditional Indian garb (including *salwar khameez*, nose ring, heavy makeup, and a *bindi* on her forehead). Nor were all the changes on the surface; when with her Bengali friends, she said, "You just have to carry yourself differently." At home, her area of expertise was dance, and law was fairly irrelevant, while the reverse was true at Boalt.[13] When she returned to school, she reassumed her lawyerly dress, language, and posture. She said that "the separation comes more naturally now," and she was determined not to let her Bengali self "leak" into her lawyerly self, for example, by forgetting to remove her nose ring. She said, "I've actually seen a couple of girls wear a nose ring, but I don't think I ever will. That's kind of my personal opinion about how lawyers should look," a perception that of course was not hers alone.

A less psychologically exotic method of trying to maintain dual identities involved concealing a stigmatized identity. Unlike the students with split identities, who made no effort to conceal the split, students who kept a stigmatized identity in the closet attempted to pass as individuals with integrated consonant identities. This is a classic management technique for lesbian and gay individuals who wish to reap the benefits of concealing their homosexuality, and at the Law School, a fairly large percentage of gay men and lesbians were in the closet. (I know this because a couple of openly LG-BTI individuals I interviewed spoke to me about numerous classmates who had revealed their sexual orientation to them but demanded they keep this information private.)

Passing as a member of the hegemonic order has also historically been a route to power for individuals of mixed race. Only one student discussed this with me, but that of course does not mean that there are not more mixed-race students passing as white. The student with whom I had the discussion was Rosemary, a blond, blue-eyed student who was half Navajo and half white. Her grandfather's family had changed the family name "because you couldn't get a job" otherwise, and so "no one expects it at all" that she is Native American. Rosemary did not identify herself to the Boalt administration as Native American, either on her application or after having been accepted. When I asked whether she frequently felt aware of her Navajo background at the Law School, she replied that "no one knows I am." But Rosemary did not consider herself to be purposely passing; she attributed people's not being aware of her racial and ethnic status to "the fact that I look just like my [white] mom." She had in fact recently joined the Native American Law Student Association, and she said, "I'm open about the fact that I'm involved in it." In some sense, Rosemary was coming out of the closet at law school, and it was probably for this reason that she discussed the matter of her racial and ethnic status with me.

A third group that concealed a stigmatized identity was composed of students with invisible disabilities. I defined a disability to my interviewees as any condition that sometimes made it difficult for them to work or attend class, and thus I got information about disabling conditions from students who did not identify themselves disabled. Some students attempted to conceal their condition altogether, hoping thereby to appear competent rather than impaired. I had to probe persistently to discover the extent of such closeted disabling conditions, as is evident in this exchange with Sharon, a law student:

CYC:        Do you have any disabilities? It doesn't have to be a big, formal, official disability, but any condition that makes you occasionally unable to go to class, or to have trouble working?

Sharon:     Nothing major. I guess I have migraines, which sometimes really do interfere with studying and things.

CYC:        Have you had a migraine since you came here?

Sharon:     Yeah.

CYC:        Have you had multiple migraines since you came here?

Sharon:     Yeah. That's the thing—I had one that lasted two days that was kind of bad. Otherwise, it's gotten better this week, but the first two weeks, I had a migraine every day.

CYC:        Did you feel that you had difficulty doing your work because of that?

Sharon:     Yeah, it was difficult.

CYC:        Did you talk to any of the professors about your having migraines?

Sharon:     No.

CYC:        Did you talk to any students about it?

Sharon:     No.

CYC:        How come you didn't talk to any students about it?

Sharon:     Because . . . it's my own problem. I guess it's something that I just have to deal with. Everybody has things that distract them from their work, and so why is mine special?

Other students did not go so far as to conceal their pain, but they refrained from identifying themselves as people with disabilities so as not to be seen as "whining" or as seeking special treatment for a problem no one could perceive. An example was Jessie, who had been in a car accident the previous summer that resulted in a back injury that made it very painful for her to sit. Jessie had explained to her professors that she would need periodically to get up and stretch and said that "they have been very accommodating," but she was in almost constant pain. Nevertheless, she did not identify as disabled or even temporarily disabled "because that would sound way too serious . . . I don't want to look like I'm trying to milk it!"

Another way in which students coped with dissonance at the level of worldview and comportment was to resort to acting—that is, to engage in role play without internalizing as identity the role played. Often this was done by manipulating physical appearance. Most of what constitutes habitus exists at a nonconscious level, but many of the students I studied—particularly women—were aware of the elements of habitus which related to physical appearance. One of the questions I asked the students I interviewed was, "Do you think you look like a lawyer/social worker?" Men typically gave rather short and uninteresting answers to this question, such as Aaron's "I guess so, why not?" But women usually gave longer and more interesting responses, such as Tarrah's:

> Look like a lawyer? Well, to the extent that I'm not middle-aged, white, and male, no. Given that that's the norm. Other than that, I mean, I think I look rather young . . . although I think I look my age. If you're talking about whether I should have a tailored suit and go into court with my hair done, yes, I can see that image. But as far as just look like a lawyer, I can't really conceptualize that.

Like many identity-dissonant students, Tarrah was unable to grasp the fullness of her habitus problem but was able to compile a list of physical appearance and fashion dos and don'ts to describe the problems of which she was aware.

Since female students tended to be aware of discrepancies between their appearance and that of an ideal-typical professional, many tried to adjust their appearance to better fit that ideal image. Sharon, for example, who had previously worn her reading glasses only at home, took to wearing them to class, as her aversion to looking geeky was replaced by a desire to look mature and intellectual. Jessie toned down her "butch" look, saying: "I guess I don't need to out myself. I *do* want to look professional." Bobbi got a haircut and a perm, thinking to herself, she said, "I've got to get something done with my hair before I can do my interviews, because they'd think it was out of control." These gestures toward professional grooming were not limited to women; Neal, who as an engineer had shaved only once weekly, took to shaving daily. However, women were much more likely than were men to report such efforts, because our gender norms lead women to focus on their appearance and men to avoid seeming overconcerned with their looks.

The attempt to manage life changes with a makeover is commonplace in our culture of talk shows and fashion magazines (Tharp, 2001). But one's habitus cannot be altered simply by changing one's clothes, and students often felt artificial in their new looks. Susan, who hated makeup and claimed to be "allergic to frills," tried to conform to a more made-up professional ideal by wearing nail polish for the first couple of weeks of class, "but then I just sort of lost the energy to keep it up, and it just chipped off and looked ten times worse than if I hadn't tried to wear it in the first place." Stacey, the former athlete, also had a failed makeover. She related how her moot-court advisor, who was "over the top," and whom she described as a potential future host of the show *Fashion Emergency!* told her that she would need to get a darker suit, wear glasses instead of contacts, and "lose the hair." Stacey did cut her long, unstyled hair into a chin-length bob, which had to be blown dry so that it would curl under—but, she said: "I just hate it. It isn't me, and I feel stupid in it. I'm letting it grow out." "It isn't me" is a phrase which captures the feeling of habitus dissonance remarkably succinctly.

There is more to acting than wearing a costume, and I observed students role-playing by attempting to alter their posture, pattern of speech, and other aspects of habitus, but few students described these aspects of role play to me. This is likely a result of their embarrassment about attempting to act a role that is supposed to come naturally. A few students did articulate their role playing, as Erin did when she told me, "When I have to go to an interview or moot court or something, I put on my legal look, but I don't want to become the dark suit." But only one student confessed to me that his entire professional school life was an act, and that was Jed.

During our interview, Jed relished telling me the fascinating story of his Law School act—a tale reminiscent of an undercover spy thriller. Coming from generations of poverty in the Ozarks, Jed knew nothing about the life of a lawyer "other than what I saw at the movies or on *L.A. Law*," and so he decided to "play the part like they do." Before matriculating at the Law School, he "bought a bunch of *G.Q.* magazines and studied them." He then spent what was for him a large sum of money to buy clothes in which he would look the part of a lawyer. (At our interview he wore a starched white button-down shirt with taupe hairline stripes, an undershirt, khaki slacks, and black leather shoes.) Next, he cut off his ponytail and had his hair trimmed "short on the sides, so that the gray would show at the temples—I thought that would be a nice touch."

Jed revealed that he had done more than change his look—he was playing the role of the perfect law student to the hilt:

I try to act hypermasculine: I do a lot of posturing [he puffs out his chest] and speaking in a loud, powerful voice. At first I used to worry a lot that I would let my guard down and forget to put on my manly act and get caught out or something, but I've got the act down now. I act really impersonal and goal oriented, like a man with a plan who's not going to get distracted. And I totally conceal my leftiness [sic]; I act as though I just want to cut to the chase and avoid any distractions like politics. And I only use a limited part of my analytic abilities—only the hyperrational part. I never let on that I actually have feelings and that I care—I'm just Mr. Hyperrational. And you know what? It works.

Jed's role playing was quite successful: he was doing well when cold called in class and felt he was learning "the tools of the trade." The problem was that his method acting was working too well, and he realized that his lawyerly act was oozing into his reality. He worried that his "true core self" was being altered, and that he was in fact becoming more hyperrational, hypermasculine, and politically centrist.[14] He also worried that his self-interested, goal-oriented lawyerly act was, as he put it, "contaminating" his relations with his wife. And, in fact, his wife had begun to complain that he was becoming "mean" and "too serious." This is the essential problem with role playing: it is either artificial and unconvincing, or, if it seems natural and convincing, it is because it is becoming embedded in habitus and is no longer an act at all.

None of the improvised strategies for managing habitus dissonance was terribly effective. For this reason, most students with demeanor problems wound up deploying more than one strategy, and some employed an impressive number of them. I found that Cecilia, for example, was employing the overcoming strategy, denial, alienation, and role play to manage her habitus problem, which she remarkably termed "cognitive dissonance." In addition, she was using the translation strategy to manage her emotional dissonance, and alienation and solidarity to manage her ideological dissonance. Juggling so many management techniques just to endure daily life at professional school, as so many students did, it is no wonder that identity-dissonant students like Cecilia were underperforming academically.

## The Reported Effects of Negative Dissonance

I have already discussed two central difficulties suffered by negatively dissonant students: underperforming academically and being starved for time. These effects were exacerbated by students' general lack of awareness of how to improve their grades and in-class performances, and by the futile attempt of many to better their performances by devoting longer and longer hours to their studies. While this extra study did not improve their performances much (Katie lamented, "Sometimes it seems I can stay up all night studying, and then if I get called on I just get flustered and mess up anyway"), it did exacerbate their time binds.

As a result of receiving mediocre grades instead of the exemplary marks to which they were accustomed, many negatively dissonant students felt keen disappointment. Getting mediocre grades was a threat to their egos because so many students shared the self-identity "academic overachiever" when they arrived on the doorstep of professional school. Of course, most matriculants have heard that professional school is much more challenging than college and that they should not count on stellar grades, but their very identities told them they would prove the exception to the rule. The identity-consonant students were generally affirmed in their identities as academic stars, while the identity-dissonant students generally had this self-identity undermined.[15]

If the result of negatively dissonant students' lower grades was injured egos, the result of their time bind was injured interpersonal relationships. Like the positively dissonant students, many were suffering relationship troubles. Ana, for example, said that the reduced time she had available to spend with her husband was "a real issue" to him, and that she too felt "I'm missing out on something that I need to have." In addition, she was unable to keep up with the domestic chores that she had taken responsibility for previously, and her husband was not willing to take over: "He's been more helpful, but he also works long hours and he works six days a week, so he doesn't have a lot of spare time." Ana tried to excuse her husband's refusal to do more around the house, but she was working seven days per week with no day off to relax and pursue other interests. In addition, while Ana was quick to point out that her husband was "extremely supportive of me doing this," she also sounded miffed that he took no interest in her studies: "He works, and he wants to come home and do the things that are important to him—sitting around and reading and discussing [social welfare issues] are not his cup of tea."

A significant number of negatively dissonant time-bound students were having serious problems in their relationships. Tsong-Min, who was working every night until one or two, basically ignored his family, leaving his wife to work to support them and to pay his tuition, as well as to be responsible for all the domestic work, including the care of their young daughter. Tsong-Min reported:

Before we came here, my daughter would turn to Mother or turn to me, equally. But after we came here for a while, she would only want "Mama, Mama." Now this semester she is in China with my parents, so it is less work for my wife, but still she miss our daughter. And my wife would always ask me to do things with her, and I felt she did not need so much time from me. Now I realize my wife was lonely. We had many fights. She asked me to go to mountains with her, go to this dinner party, that restaurant, but I would not go because I have to work. She would complain but I would ignore her. Then she started talking of divorce. We even discuss child custody. I did not know what to do. There is no one to talk with about my problem; I realize I have no friends. I decided my family is my obligation, and time with my wife must be my sixth class. She is still unhappy but she is no longer talking of divorce.

Tsong-Min's family relationships were damaged; other students' relationships broke off completely. Erin's long-term relationship with her boyfriend did not survive the first semester of law school. She said caustically that "the law is a jealous lover," and that her boyfriend could not understand "my mindset and my focus on my goals and on school, which I had to have to survive here."

I was interested to discover that a significant number of identity-consonant students also had relationships attenuate or terminate during the first year of professional school. What was remarkably different about the consonant students' experiences was that the deterioration of their relationships did not bother them. When I asked Meredith if she had a significant other, she replied:

Well, I had been in this relationship with a guy—he's pretty much of a slacker—for a pretty long time when I came here. He's really laid back—he teaches gardening to young children, and he's not interested in anything more high-powered—and he didn't really like my decision to come to law school. He kept calling me to tell me I shouldn't work so hard, and he couldn't get it that I wanted to work this hard. So I basically used the fact that I had come to law school as an excuse to end the relationship. He's a nice guy, and I didn't want to hurt his feelings, so I just said that I didn't feel like a long-distance relationship could work. He's still calling me every day anyway. But I'm on the market for someone with some more energy. Not a slacker.

Carlos, a social welfare student, sounded equally nonchalant about having broken off his engagement with his fiancée:

Carlos:    I think in the process between the time we got together and now, we kind of grew apart, and she realized that she wants more than being number two, and I can't give her all the attention for her to be number one right now, because I'm focused on my school, and I honestly want to be the best at what I do. . . . But in a weird way, when she was with me I got the highest grades I've ever gotten.

CYC:    Why do you think that is so?

Carlos:    I think the more she wanted me to spend time with her, the more I had to go away and study more.

Rather than experiencing his relationship difficulties as an agonizing distraction from his studies, as negatively dissonant students like Tsong-Min did, Carlos felt that his relationship problems only sharpened his focus on school. It seemed that for consonant students like Carlos, whatever obstacle they faced turned up academic roses for them.

For many negatively dissonant students, however, facing disappointing grades and disgruntled partners led to depression. Julia, for instance, might have approached her two Hs and two Ps with optimism—they were, after all, above the median. Instead, she said, "Lately I've been getting depressed" because her grades did not put her in contention for a top summer job. Sitting on the sidelines, she said bitterly, "Summer jobs, you know—that whole process is just ridiculous, watching people fight it out and talk about it and everything." Bobbi, too, was feeling "very stressed" and "very frustrated" and said, "I don't know if I can take this sterile environment for three years." And Rina had found it necessary to seek therapy so that she could manage what she termed the "rocky road" of her social welfare training.

Certainly not every negatively dissonant student was depressed. Some relied on the determined optimism of the overcoming strategy to manage their dissonance, others employed the strategy of alienation and claimed to feel little at all, and a small number even relished their experiences. But no matter what the effect, the experience of negative dissonance threatened students' sense of self. Even Jed—who relayed with zest his cloak-and-dagger story of going undercover at the Law School—experienced his dissonance as threatening. While he enjoyed the game of acting the role of a lawyer, he acknowledged that he was "playing with fire" and feared that he would become the part he was playing, losing his principles and risking his relationship with his wife.

While some students who endured identity dissonance were depressed and others displayed determined optimism, almost all suffered from anxiety. By its very nature, the discordance between two different identities seems to produce, like nails scraping a chalkboard, anxious discomfort. Complaints of feeling stressed and nervous were ubiquitous. Lindsey, a social welfare student, reported:

> I work hard, I really do, and then after I've stayed up late to finish a paper I can't fall asleep. I've just got a lot running through my mind, and it's giving me insomnia. It drives me crazy. I didn't used to be so anxious, and I'm really considering whether I should look into getting some sleeping pills or anxiety meds or something. Because I tend to be anxious in class as well. I don't know what I'm afraid of—like the professor is going to catch me out not knowing the answer to something, or I'll say something wrong and everyone will act all nice about it but inside they'll be, like, what's she doing here? Like that would happen. I know it's silly, which is why I've been thinking about asking for meds.

Feelings of inauthenticity in role playing and the fear of being caught out contributed to dissonant students' anxiety.

A final typical result of negative dissonance was students' reasonable fear that they would not do well in their chosen professions. For social welfare students who were already having problems at their clinical placements, this fear was not theoretical. Why should Rina's conflicts with her supervisors or Grace's lack of authority over clients or Jessie's tendency to cry disappear when they were handed their MSW degrees? The law students' impressions of professional practice were much more vague and unformed since they did not do clinical work, but they too raised reasonable concerns. Rosemary said:

> I have definite misgivings about [professional practice]. When I think about the big law firms they tell us about, it's like nothing I even want to get involved with, because it's too cold. Things I've read and things they've told us about it, it's like you're just their worker, and you don't bring in the personal side . . . you're just a blue suit or something.

Bobbi said something similar.

| | |
|---|---|
| CYC: | Do you think you're going to make a good lawyer? |
| Bobbi: | Do I want to make a good lawyer? |
| CYC: | Why do you say that? |
| Bobbi: | There's this idea around here that the good lawyer is the very rational, the very "I can make an argument, no matter what you give me" kind of person, the very professional, the very kind of cold, I think, person that's more of a "I do my job" kind of thing. Could I do that? Maybe. Would I be very happy at it? Probably not. |

For suffering students, negative identity dissonance had multiple detrimental consequences. It negatively impacted students' academic lives, leading to poorer grades. It adversely influenced their personal lives, leading to a drought of time, to domestic disarray, and to strained and fractured personal relationships. It left them prone to anxiety and depression. It negatively impacted their professional success, which would depend upon the full internalization of an appropriate professional identity. And the tendency toward experiencing identity dissonance was patterned in ways that reproduced patterns of social stratification, as we explore in the next chapter.

# 7    Patterns Observed

*The Reproduction of Social Stratification*
*at Professional Schools*

In the previous chapter, in which we explored identity consonance and dissonance from an experiential perspective, that consonance and dissonance are not randomly distributed experiences began to become clear. For example, being positively dissonant was associated with being a woman of color and with having strong religious commitments. In this chapter I focus on the patterning of identity consonance and dissonance that emerged through my participant observations. What surfaces is a distribution of identity dissonance that often mirrors patterns of social stratification—which is what makes the study of identity dissonance important.

## Early Evident Identity Problems

In the earliest days of professional school, most students displayed habitus problems as they found themselves in an unfamiliar environment, and strong patterns of dissonance were not yet apparent. For example, the students lounging in the Bordon Family Courtyard before the first day of classes at the Law School had widely varied styles of dress; norms of attire had yet to emerge. Several students, particularly women, were dressed glamorously, apparently inspired by the wardrobes of attorneys on television dramas. Some students wore casual shorts and T-shirts, and others wore somewhat more formal khakis or jeans with button-down shirts. A few returning 2Ls and 3Ls were displaying their summer-associate attire, wearing pressed shirts or blouses with linen or tropical-weight wool jackets. The general impression I gathered was of a hodgepodge of styles; however, during my second year of observations, I could see that the students who were most likely to be wearing what would emerge as the law-student norm (khakis or jeans with unadorned neat shirts) were disproportionately white and male. But this was only a tendency and hardly a strong pattern.

The pattern that did emerge among the law students gathered before the first day of classes was the difference between the incoming students and those who were returning. The novice professional students were an awkward lot compared to their elders: they looked nervous, engaged in stilted interactions, and laughed too loudly, while the 2Ls and 3Ls appeared relaxed and confident. Almost all the first-year students seemed off balance, whatever their gender, ethnicity, or background.

Feeling friendless and unsure of what social norms apply is a highly anomic and uncomfortable state, and I observed the first-year students engaging in a frenzy of socializing in an attempt to regain their social footing. When, the day before classes began, I met an acquaintance in a Boalt lobby and said hello, the two new beskirted students with her quickly began a conversation with me, seeking to find mutual acquaintances. I wrote in my field notes: "The conversation was forced, upbeat, well-mannered, and net-worky." At both schools, numerous new students approached me in the early days of the year, assuming I was one of their peers, and there was a lot of handshaking and insistent cheer. I received contradictory impressions from these interactions: they felt simultaneously friendly and calculating, open and appraising. I believe this was because the unsettled first-year students were approaching me both as an end in myself (a potential new friend), and as a means to an end (a source of information about norms, or even a potential competitor).

The intense socializing on the part of the first-year students, both with each other and with upperclasspeople, led to the establishment of group norms with remarkable speed. For example, on the first couple of days of classes at the School of Social Welfare, students took copious notes. Within days, however, note taking was tapering off, and students were scribbling furiously only when the professor wrote something on the board. By the second week, the students in Professor Alverson's Practicum were taking almost no notes, although they were engaging in affirmative listening techniques with great vigor. Students were evidently paying intense attention to one another's behavior, because I observed some trends sweep through classes over the course of twenty-four hours. One day in early September in Professor Tate's Torts class, I noted that a few students had taken to raising a pen instead of a hand in order to volunteer. By the very next day, raising a pen instead of a hand had become a majority practice in that classroom. The replacement of junk-food snacks with healthy ones at the School of Social Welfare proceeded almost as quickly.

Because of the intensity and speed of norm establishment at the schools I observed, early habitus problems soon became evident. Some students came to stand out because of their style of dress. For example, women at the Law School quickly adopted an androgynous style of dress, and the few women who did not follow this trend swiftly came to appear overly feminine, as did a white woman who wore a bubblegum-pink outfit during the second week of classes. Other students who stood out sharply because they departed from the ethnic and gender norms of law-student dress included an Indian woman who wore a *bindi* on her forehead, and a man with long gray hair pulled back in a fabric scrunchie. At the School of Social Welfare, the norms of dress were more flexible, but students still managed to violate them. Ugo looked overly formal in a charcoal suit, and a woman with neon magenta hair and numerous piercings was conspicuously a cultural outlier.

Some of the students who stood out visibly from the crowd in the early days soon modified their appearance and blended in—Ugo, for example, bought himself some less formal clothing for school. Others did not achieve consonance so easily. At the Law School, students literally had their marginality locked in when seating charts were drawn up after a few days of classes. In both the Torts and Contracts classes that I regularly observed, every single Asian American male was sitting on the periphery when this happened. There was a marked tendency for students of color in general to seat themselves away from the center of the class in the early days of the semester, and this decentered position was petrified by the seating charts. The front row was disproportionately occupied by students with visible comportment problems, including an Asian woman with poor English skills, the man with the ponytail in a scrunchie, and a white woman who wore outfits that I noted looked "floofy" and "secretarial" in comparison to those of her peers. Students who sat in the front row apparently hoped to signify their academic eagerness to the professors, and yet they were often overlooked, due, I believe, to their inappropriate habitus. For example, I noted that the "secretarial" woman raised her hand several times in Professor Santana's class and was not called on.

Sometimes students were physically unable to conform to the norms of habitus which were established. Having a daily fresh shave was a norm at the Law School, but when one African American man tried to conform to it, he developed a terrible case of razor bumps due to ingrown curly hairs.

Another African American man looked awkward in his interview suit, which was too short in the leg and gaped at the back vent, having been designed for a body with a flatter posterior; his habitus failure was built into the suit by designers who shaped their clothing to white male proportions. A female student with a large bosom made a related point to me when she complained that she could not find a suit which did not gap or pull at the chest. The norm of androgyny for women in the professions found an expression in the construction of women's suits to fit slim, boyish frames.

Another group that was physically unable to conform to habitus norms included students with visible disabilities. For example, social welfare students quickly found that in the bare corridors of Haviland Hall, sounds echoed and reverberated, and they tried to avoid making undue noise in the central hall while classes were in session.[1] But a white male student with a motor disability was unable to avoid violating this norm when he walked down the hallway, the metal taps on his orthopedic shoes sending out loud, syncopated, ringing echoes, calling attention to his uneven walk. And at the Law School, students sitting in the amphitheatrical lecture halls responded like a theatrical audience to professors' comments, laughing and frowning and nodding in synchronicity—except in the case of Beverly, a deaf woman, who received a transcription of the comments with a five-second delay, and whose laughter rang out awkwardly in the middle of later remarks.

Another way in which identity dissonance became evident to me as an observer was through students' awkward attempts to hide it. Students attempting to manage dissonance through closeting sometimes called more attention to the information or behavior they were trying to conceal than would have been the case had they made no attempt at concealment. I encountered a classic example relating to the closeting of homosexuality when a man and woman who sat near one another in Professor Tate's class had an awkward conversation in which she attempted to ask him about his attachment to another student without making reference to that student's gender, and he attempted to discuss the relationship with "this person that I can't name because the person's not comfortable."

Closeting or passing was a technique students used to manage dissonance relating to many things besides sexual orientation, and I regularly observed physical attempts to hide nonnormative behavior at both schools. I saw a student at the School of Social Welfare hide Doritos in a bag under the table, sneaking each chip to her mouth behind her hand—brown-bagging it with no less guilt or obviousness than an alcoholic sneaking a swig of bourbon. I watched a student in Professor Hoffert's class secretively glance at a commercial contracts outline in his backpack, as red faced as if he were risking a peek at some pornography. I also observed several pairs of female students at both schools, and one pair of social welfare males, making ongoing, obvious attempts to conceal their passing of notes.

Sometimes dissonance became apparent to me because students attempted to give it voice, rather than conceal it. During the first weeks, I occasionally heard from students' comments that they were becoming aware of the conflict between their conscious identities and the professional role they were encountering. For example, on the first day of his Property class, Professor Santana gave a brief introduction to stock arguments and counterarguments, presenting legal cases as indeterminate and legal practice as gamesmanship. When he asked students what they thought of this, some responded with excitement, but a few gave replies that revealed incipient ideological dissonance: "It makes me worry we might lose sight of why we're here in the first place"; "It's like taking an ethics class when the professor says, 'There are no right answers'—it sounds immoral." The first remark raises a student's fear of losing herself, and the second raises the social justice orientation that led to much of the ideological negative dissonance at the Law School. (Both of these respondents were white women.)

In my observations of early audible or visible identity problems, patterned trends did emerge. Female students, members of racial/ethnic minorities, and students with visible disabilities made up the bulk of those who displayed obvious identity problems. This was by no means a universal rule, however—consider the white man who wore the ponytail and scrunchie, and the white male whom I caught sneaking a peek at the commercial outline.

## Disparate Professorial Treatment

While I argue that patterns of underperformance can be explained by identity dissonance in the absence of overt professorial discrimination, I do not wish to ignore the reality of disparate treatment of students by professors. In fact, I noted disparate treatment upon a significant number of occasions. The two groups who seemed most likely to face disproportionately negative treatment were students of color and students who made relatively radical fashion statements.

Two of the teachers I observed, Professors Hoffert and Tate of Boalt Hall, were most likely to give disproportionately negative treatment to students of color. Professor Hoffert seemed to be somewhat less likely to be favorably impressed by the comments of students of color than by those of white students. During one class, for example, he asked an African American woman to state the facts and respond to questions on one case, and then asked a white woman to do the same for a second case. In my estimation, the first woman gave a much stronger Socratic performance: she spoke confidently, recited the facts smoothly, and answered all the questions correctly. The second woman's responses were vague and filled with hedges such as "I think . . . " and "It seems like . . ."—the sort of responses of which law professors typically disapprove. Yet Professor Hoffert reacted much more favorably to the white woman than to the African American woman. His responses to the African American woman's comments consisted of saying, "You'll have to speak up" and some unenthusiastic nods and uh-huhs. His gave the white woman a much more cheerful and enthusiastic reception. I do not believe Professor Hoffert chose intentionally to discriminate. It seems likely that he was unaware that he reacted to different categories of students with greater or lesser enthusiasm. His behavior, that is, was driven by nonconscious habitus rather than by a conscious, ideological identity such as "white supremacist."

If Professor Hoffert reacted with less enthusiasm to the comments of students of color than to those of white students, he gave disproportionately positive responses to the comments made by white men in his class. For example, Professor Hoffert knew the names of his white male students better than he did those of other students. In one incident I described earlier, Professor Hoffert kept comparing an existing contract rule with two alternate possibilities, which he named after the students who proposed them: one was called "Mr. Froebel's rule" and the other "her rule." Mr. Froebel was a wealthy foreign student from Germany, while Yesenia, the other student, was Latina. Yesenia's proposal proved much more memorable to Professor Hoffert than did Yesenia herself, and he forgot her name moments after reading it off the seating chart. The only students whose names Professor Hoffert knew this early in the semester were all, like Mr. Froebel, white and male. Yesenia was a sharp student, unafraid to ask questions, but the rewards for her behavior were mixed. During a class discussion of unilateral contracts, Yesenia raised her hand to ask a question, and Professor Hoffert's response was to propose a hypothetical in which Yesenia was presumed to be a kleptomaniac. For the next few minutes, she was "the shoplifter" to the rest of the class, an outlaw instead of a law student.

Professor Tate was also prone to respond insensitively to students of color. For example, when calling on a Filipina student, he repeatedly mispronounced her name, Ligaya, which flustered her but not him. When Professor Tate asked her for a particular fact from a case, and Ligaya began to scan her copious notes to locate it, he immediately called on a (white male) volunteer to take over, without giving her a chance to find it. Professor Tate seemed to consider himself an equal-opportunity insensitive, averse to "coddling" anyone and prone to sadistic joking, but while many students of various backgrounds might object, for example, to his regular proselytizing for the elimination of bans against hate speech, it is likely that students who were members of the underprivileged groups that are most often the targets of hate speech found his stance more personally threatening than did students from privileged backgrounds.

I did not observe any professor at the School of Social Welfare display a pattern of disparate treatment of students according to their race or ethnicity. However, I did note that professors at both schools were less receptive to the comments of students who made rebellious fashion statements. I recall that, when I was a graduate-student instructor, I once dyed my hair violet for a lark. My graduate advisor asked, "But Carrie, aren't you worried that your students won't take you seriously?" I replied that this was the U.C. Berkeley Department of Sociology, and my students were likely to respect me *more* with purple hair. I did not, in fact, find the authority accorded me by my students to be impaired in the least—but this only serves to highlight the differences between the norms of college students and of professional school professors at the same institution. A student at the School of Social Welfare began the program with bright magenta hair, and her professors seemed to treat her with much less deference than was typical. When she challenged Professor Dunn's apparent endorsement of the ecosystems approach, stating, "It assumes that 'adaptation' means 'good,' when what it really means is accepting cultural losses and accepting being hurt," he rebuffed her in what was, for him, a brusque manner: "I think you really need to take into account that all change involves both gains and losses; we really need to bear that in mind." There were no students at the Law School with multiple piercings or magenta hair, but the bar for determining what styles were considered discrediting was set much lower. A white male student who wore a couple of big silver rings, an earring, and his hair in a chin-length bob probably had the most radical appearance in the Torts class I observed, and he was repeatedly treated dismissively by Professor Tate.

In sum, patterns of disparate treatment on the part of professors did exist. Yet I could observe only a limited tendency toward regular patterns of discrimination. While this limited dissimilar treatment may have heightened identity dissonance, it is insufficient to explain it. For that, we must turn to an examination of how consistent treatment by professors led to differing outcomes depending upon the personal identities of students.

## Differing Outcomes of Consistent Professorial Treatment

### *The Score*

All students hope their comments will receive professorial respect. At the Law School, where professors employing the Socratic method gave swift and public positive or negative feedback on student commentary, this hope was particularly fervent. The law students employed a variety of terms to refer to doing well under Socratic questioning: they spoke, for example, of "nailing it," "acing it," being "right on the money," being "right on target," and "scoring." Occasionally, students displayed their respect for an especially impressive peer performance with the sort of gestures often made to celebrate an impressive athletic performance—pumping their fists and saying "Yes!" fanning their faces dramatically, or sketching a few little "I'm not worthy" bows. This was the case when Valerie, the person first cold called in her module, reviewed her successful performance with peers in the courtyard at lunchtime. She received high fives from the circle that gathered around her, exactly like an athlete who has made an important score.

Law students were all aware that, to score, they had to be substantively correct. But they were less aware that being substantively correct was insufficient to secure a score—one had to have the correct habitus as well. I observed on numerous occasions that the success of a law student's performance was undermined if he did not display steady upright posture, easy eye contact with the professor, a dry bantering tone, hyperarticulate syntax, a refusal to be cowed under questioning, and a voice whose volume began and remained fairly loud.

In the early weeks of classes, students' comments during Socratic questioning tended to be somewhat off target substantively, yet students who displayed the appropriate habitus managed to score nevertheless, because their performances hit the right note and therefore received professorial approval. For example, during an early discussion of fraud in the Contracts class I observed, Professor Hoffert peppered Jeremy—a white man wearing a charcoal sweater-vest over a white T-shirt—with a series of questions. Jeremy sat upright and still, holding a thoughtful hand to his chin, maintaining eye contact with the professor, speaking in a confident tone, and refusing to back down from his argument. In the end, Professor Hoffert conceded the point admiringly, despite Jeremy's failure to come up with the legal rule the professor wanted. He said, "Okay, that sounds like a good rule. It's not one I've ever seen before, but it does sound good." The students who entered the Law School with the approved confident habitus already in place were disproportionately white and male, as Jeremy was, and therefore white male students experienced a disproportionately large percentage of classroom scores. (Note, however, that even privileged white men fairly often failed to score, and that few found being the subject of Socratic inquiry pleasant.)

A characteristic of students who were likely to score was their refusal to treat anyone as having greater authority than their own. For example, when Daniel, a white male student, proposed a rule in Property class, and Professor Santana counterproposed a compromise rule, Daniel replied, with unselfconscious arrogance, "That's not good enough." Similarly, rather than deferring to a court decision, Brad called its reasoning "inappropriate and unconvincing." Most individuals in our society are negatively reinforced from a young age if they display such egotism and indifference to others' authority, but those who come from a position of privilege (particularly ruling-class white males) are most likely to be permitted to develop such habits. (As always, this is a trend rather than an absolute rule; students other than upper-middle-class white men displayed a lack of deference at times. For example, when Sylvia asked Professor Santana a question, he reformulated it and asked her, "Is that a fair restatement?" Her friendly yet not deferent reply was, "No, that's a different question, but it's also an interesting question.")

Another habit likely to contribute to scoring in the Law School classroom was to employ the sadistic humor toward which the professors were inclined. This was something women rarely did, although it seemed to come as naturally to men of color as to white men. After Adam, an African American student, gave a long and complex exposition of the facts in a torts case, Professor Tate asked, "Can you put that in a nutshell?" Adam's reply—"The plaintiff drove on the tracks and got smacked by a train"—had Professor Tate nodding and chortling. Similarly, Miguel, an Asian Cuban student, recited a fact pattern involving drinking, harassment, beating, and death in a light, comedic tone that reduced the entire class to laughter and made Professor Tate beam.

A few abilities that increased the likelihood of a score were evenly distributed among all students. These were cognitive habits of mind.[2] One of these was the ability to pay exquisitely close attention to procedural de-tails—the sort of details many people find boring or technical upon which legal cases so often hang. For example, Paige, a white female student, raised her hand in an early Torts class to inquire: "May I ask a procedural ques-tion? This case is before the Supreme Court and the opinion discusses the trial disposition, but was there an appellate review?" Professor Tate replied: "*Good* question. In Washington State at the time, there was no appellate level." (The class found this early score so impressive that it gave out a col-lective "oooh.") Another score-promoting characteristic was the capacity to memorize great quantities of minutiae. Jason impressed all with his recall when, having been cold called to give a recital of facts, he mentioned the ex-act date in 1905 when the defendant's ship damaged a dock during a storm, without ever glancing at his notes.

At the School of Social Welfare, students never spoke of scoring, and the competitive drive to perform well in class was much reduced. Never-theless, students did hope to be well received by professors and peers. As I discussed earlier, students played a greater role in monitoring the behavior of their peers in the social work program than at the Law School. What I found interesting is that professors at Haviland Hall tended to focus upon different aspects of student commentary than students did. While the social welfare professors modeled affirmative listening for all student comments, I observed that they tended to respond most positively to students who made articulate and insightful intellectual points. In this focus, they responded very positively to students with rational emotional identities and strong cog-nitive analytic skills, and these students were disproportionately male.[3] For example, the hyperarticulate comments made by Peter, who was introduced in Chapter 1, were treated with professorial deference upon every occasion I observed him speak in class.

Social welfare students themselves, however, gave positive and negative reinforcement (by giving or withholding affirmation) according to a differ-ent set of criteria. They rewarded expressions of empathy and sensitivity and punished politically incorrect, insufficiently sensitive utterances. They also rewarded deference to communal authority and punished failure to acknowledge communal authority.

Because the matriculating student body at Haviland Hall was largely fe-male, highly empathically oriented, and generally left-liberal, peer feedback centered on the sensitivity of students' comments in a way that professorial feedback did not. For example, when Ugo complained about the need to "restrain the jaws" of teenaged female clients "who say, 'I can do whatever I want and I can say whatever I want,'" and Luis issued his comment about "sneaky" Hmong and Laotian clients, Professor Alverson said nothing about their insensitive phrasing but simply addressed their substantive concerns. Ugo's and Luis's classmates, on the other hand, gave them negative feedback in the form of bristling and shunning. This sort of negative peer feedback affected students with conservative social ideologies (who were disproportionately Christian) and students without strong empathetic orientations (who were disproportionately male).

While the professors I observed at the social welfare program all told students that they should learn from one another, they maintained control of the classes they taught and took it in stride if a student addressed a comment directly to them. The students, however, generally held to a communalist ethos, and in all but the large Introduction class, they subtly discouraged students from addressing remarks to the professor instead of to the class as a whole. For example, in Professor Alverson's class, two students gave reports on the Foundation Center Library. When Rachel made her report, she made eye contact with various classmates in turn, explaining to them what materials and services they could access at the library. Her peers responded with many nods and "mm-hmm's" of affirmation. Margaret, who reported next, directed her report to Professor Alverson, making no eye contact with her classmates (although they, not the professor, were unaware of the library's policies). Her peers responded by greeting her comments with dead silence. Students who were especially authority conscious were often subject to shunning for their noncommunalist behavior—sometimes including, interestingly enough, Peter, who was often received especially well by professors.

That Peter was sometimes received frostily by his peers raises a provocative possibility. Theoretically, a social welfare student could make a comment that scored with a professor while being treated negatively by his or her peers. Would such a student likely be identity consonant or dissonant? That Peter was a comfortably consonant student suggests that the socializing effect of professors was more important than that of peers.

## The Scrub

We have seen the patterns of identity consonance which emerge when we consider classroom performances that are treated as exemplary. Related patterns emerge when we consider classroom performances that fall flat. At the Law School, what students desired much more than to score was to avoid embarrassing themselves with a poor performance. Boalt students referred to such a mortifying experience as a "flub," a "strikeout," a "freeze," a "crash"; as "blowing it," "losing it," "being wasted," "tanking," "bombing"; and as a "scrub." The fear of enduring a scrub before an audience of a hundred peers was strong and existed from the first day of classes. This was evident from the tense atmosphere during the first class meeting when, although Professor Tate used a friendly tone, he subjected a student to prolonged Socratic inquiry; when he attempted to lighten the mood by phrasing his questions as bantering jokes, the students' laughter sounded forced and brittle.

If students who scored had a hyperarticulate and highly self-confident self-presentation, students who scrubbed generally did not. Habitus failures which undermined the success of a Law School performance included a posture that shrank back under challenge, a gaze that dropped, syntactical habits that differed from those of the WASP upper class, a tone of voice that betrayed fear or hurt feelings, a rising or questioning tone, or a voice whose volume dropped over time. These sorts of professionally inappropriate habitus were displayed much more frequently by students who were female, people of color, or individuals with lower-class backgrounds.

Law professors told their students that they needed to learn to "think like a lawyer," and that the Socratic method would teach them to think on their feet. In fact, the classroom performances which received positive reinforcement from professors were distinguished from poor fledgling professional performances by style more than by content. For example, Professor Santana asked students to argue the two sides of a case. Brad argued firmly and confidently for the plaintiff, retaining his composure under questioning. At the end of his argument, the professor beamed and commented, "Beautifully done." Trisha then argued tentatively for the defendant, and although her legal points were correct, she demurred deferentially under questioning and ended by stating in a rising, questioning tone, "I'm not sure if I expressed that so well?" Professor Santana cocked his head and stared silently at her in disapproval. What is important to note from the perspective of identity dissonance is that Brad's style involves a demeanor typical of men in our culture, while Trisha's style involves a style typical of women. The female law students I observed were more than twice as likely as the males to have their substantively correct answers dismissed because of a "weak" presentation, although men gave "weak" performances too, especially in the early weeks.

The vocal habit that I frequently observed led women to scrub despite being substantively correct in their answers was the tendency to phrase their answers in questioning tones. In Professor Santana's class, Nicole volunteered to make a point; she phrased the point as a question and received a lukewarm response from the professor. Bryan, a white male student, then volunteered essentially the same point, articulately phrased it as an argument, and received professorial affirmation. (The woman seated beside me whispered admiringly, "He nailed it.") What distinguished Nicole's scrub from Bryan's score was the gendered tendency for women in our society to use questioning tones to indicate either vulnerability, lack of complete confidence, or a desire not to sound presumptuous, whereas men generally bluster through, making self-confident statements despite feeling the same vulnerability, lack of complete confidence, or lesser expertise (McFayden, 1996).

I know from my interviews that both women and men often lacked complete confidence in their responses, and that both at times felt stymied by a professor's Socratic questioning. The distinguishing difference in their habitus is that women tended to own and expose their anxiety and confusion, whereas men tended to disown or conceal their confusion. A striking example of the disparate outcomes of these styles was provided one day in the Contracts class I observed. Professor Hoffert first cold called Robin, a white woman, and asked her to recite the facts of a case, which she did calmly and comprehensively. He then diagrammed several contracts on the board and asked Robin to relate the case at hand to the various diagrams. She became flustered and said, "I'm so confused by all the boxes and letters on the board." Professor Hoffert said, "Okay, I'll walk you through it." His hand-holding allowed her to answer the question, but at the cost of looking weak and losing "points." Professor Hoffert then asked Thomas, a white man, to recite the facts of a second case, which he did with ease. When Professor Hoffert next asked Thomas to relate the content of the acceptance in the case, he did not give the answer the professor was seeking. Professor Hoffert then asked, "What else does the acceptance say?" Thomas clearly had no idea of what Professor Hoffert was looking for, but rather than becoming flustered and saying "I'm confused," Thomas assertively placed the blame squarely on Professor Hoffert: "What else does it say? The acceptance says numerous things. You'll have to let me know what you're aiming at." Instead of responding with hand-holding condescension, Professor Hoffert responded with respectful clarification. Internalizing the awkwardness of Socratic questioning led to scrubs; externalizing it led to scores.

Another gendered habit that tended to undermine classroom performance was nervous giggling, engaged in fairly frequently by women but only rarely by men. For example, Cindy, an Asian woman, gave a long, technical, accurate response to one of Professor Hoffert's questions, which probably would have earned her a score—had she not paused twice and filled her pauses with high-pitched giggling. When men needed to pause to collect their thoughts, they mostly did so in unapologetic silence and lost no "points" thereby.

Even if they were able to avoid using a questioning tone or giggling, women at the Law School were more likely than men to have their points fall flat because they sought to explain rather than argue their position. Tarrah explained her take on a property case without phrasing her position as a question but nevertheless failed to secure an affirmation from Professor Santana, whose response was, "Okay, now make that argument." In fact, even when making an argument, women were still more likely to scrub, because of their tendency to defer to the professor's greater authority. For example, when Professor Tate stated as a fact that it was poor policy to employ tort law as a form of economic redistribution because the injured poor would unfairly benefit, a white woman, looking disturbed, raised her hand to disagree:

> Eliza:    But often when large corporations take actions that will lead to injuries, the poor are unaware that they have been wronged. They don't know that they have the right, the legal right to sue, unlike the wealthy or corporations.
>
> Prof. Tate:    Well, all you have to do is watch late-night TV to see tort lawyers advertise.
>
> Eliza:    Yes. Well. That isn't . . . maybe I don't necessarily agree.

If Eliza's habitus had allowed her to defy Professor Tate's authority over her and disagree with his assertion, she could have scored despite the professor's disagreement. But by being a "good girl" and deferring to his authority, Eliza scrubbed.

Lack of self-confidence was the factor that underlay women's greater tendency to scrub. It was the characteristic that led to some of the most spectacular classroom failures, which I termed in my field notes the "deer-in-the-headlights incidents." In one such incident, Professor Santana asked Joanne, a white woman, to use the precedent in one case to argue for a certain outcome in a second, and then to distinguish the precedent in the first case to reach the opposite outcome in the second case. Her response was to freeze, staring at him for an increasingly awkward period of time until chairs around the classroom had begun to squeak, and Professor Santana permitted a volunteer take over. Released from the figurative spotlight, Joanne was able to sit back, trembling slightly. Frozen by her fear of failure, she had failed even to try to respond.

Two vocal mannerisms that varied by race and class affected the outcome of Socratic performance. The first was the use of verbal fillers such as the ubiquitous "like." The use of fillers was more common among students of color and students with working-class backgrounds, such as Tracy, who gamely responded to a series of debating questions from Professor Santana with answers that were adequate in substance but marred by her repeated use of the phrases "I mean," "I think," "it's like," and "you know." A second speaking prop which undermined performance was the habit of reading one's notes aloud rather than speaking extemporaneously. I noticed that women of color were especially reliant on note reading.

Sometimes identity dissonance did not impair classroom performance. Ideological dissonance did not lead directly to scrubbing, because ideological differences which led law students openly to debate professors actually enhanced their professional image at the Law School. But I observed that classroom performance at Boalt was often undermined by emotional dissonance. Students with empathic orientations were often dismissed sarcastically by professors who saw them as failing to reason with mature moral logic. When Professor Hoffert asked Betsy, the white woman who sat next to me, what she thought of the result in a case under discussion, she said she agreed with it. He then asked her why she thought the rule was a good one, and she replied:

> Well, I think . . . I think this particular case is fair on the facts. I feel the plaintiff got what he deserved. But I don't necessarily think that this should always be the rule.

Professor Hoffert shook his head at this use of particularistic, empathy-driven moral reasoning and responded mockingly:

> So we'll have one rule when people lose grain, but another when they lose their foot! But if you look at the rule, it's supposed to apply to all cases equally. So let's play the game of sticking to one rule and see what results.[4]

Students who scrubbed as Betsy did because of their reliance on empathy were primarily women but sometimes men, among them Hector, a Latino student, in this discussion of a case with Professor Santana:

Prof. Santana:    In a way, this is a pragmatic decision: "Conquest gives a title which the court of the conqueror can't deny."

Hector:      It's a "might makes right" doctrine.

Prof. Santana:      What do you think of that?

Hector:      It sucks. [*class laughter*]

Prof. Santana:      Why?

Hector:      I . . . it . . . I just have a gut feeling that it's wrong.

Prof. Santana:      [*purses mouth in dissatisfaction*]

Considered in overview, it is apparent that most of the elements of habitus that negatively impacted Socratic performance in the Law School classrooms were disproportionately displayed by women. Women's tendencies toward deference, toward admitting lack of self-confidence, toward nervous giggling, and away from confrontation all inclined them toward scrubbing. Women were also more likely to suffer professorial disapproval for displaying an orientation toward empathy. The performances of law students of color or of impoverished backgrounds were disproportionately undermined by non-WASP speech patterns and the use of verbal fillers, and by reliance on note reading. The only factor that detracted from the classroom success of all students equally was lack of substantive knowledge; that is, the tendency simply to get an answer wrong was an equal-opportunity stumbling block.

While students at the School of Social Welfare hoped for professorial approval just as law students did, they did not have to fear the public humiliation of a scrub. Social welfare professors, even at their most irked or least impressed, never resorted to employing a stronger corrective than withholding affirmation. Social welfare students did express discomfort during their interviews due to not receiving the support they desired, but they did not convey the level of anxiety that law students did. Students who did report feeling that they were not receiving deserved faculty support felt this largely on ideological grounds—that is, they felt that the curriculum was heterosexist or that their professors were not sufficiently committed to antiracism or that the rights of unborn children were not being adequately addressed. But I did not observe patterns of classroom humiliation based on deportment problems or emotional dissonance as I did at the Law School. Social welfare students might fail to score, but they did not scrub.

Students at the School of Social Welfare did face negative reinforcement from peers. Students who made insensitive or politically incorrect statements were subject to peer correctives in the form of withdrawal of affirmation or, in more severe cases, shunning. Social welfare students were sensitive to these correctives in a way their law-student counterparts were not (since the former were trained to sensitivity and the latter away from it), and so they might experience them as akin to scrubs. For example, when Maureen, a working-class white woman, used the terms "black" and "Mexican" early in the semester instead of the more politically correct "African American" and "Chicano," she received a rather stiff reception from her classmates, which she was sensitive to, as I could tell by her increasingly tentative tone. (She later adjusted her vocabulary.) It appeared to me that, in general, middle-class white women, who were in the majority, were the least likely to suffer peer correctives.

### Saved by the "Balls"

In addition to the language of "scores" and "scrubs," law students introduced the additional evocative concept of converting a potentially failed performance into a successful one through a "save." Being assertive and confident in one's responses in the face of professorial challenge could secure a law student professorial admiration even when his or her theory was substantively wrong. For example, Joel made an argument for the defendant's case which he mistakenly structured around the plaintiff's case. When Professor Hoffert snidely stated, "Did you by chance mean to argue for the plaintiff?" Joel confidently stated, "Of course," without embarrassment or hesitation, and then had his argument treated with respectful consideration by the professor. A student who brazened out a Socratic situation this way was referred to casually by other students as "having balls," which serves to underline that it is a normatively masculine characteristic. And, indeed, it was demonstrated almost solely by men.

When unable to answer a professor's question, the reaction of most women (and of a fair number of men) was to become apologetic or embarrassed. Rather like the dominant wolf who stops attacking a pack mate when she turns up her belly in submission, the professor would then back off from Socratic inquiry, but the student would be left looking weak and defeated. But students who were able to brazen out a situation in which they did not know the answer retained their unsubmissive honor. For example, Professor Santana questioned a number of students about the *Pierson* case, attempting unsuccessfully to extract a legal concept from them. The students all flailed about, becoming flustered and apologetic. When Professor Santana turned to Ted, he too was unable to come up with what Professor Santana wanted, but instead of becoming flustered, he stated with self-possessed irritation, "It really seems like you're looking for a particular answer, but I can't find it." It was then Professor Santana who became apologetic. That Ted responded with "balls" on the second day of classes indicates that he arrived with this consonant manner in place. Over the course of the first year, I did not observe many women acquiring the ballsy response through socialization, probably because it conflicted strongly with their deeply ingrained feminine habitus.

### Bodily Betrayals

At some times, especially in the early months, students at both schools made excellent comments with the appropriate demeanor and yet found their performances undermined by physical symptoms that betrayed their discomfort and anxiety. A visible bodily betrayal was the flush. For example, when Professor Tate called upon Lisa on the first day of Torts class, a bright pink flush spread dramatically from her face to her neckline. Social welfare student Margot blushed as brilliantly when she volunteered to speak in the Foundations of Practice class. And when Professor Hoffert called upon Jack, the consonant habitus implied by his evenly paced and smooth answer was belied by his glowing red face. Whether this physical betrayer was demographically patterned or not, it could be readily observed only among the fair of skin.

Students also suffered bodily betrayals in the form of nervous gestures and tics. Students of every stripe displayed nervous tics of all kinds, again particularly at the start of the school year. Some, like the law student Tim, stuttered; others nervously pulled at a lip or a lock of hair; still others shook a foot or twisted anxiously in their chairs or gestured wildly. This behavior was more discrediting at the Law School than at the School of Social Welfare, and perhaps for this reason persisted longer into the semester at Boalt. Nervous twitching was not demographically patterned, but I did not often observe extravagant hand gesturing on the part of students with more patrician WASP backgrounds.

### Rehashing

Law students whose performances were treated negatively by a professor received their negative reviews before an audience of about one hundred peers, a typical class size. Students often remarked to me that they felt as if everyone was watching them, and they clearly found this stressful. During interviews, Boalt students sometimes reported reactions similar to posttraumatic stress disorder: they reported finding themselves playing a classroom incident anxiously over and over while trying to think what they could have done better. As Sharon put it, "The first year, everyone goes home and rehashes everything that they said, and everyone thinks that they're so stupid for saying this." Such rehashing detracted from students' learning experiences inside and outside the classroom. For example, I watched Nora, who volunteered to speak on an issue, begin well, giving a clear, seemingly well-rehearsed answer, maintaining eye contact with the professor, and sitting with an upright and still, if rather stiff-looking, posture. But as the professor pressed her further and further to defend her position, Nora's answers, which continued to be adequate in substance, were undermined by her inability to maintain her lawyerly demeanor: she giggled, snorted, looked down at her notes, and gestured nervously with her hands. I noted that minutes after the professor had turned to other cases and students, Nora was completely distracted, mumbling to herself under her breath as she rehashed her performance.

Students who scrubbed lost out not only because they felt professionally invalidated during their failed performance, but also because they did not learn anything during the period in which they rehashed their inadequate responses, and this period could be surprisingly extensive. For example, when a Chinese American student, Harold, was pressed by Professor Tate, he stuttered to a weak surrender ("I . . . it . . . I really don't know. Next?"). I timed him to see how long he took to become fully involved in following the class discussion again: he spent three minutes muttering to himself, then two minutes flipping through his casebook to look at the case, which was no longer under discussion, then about four minutes fiddling with his pen and doodling. By the time Harold returned to note taking, almost ten minutes had passed.

Because law students who were female, people of color, or of underprivileged class origins were more likely to scrub in the first place, these students were most negatively impacted by such rehashing. Thus we can see how having a dissonant identity crossed over from being a problem only of professional identity to a problem of knowledge acquisition as well. While the identity consonant and identity dissonant might have the same intellectual capacities, the identity-dissonant student suffered greater levels of distraction in the classroom.

## Role Play

While students tended to react without conscious volition by blushing, deferring to authority, or giggling when nervous, other aspects of their behavior were under greater conscious control, and students manipulated these vigorously in an attempt to secure a professional reputation via role play. They altered their appearance and their vocabulary, their opinions and behavior, in an attempt to look more professional—to engage, as Robert Granfield put it in describing the behavior of underprivileged Harvard Law students, in "making it by faking it" (1992). Sometimes these actions were convincing, but many times they were not, which served only to throw the students' dissonance into further relief.

### Appearance Management

As I have mentioned, in our makeover-obsessed culture, people often attempt to deal with life changes by altering their "look." Certainly the professional students I observed were no exception. A good illustration is provided by hairstyles. A substantial number of students at both schools changed the way they wore their hair during the first semester. Because women's hairstyles vary more than men's in our culture, these changes tended to appear more dramatic on women, although men in droves also got their hair cut—four men sported fresh haircuts on a single day in Professor Lipman's class.

Women changed their looks in a number of ways by manipulating their hair. At the Law School, women sought a simple, elegant, WASP look, having their hair styled in plain blunt cuts. For example, Stacey got her hair cut from its scraggly midback length to a neat above-the-shoulder blunt cut. Women affected a casual elegance by giving up the scrunchies and claws that they initially used to hold back their hair, instead putting their hair into a simple French twist or bun, often secured casually with a pencil.[5] Women of color also adopted the WASP look. After just one week of classes, an African American student, Camille, had removed her many cornrowed extensions and wore her hair short and straightened, styled into a small bun with gold pins. Roshida, who was also African American, similarly shortened and straightened her hair. And Susie, who was Asian American, had her hair lightened to a medium auburn brown, which gave her a more Anglo look.

Susie cannot have been the only woman dyeing her hair at the Law School, because I noticed that while a good number of men in Professor Tate's class sported graying temples, none of their female peers did. Men benefited from looking mature, but women apparently did not think this look would give them a similar advantage.[6] Law-school men did little fussing with their hair, in generally wearing it in short and unremarkable styles. The few men who did come to the Law School with longer hair attempted to lessen their style's drama, either by pulling their hair back into a ponytail or by cutting it somewhat shorter—but if their hair remained chin length or longer, these modifications did little to remediate their nonconforming habitus. The vast majority of men at the Law School kept their hair short, got regular trims, and came to class freshly shaved every day.

At the School of Social Welfare, people of all genders wore their hair longer. Whereas law-school women sought to shrink and control their hair, social welfare women sported fuller, more feminine styles. This is not to say, however, that women at Haviland Hall did not cut and restyle their hair. Luz, for example, had her longer, wilder hair styled into shorter face-framing curls that looked more mature and more conventional. This proved to be a popular move; two more women in the same class (one white and one Asian) followed Luz's lead and cut their long hair into shorter, more full-looking styles. African American women, like their peers at the Law School, also adopted white-looking hairstyles, as did MSW student Shandra, when she had her elaborate curled extensions removed and her hair straightened and styled into a French twist, and Ivette, when she adopted a straightened, chin-length bob.

Besides manipulating their hairstyles to give a professional impression, many students regulated their appearance through careful wardrobe management. Just as an actor seeks to get into character by assuming an appropriate costume, so the professional students I observed sought to enhance their professional role playing by dressing the part. The law students quickly adopted a more formal and subdued look, while the social welfare students tried to appear more casual and funky, in a calculatedly limited fashion.

A garment whose use illustrates these trends well is the T-shirt. Among the U.C. Berkeley undergraduates, T-shirts were the garment of choice during the warmer months and were often emblazoned with commercial motifs such as athletic shoe logos (Adidas, Puma) or cute characters such as Hello Kitty. At the Law School, a much smaller percentage of students wore T-shirts, often unornamented. On 9 September of my first research year, the temperature was unusually hot but the number of law students wearing T-shirts continued to decrease. Most of the T-shirts I did see were unadorned, and of those that were ornamented, only one bore a commercial logo (an Asian American man wore an Ocean Pacific–brand T-shirt); the other ornaments were two college names (UCLA and Dartmouth), one Monet art-exhibit souvenir shirt, and two striped T-shirts. Instead of wearing T-shirts, law students favored more formal polo shirts and preppy button-downs, particularly in plain white. During a single typical Torts class I counted twelve plain white shirts—the equivalent of camouflage in the Boalt Hall classrooms.

Students in the MSW program were much more likely to wear T-shirts than were their Law School counterparts, particularly on hot days. In addition, while law students eschewed T-shirts with slogans, social welfare students wore them frequently to display ethnic sensitivity and a commitment to social justice. On the same hot 9 September, the T-shirts social welfare students wore included an iconic Che Guevara T-shirt, one advertising the "Books in the 'Hood" project, one emblazoned "La Raza," and one that proclaimed "All One People" over a view of Earth from space. In addition, whereas law students clad themselves in snowy white, social welfare students rebelliously preferred the more edgy black, even on this hot day.

In addition to attempting to signify their social justice orientations by wearing political T-shirts, social welfare students sought to signify cultural sensitivity by wearing assorted ethnic paraphernalia, including Native American jewelry, Central American textiles, Kente-print accessories, and Chinese coin necklaces. The law students, on the other hand, abjured wearing anything ethnic and instead attempted to signify a cultural affiliation with the patrician class by wearing cardigans, sweater-vests, and turtlenecks in quiet, subdued hues such as navy, burgundy, and charcoal.

Whereas the social welfare students favored ethnic jewelry as the role-defining accessory of choice, law students were restrained in their jewelry choices. The men wore little if any jewelry apart from the nontransgressive wedding ring, and the women wore mostly small gold earrings, a gold ring or two, and perhaps a gold chain necklace. The preferred accessories for law students signified intellectualism and class status. Favored among these were eyeglasses, associated with intellectualism in our culture—half again as many law students as social welfare students wore glasses. In September and October, I observed a rash of law students who had previously worn contacts starting to wear glasses to class. In fact, two female students came to class on a single day wearing new, very similar glasses with tortoiseshell frames that looked sophisticated and expensive. A few students went so far as to wear glasses that had the look, if not the function, of half-glasses in an attempt to signify not only intellectualism but maturity. And of course, professionalism was advertised by the use of the most up-to-date, lightweight, sexy laptop computer. Technological toys served role-signifying ends perhaps even more than they served functional purposes.[7]

It appeared to me that male social welfare matriculants feared that they would have to share the understanding of masculine appearance to which law students adhered. I came to this conclusion because I was struck by the large number of new male MSW students I observed whose pierced ears were empty of earrings. After a couple of weeks had passed, I gathered that the social welfare men had come to understand that wearing earrings need not hurt them in a "feminine" profession, because those empty ear holes began to fill. Still, I could tell that social welfare men continued to manage their appearances carefully when I noted that a number of men had multiple ear piercings yet wore only one earring. The subpopulation of men who had pierced ears before attending the social work program had to engage in a balancing act, adding enough earrings to appear suitably sensitive and nonthreatening, yet not so many as to appear deviant.

All women (rather than a subpopulation) at both schools had to engage in a similar balancing act, appearing feminine enough not to look ugly, yet masculine enough to appear professional. At the Law School, women adopted a bland androgynous look, as if attempting to erase any gender markers from their appearance and to look neither feminine (weak) nor masculine (offensively butch). Law School women generally wore khakis or jeans with a simple turtleneck, shirt, or blouse, minimal makeup and jewelry, and simple, restrained hairstyles. At the School of Social Welfare, in contrast, women adopted an androgynous style of dress characterized by exuberant combinations of masculine and feminine elements, appearing both feminine (empathetic) and masculine (authoritative). Their footgear was usually masculine (Doc Martens, hiking boots, Converse high-tops, or fat-strapped Birkenstocks); their tops tended to be feminine (embroidered shirts, Indian-print blouses or low-cut tank tops). Women at both schools thus had to balance masculine and feminine elements to create an androgynous impression, but the Law School women were in flight from gendered characteristics, while the social welfare women were drawn toward both genders' associations. The women law students displayed a negative, subtractive androgyny, the women social welfare students a positive, additive one.

I found it thought-provoking to note that when women at the Law School prepared for professional practice by interviewing for summer associateships, they wore much more feminine garb—dark navy or black skirted suits with ivory or white silk blouses, pantyhose, pumps, and a moderate amount of makeup. In fact, the only time I saw women at the Law School fussing with their appearance at the bathroom mirrors was when they were preparing for interviews. The androgynous norm of avoiding feminine primping was displaced during interview season by displays of femininity. I also noted that second- and third-year female law students were more likely to wear skirts and other feminine attire than were the first-year women. This led me to suspect that different norms controlled the Law School and legal practice, and that female law students would have to undergo another resocialization when they began to practice law. When women at the School of Social Welfare went to their placements, in contrast, they dressed in a style nearly as androgynous as they did when going to class, leading me to believe that the School of Social Welfare and social work agencies held similar norms.

Life appeared simpler for men at both schools I observed. They did not have to balance masculine and feminine elements in their dress to avoid looking unprofessional or unattractive. Men *were* constrained in their dress and could not adopt too radical an appearance, but as for their positive obligations, all they needed to do was wear jeans and a simple shirt, and no one would take any note of their clothing. Men at the School of Social Welfare were more free than were the male law students to vary their appearance, for example, by wearing longer hair, an earring, or a political T-shirt, but they were certainly not obliged to do so. It appeared to me that women had to do a lot more work to manage their appearance in dressing the part of a professional than did their male peers.

Other groups of students besides women had to do a notable amount of work to manage their appearances as well. Students who were lesbian, gay, or bisexual took great care to manage the queerness of their appearance. Students who entered the Law School with the demeanor of queer activists quickly toned down their style. For example, Fred, who during the early days of his first semester in the Law School wore a rainbow flag on his backpack and a T-shirt with a Gay Pride slogan, within three weeks had taken to wearing a Boalt T-shirt and a Cal Bear pin on his backpack. Similarly Nikki, a lesbian who had initially sported a butch look, by that date had toned down to a white polo shirt and cargo shorts.

At Haviland Hall, LGBTI students underwent an inverse transformation. To attempt to appear professional, they were initially careful to remove earrings, avoid rainbow paraphernalia, and dress fairly "straight." But as the early weeks progressed, LGBTI students cautiously added more queer signification to their appearance until they apparently felt they had achieved an appropriate balance between LGBTI ethnic identification and professional nonradicalism. Richard, for example, arrived clean shaven with his hair at a neutral length and his ear pierce empty. After a couple of days, he put his stud earring back in; after the second week, he got a trendy haircut; and a month later, he was sporting dramatically pointed sideburns and a fashionable goatee.

I observed that students with disabilities also had to work hard to manage their appearance. Beverly, for example, was a deaf law student who needed to have lectures interpreted for her. During the first week of classes, her interpreters employed American Sign Language. That they were unapologetic in their support of the rights of people with disabilities proved a liability for Beverly. Two interpreters came to class with her, and every half hour one would relieve the other. The fresh interpreter would walk up front and place a chair directly beside the professor, a process which attracted attention and which Beverly apparently found mortifying, for with each unapologetic switch she blushed deep crimson. Beverly wasted no time changing the arrangements for her accommodation, and by the third week of classes the ASL interpreters were replaced by a stenographer who transcribed the lecture so that it appeared on Beverly's laptop screen after a delay of several seconds. Now, instead of the embarrassingly political interpreters, Beverly had secured the aid of a legal-looking stenographer, less visible help that gave her a more professional air.

In the course of my research I found that most students with disabilities sought to make their disability less visible to appear more competent and professional. Some students with disabilities who suffered from a related ideological dissonance, however, sought instead to make their disabilities *more* visible, because they were offended by the grudging nature of the schools' efforts to accommodate them. Nicole, for example, faced resistance from the Law School's administration when she sought to change her class schedule to fit in her breathing treatments for asthma.[8] As a result, she had taken to using her inhaler in a very public manner:

> Like, this is the first time in my life where I actually had to do, like, "I'm disabled!" Whereas before I would try to play it down. I would only take my inhaler in the bathroom. Now I take it whenever, because I feel like I almost have to prove that I'm an asthmatic. Which is really unfair.

I found that students who concealed their disabilities to the extent possible were those most likely to approach identity consonance. These students understood that "professional" was tacitly and unfairly assumed to mean "nondisabled," and they sought to manage their appearance accordingly.

Students of color also took special care to manage how they were perceived. As I have mentioned, women of color emulated the hairstyles and hair colors and textures of their white female peers. But this is only one example of the numerous ways in which many students of color sought to approach a white look. Unsurprisingly, few described this in my presence in overtly racial terms (although Jasmine did so when she told me that her friends referred to her Law School persona as "whitewashed"). Yet it was apparent to me as an observer that the professional students of color differed much less in their self-presentations from their white peers than, for example, did the students of color from the white students at the local Berkeley High School.

I noticed that African American students appeared to be especially careful about managing how they were perceived. At both professional schools, African American students paid meticulous care to their grooming and dress; for example, at the Law School they were more likely than were other groups to wear clothes that were obviously pressed and starched. At the School of Social Welfare, a student who wore starched clothing deviated from the calculated casual norm, but that African American students carefully managed their self-presentations was made evident in an incident I observed when students' photographs were taken.

In the central corridor of Haviland Hall, display cases held alphabetically arranged photographs of the social welfare students. Of all the photographs of first-year students, two—both of African American women—were different from the rest. These two photographs pictured students who were in Professor Alverson's class. On the day the pictures were taken, I observed these two women leave the room before class began, seeking to arrange to have their photographs retaken because they deemed the initial results "ugly." One day much later while I was walking down the hall, I was struck while I was still halfway down the hall by the way these two women's photographs stood out from the rest. Unlike the casual, generally unflattering photographs of the other students (worthy of any Department of Motor Vehicles), these two were carefully posed and pictured women with perfectly groomed hair. One woman's glamorously made-up face was in closeup, in contrast to the shoulder-up shots of her peers, and the other's was displayed in three-quarter profile, in contrast to all the others, which were full-face photographs. These two women had taken extraordinary measures to manage their self-presentation, presumably because they felt they could not afford to appear unattractive or unprofessional.

At the Law School, students of color appeared most professional when they had erased their ethnicity as much as possible. But at the School of Social Welfare, students of color had a less clear path to follow because they needed to balance definitions of professional appearance and demeanor that assumed a white cultural norm against signifiers of their special abilities to provide service to their ethnic communities. They had to worry both about looking professional, and about "keeping it real." That this balancing act was difficult and triggered anxieties seemed evident to me as I listened to Luis report on his site visit to his potential clinical placement agency. After describing how he had dressed for the visit (in nice slacks and a "professional-looking" jacket), Luis went on in his report to compare the "nice suburban program" to "our kinda situation in da 'hood." It seemed to me that Luis chose to speak from a position of oppression, to balance his prior speech from a position of neutral professionalism. The balancing act that the social welfare program required for the socialization of its students of color was a difficult one—although the more straightforward cultural erasure required of law students of color seemed to lead to even greater levels of identity dissonance.

I observed some students of color struggle without resolution with the issue of self-presentation during the entire first year of professional school. For example, Laksha was an East Asian law student who first appeared at Boalt wearing a *sari*, Indian jewelry, and a *bindi* on her forehead, looking very different from the rest of her Law School peers. Apparently feeling uncomfortably visible, she soon took to wearing standard Western clothing—although she wore her *bindi* still. But it seemed that Laksha did not feel comfortable discarding her Indian garb, and halfway through the semester she wore a *salwar khameez* to class, partly concealed under a J. Crew jacket with a plaid lining. Laksha continued throughout the year to seek a balance in her self-presentation, but her combinations of Indian and WASP Western garments made her stand out no less than did Indian garb alone, and the mixture often gave a much more awkward impression than would an unadulterated *sari* or *salwar khameez*. I believe this outer awkwardness reflected the inner awkwardness of identity dissonance.

Students from all backgrounds, not only students of color, failed in their attempts to modify their appearance. For example, before Professor Tate's class began one day, I overheard Erin ask Shane, a white man, if he was growing his hair—a comment which struck me, because Shane's hair was a scant two inches long. Shane replied, "Yeah, I'm just trying to get it back to normal again, like it was before I cut it for law school." Clearly, Shane did not feel like himself in the hairstyle he had adopted to look the part of a law student. Other attempts at looking the part failed because they were unconvincing. Luke, for instance, wore a conservative outfit of navy slacks and blue button-down shirt to class, but a bold tattoo peeked from under the edge of his rolled-up sleeve, and his white-blond hair was bleached. It required no impressive act of deduction to conclude that Luke looked very different when he was away from the Law School. And because the tattoo was literally closer to Luke's inner being than was the button-down shirt, his conservative clothing looked like an obvious cover or costume rather than like "the real Luke."

On a few occasions, I even observed students adopting visibly *less* normative self-presentations. These were uniformly identity-dissonant students. Over the course of her first year, I observed Christine, the positively dissonant Asian American social welfare student whose fiancé had terminated their engagement, playing with her appearance. Presumably feeling empowered to develop a new sense of self, Christine shed her long acrylic nails and big hair and took to wearing dominatrix-style high black boots and a leather jacket. Her new look was not outrageous in the social welfare program context, but she did push the envelope.[9] Tasha, a negatively dissonant mixed African American law student, also altered her appearance away from the normative. When I encountered her at the start of her second year at Boalt, she was sporting a newly pierced nose. Her nose ring was quite small and delicate—a silver stud not much larger than the head of a pin—but it nevertheless marked her as straying from the Law School's conventions, which abjured piercings (other than of women's earlobes).[10]

Students like Christine and Tasha were rare, however. Most professional students I observed were trying quite hard to manage their self-presentations in a way that would make them appear at the center of professional convention rather than at the margins.

## *Use of Jargon*

Just as the students I observed attempted to look like lawyers and social workers, they tried to use the vocabularies of lawyers and social workers. In the early weeks, this was patently obvious because students often lobbed professional malapropisms into their sentences like rocks, causing their attempts at professionalism to sink swiftly. This is what Jon did on the first day of Torts class when he was cold called and began to stumble: he threw out a stream of irrelevant tort terminology as if he were trying to propitiate the legal gods with magic words. This sort of early semester behavior began to get on Professor Tate's nerves, and after several students in a row blurted out inappropriate legalisms, he scoffed, "Well, you're all fooling around with terminology you know nothing about."

Jargoning did students no good when the jargon they used was inappropriate, but the rewards of using appropriate professional terminology were high, leading students to continue to use jargon in hopes of scoring. For example, after a white female student, Paige, raised her hand in Torts class and issued her scoring inquiry ("May I ask a procedural question? This case is before the Supreme Court and the opinion discusses the trial disposition, but was there an appellate review?"), students engaged in a spate of jargoning in an apparent attempt to capture the glory that had redounded to her.

Students at the School of Social Welfare engaged in jargoning no less than did their Law School counterparts. In the large Introduction class, which was closest in atmosphere to a Law School lecture, MSW students were especially prone to use psychobabble and bureaucratese. Whereas law students were apt to use Latin phrases and legal terms of art, social welfare students were prone to attempt to sound knowledgeable by using acronyms and initials with which their peers (and I, and even, at times, apparently they themselves) might not be fully familiar.[11] For example, in reporting on her site visit, Shandra spoke importantly of "meeting the needs of SED kids," forcing a classmate to have to ask the meaning of "SED." (It stands for "severely emotionally disturbed.")

Students of all types at both schools were prone to jargoning. At both schools, students with more professional experience had an advantage in their ability to use terms of art appropriately. In addition, hyperarticulate students with some knowledge of Latin, who tended to be students from relative wealth, were advantaged at the Law School.

## Ideological Rebound

It is my impression that the students I observed tried on what they considered professionally appropriate ideologies just as they tried on what they considered professional attire. While students' ideological position-play may have ranged across the ideological spectrum and occurred at both schools, it was visible to me only in cases where law students took positions so conservative and dismissive of social justice concerns that their professors objected. These positions tended to be so extreme that I termed them "ideological rebound" in my field notes, feeling that they were probably reactive against an anxiety about the lack of concern for social justice at the Law School.

Let me give a few examples. A group of students in Professor Hoffert's class took to arguing that no contract should be considered unconscionable, and that the doctrines of reliance and unconscionability "destroy personal responsibility." These positions were so extreme in their nineteenth-century approach to contract law—holding that it is fine for knowledgeable corporations or wealthy individuals to trick people through the use of a contract's fine print into obligations they had not intended to assume—that Professor Hoffert objected vigorously. In another incident, Professor Tate asked his class whether it was tortious for an individual to see someone drowning, to see the life preserver on the dock nearby, but not to throw it in. He was taken aback when not a single student would argue that it was. And on another occasion, during a discussion of a case in which an ex-wife was awarded money from the earnings of the ex-husband she had supported through medical school, Caroline argued to Professor Santana that the case was wrongly decided:

| | |
|---|---|
| Caroline: | Now we all know that marriages aren't permanent, and it seems crazy to me that people should be allowed to assume that their current support of a spouse will be repaid later. |
| Prof. Santana: | [*sarcastically*] So it would be best for people to enter marriages as arms-length negotiators. |
| Caroline: | [*nodding earnestly*] I think that people should assume that if they break up, they'll get screwed. |
| Prof. Santana: | But should the law, as you so colorfully put it, be part of the "screwing"? |

Considering how sympathetic the facts in this case were for the ex-wife— she slaved to pay her ex-husband's medical school tuition and put food on the table, only to be divorced out of the blue on the very day he finished his training—I concluded in my field notes: "[Caroline] is going overboard in her attempt to adjust her ideology."

For men who underwent ideological rebound at the Law School, the penalties were few. The worst they had to cope with was their professors' exasperation. But for ideologically rebounding women, the penalties were often higher. In class discussion of a case in which a sympathetic plaintiff lost, Professor Hoffert called upon Pauline to ask if she agreed with the result in the case. Pauline's reply was emphatic: "Yes, absolutely." Professor Hoffert's response was to drawl, "Well, many of you may be sympathetic with the plaintiff, even if Pauline is not." The class erupted in laughter, causing Pauline to blush. The irony here is that Pauline was the victim of a catch-22, because her response, if unduly emphatic, was legally correct. Professor Hoffert had assumed that she would give the empathetic but incorrect response. In attempting to avoid a scrub for giving an unprofessionally empathetic response, Pauline in effect scrubbed by giving an unfemininely cold, legally correct response. Ideologically rebounding Law School women were apt to receive disapproval for ignoring social justice in a way that their male peers were not.

### *Acting the Professional Part*

Sometimes students engaged in full-fledged role play, acting out the professional role rather than merely looking the part or using the jargon. At times, professors initiated such situations by requiring students to act as practicing professionals in an exercise. This was common at the School of Social Welfare and occurred occasionally at the Law School. Such was the case when Professor Santana had Brad and Trisha argue the two sides of a case, as I have previously discussed. Recall that Brad's star performance and Trisha's flop occurred because of their gendered habitus; this was a fairly common pattern at the Law School.

At the School of Social Welfare, where role-playing exercises were frequent, there was no gendered pattern of success. Instead, race and class seemed to account more than did gender for the relative success rates. Students engaging in social worker role-play exercises needed to project the right balance of authority, empathy, and authenticity, and this approved balance seemed to come most naturally to white middle-class men and women. Marisol, a Latina student from a working-class background, stumbled and became so uncomfortable trying spontaneously to act the part of a social work supervisor who was authoritatively proposing a new program to a funding agency that she fell back on reading her written proposal in an un-inflected, quiet voice. (She received no stony glare, but students became bored and began to rustle.) And if Marisol had trouble mustering sufficient self-confidence and authority, Luz faced criticism for the opposite problem, being deemed insufficiently sensitive and too pushy when she insisted to the other groups in a role play that they all wanted to build housing for the homeless. Professor Dunn had to interject gently, "I'm not sure all these groups are there yet," but instead of backing off apologetically, Luz raised an eyebrow and challenged, "Oh?" The professor then waved her quiet to allow the other groups to speak for themselves.

Students of color at the Law School also had more difficulty staying in character during role play than did their white peers. Like Marisol, they were prone to dropping out of role. Nicole did this when she dropped her legalese midstream with a nervous laugh: "Any changes would interfere . . . would mess it all up." Similarly, Darrius, an African American man, attempted to make an argument on behalf of a Benneton store that wished to discriminate racially, but he couldn't maintain the role play and dropped it like the awkward act it was to stutter, "Look, what I want is . . . what I'm trying to say is, is it's like a residence . . . the Benneton's." Professor Santana responded scathingly, "You're risking your credibility."

Comparing role playing at the two professional schools, I found the social welfare students in general more convincing than the law students in their performances. There were two reasons for this: first, since they had a clinical placement requirement, they participated in and observed professional practice, while the law students generally did not; and second, because they were at least partly responsible for client care, the stakes were much higher if they were to fail. Law students whose professional role plays fizzled failed to impress their professors, but MSW students who failed to act like professionals could negatively impact the lives of people who were depending upon them. The seriousness with which the social welfare students took their obligation to provide professional care was evident to me when they met after beginning their new placements; they projected competence, confidence, and concern at fever pitch. I wrote in my notes: "They certainly seem to want to convince one another (and themselves) that they're Dr. Kildare, ready to save lives with compassionate authority."

## Conspicuous Studying

The first-year law students I observed did not take their professional-practice role playing terribly seriously because professional practice was an abstract to them. Their professors trained them to focus all their attention on their law-school performance. As a result, while the social welfare students played the role of social worker with great care, the law students tended instead to play the role of diligent student to the hilt. This was evident in the degree to which they engaged in conspicuous study.

While the social welfare students tended to study in the comfort and privacy of their homes, I observed the law students studying quite publicly in the corridors, courtyards, café, and, of course, the library. Not only did students engage in conspicuous study, they felt an obligation to participate in academic one-upmanship, as several of my interviewees complained. Hence, although most of the U.C. Berkeley campus emptied on Friday afternoons, at five o'clock on Fridays the Garret McEnerney Law Library was full of studying students. Students even engaged in conspicuous sleeping, heads down on a library table, surrounded by piles of books, giving passersby the impression that they lived in the library.

Whereas social welfare students piled Tupperware containers of healthy food before them during class (signifying self-care and self-control), the law students accrued ever-larger piles of academic impedimenta on their desks, as if these could enlarge their auras as serious students. Over the course of the semester, I noted that law students' desk spaces became more crowded as casebooks and laptops and loose-leaf binders were joined by statutory supplements, folders filled with handouts, drinks, extra pens and highlighters, pen cases, organizers, voice recorders, and assorted piles of additional books. An even more varied array of academic paraphernalia appeared during the intense period before final exams, when students ritualistically displayed their various methods of organization and preparation. Walking through the law library early in May, I observed Xeroxed and annotated cases collected in loose-leaf binders, word-processed outlines highlighted in multiple colors, flashcards of distilled rules of law arranged in piles, and casebooks blooming with colored Post-it flags. Dozens of laptops were clicking, while others were kept locked with little chains while their owners paused to chat or visit the bathroom. Books were held at the perfect angle by special stands. Academic props were displayed everywhere by students of every variety.

There was little pattern to law students' displays of conspicuous study. Identity-consonant and -dissonant students alike sought to bolster their professional image with their props and performances. But this lack of patterning was unusual; over the course of my observations, I noted that students' successes and failures generally did follow demographic patterns.

## Observed Patterns of Consonance and Dissonance

### Observed Patterns of Consonance

The demographic characteristics easiest for me to observe were race and gender. At the Law School, consonance was clearly gendered and raced. White men demonstrated a greater proclivity for achieving identity consonance from the first days of their law-school careers. They were more likely to enter with a habitus that enabled them to respond well in the Socratic classroom, so that after a mere week of classes, a core group of white men volunteered consistently in each of the classes I observed. (The minority of regular volunteers who were not white men were almost all white women.) White men's habitus also seemed to predispose them to pick up the Law School's norms quickly. Men, for example, seemed to swallow the anticommunitarian ethos of the law-school classroom with greater ease, so they were swifter, for example, to adopt the norm of not taking notes when peers were speaking.[12] White men also soon adopted the habit of speaking confidently despite not knowing the answer—behavior other groups found difficult to emulate.

As the semester wore on, more students began to volunteer and to banter easily with the Law School's professors. Yet white men continued to constitute a disproportionate percentage of the consonant, bantering volunteers. In fact, the more a student's habitus approached the Western European male ideal, the better he seemed to do. This was evinced concretely by the fact that the students who shared the easiest camaraderie with the professors were the European men in the LLM program. This easy camaraderie is evident in the following exchange:

Prof. Hoffert:   I don't like the unilateral contract rule—it's ugly. Nobody else does it this way but us. If you demonstrated this rule to a Frenchman or a German, they would probably laugh [*eyes Heinrich Froebel pointedly*].

Heinrich Froebel:   (*smiling tolerantly*) Ha ha. [*Class chuckles.*]

White men were also able to get away with behavior that their female peers and classmates of color could not. For example, although white men were the most likely to arrive at Boalt wearing the sort of outfit that would become normative, they were paradoxically the most able to resist the wave of conformity in dress that swept their peers after the first several days. Students of color in particular tried hard to conform to the unwritten dress code, but probably because their bearing had already secured their position, some white students, particularly men, felt free to wear ratty shorts, beard stubble, and sneakers with holes in them.[13]

Women of color had the greatest likelihood of being visibly dissonant. White women sometimes wore comfortable, faded clothing in the early weeks with confidence; men of color gave up the practice of taking notes when their peers spoke as easily as did their white male peers. It seemed to me that there was an interaction effect between gender and race, so that being at the underprivileged pole of two dimensions of identity was more difficult than being at the underprivileged pole of one.

At the School of Social Welfare, gender did not seem to me to play so great a role in determining levels of identity consonance as at the Law School, although race and class seemed central. Before beginning my research I had anticipated that women would have an advantage over men in facing socialization into a "feminine" profession, but to my surprise I saw men adapting well. Rather than running into a glass ceiling, male MSW students seemed to take a glass elevator of identity consonance to the top of their class (see Williams, 2002). I expected that men might run into emotional dissonance problems because of being overly rational, but this did not occur, due, I believe, to two factors. First, professors showed great respect for a rational approach to social welfare problems, an approach men demonstrated more often than women; and second, most of the men had a strong empathetic streak and combined the rational and emotional with ease, earning them the respect of both professors and peers. The combining of rational and empathetic problem-solving skills is evident in this statement by Kenny, a white man who said of his fifth-grade clients:

> They're probably at risk for joining gangs—they're into the talk and the clothes, and they're really angry. So I'm a sort of teacher figure to them, and I don't let them act out, so I can establish respect. But my cocounselor doesn't want to come down on them, so he lets them get away with things . . . but I want to establish boundaries and authority. So I was frustrated with the cocounselor, but we talked about it, and we agreed to work it out so the kids don't use any conflict between us to disrupt things.

Professor Alverson and her class responded with admiration and affirmation to Kenny's description of his professional problem solving. The combination of authority and care he evinced were commonplace among the social welfare men and actually seemed to present a greater problem for the women.

The male social welfare students were more likely to express confidence about their performance at clinical placements than were their female peers. I could sometimes literally hear them achieving consonance as a result of their strong clinical performance. In reporting on his positive early placement experience in the Gerontology Practicum, Fernando, a Latino, glowed. "For so many years as a specialist I've wondered, 'What do social workers do, anyway?' So being a generalist is starting to make sense to me, and—" He broke off, beaming. Women in the class were much more likely to report self-doubts along with positive feelings, or doubts alone.

Still, white women seemed to my eye to be settling into the social welfare program with much greater ease than did their Law School counterparts. Surveying the large Introduction to the Profession student audience before class one day in early October, I noted that the most bonded-looking, talkative groups of students were composed solely of white women. White women were more likely than their female peers of color to dress in a manner similar to Professor Alverson's and hence to look professional, and they tended to display the best professional props, as Jenny did when she lay on the desk before her a high-end, text-displaying pager and a peanut-butter-and-jelly sandwich in a Tupperware container. My general impression was that if one were not male, it was advantageous to be white at Haviland Hall. For men, however, being white did not seem to convey as great an advantage—men of all ethnicities seemed fairly comfortable in the MSW program.

## Patterns of Dissonance Observed

I have already addressed the patterns of dissonance I observed at the Law School as they related to scores and scrubs. Students who were female, students of color, and other students with discrediting identities were more likely to scrub than were privileged white men. I now address other ways in which I observed identity dissonance manifested.

At the Law School, identity dissonance often presented itself through silence. If, as I have mentioned, white men were most likely to speak, then, contrapositively, women and people of color were most likely to remain silent. Silence was often a signal of alienation. For example, of the students locked into the marginal back row in Professor Santana's class, only one, a woman, was white, the rest being predominately Asian, and it was not until the fourth week of classes that I noted a single one of these students volunteer to speak. Similarly, I considered it a sign of alienation that most students of color sat silent, looking detached, during a class discussion of racially restrictive covenants.

Silence could also be a sign of fear of failure rooted in habitus problems. This was the case when Professor Tate asked Mallory, a white woman, to recite the facts of a case. She blanched and said, "I'll pass." Professor Tate did not let her go so easily: "Oh, come on." Mallory said apologetically, "I haven't read *Service Merchandise* in a long time" but went on to recount the facts accurately and with good detail. Nevertheless, when Professor Tate asked her to infer a rule of law from the case, Mallory sat silent until he called on another student. Fear of failure had rendered her speechless. Like Mallory, law students might appear to remain silent because of being unprepared, when in fact their silence was based upon a habitus failure.

Because so many women feared having to debate the professor, their identity dissonance was evinced by their pattern of volunteering, as well as by their silence. Women tended to volunteer in droves when what would be required of them was to relay factual information rather than to debate points of law. Identity dissonance could also be revealed by the questions law students asked. African American women were virtually the only students who asked practical questions, as, for example, when Tarrah asked Professor Hoffert about norms of practice among subcontractors as opposed to the formal legal rules. His response was only to say dismissively, "That's a good question—regarding the real world," and to move on to cold call another student. Practical questions like Tarrah's might enhance professional practice capacities, but they were considered irrelevant and insignificant by the law professors at Boalt. The cultural tendency to ask such questions that may have enhanced African American women's educations prior to law school proved detrimental to their law-student reputations.

In addition to having other habitus problems, I observed, women students of all races suffered from higher rates of emotional dissonance. An African American student, Paulette, displayed emotional dissonance when discussing the meaning of *Brown v. Board of Education*:

> Even in a world of precedent, logic, and reason, a feeling of fairness should be able to override all of these. I'm not making any sense. It's like the justice of fighting segregation overrode the precedent, and that's the feminine side overriding the male. I guess I'm not making any sense.

Professor Santana agreed with Paulette's repeated self-deprecations, declaring that it was wrong to ignore precedent and logic to reach a conclusion which merely felt good. Similarly, Nikki, a white lesbian student, had her performance undermined by emotional dissonance in the following exchange regarding a case in which a man was killed rescuing an infant from an oncoming train:

Prof. Tate:    The train was negligent but it mounts a defense of assumption of the risk or contributory negligence or comparative negligence. There was a 50 percent chance of saving the baby and 100 percent chance he'd die. First of all, is this contributory negligence according to the Hand formula?

Nikki:    [*softly*] Well, it depends on whether and to what degree society wants babies to be saved.

Prof. Tate:    [*impatiently*] Okay, but how do you figure this policy issue into the legal argument?

Like Paulette and Nikki, female law students were prone to react empathetically and to reason toward a socially just conclusion, both of which were deemed unprofessional.

Women and students of color were also more prone to ideological dissonance at the Law School than were their white male peers, although white men, particularly those with marginal political commitments and those disadvantaged by class or disability, also evinced ideological dissonance. When students of color experienced dissonance on the basis of racial ideology, they tended to remain silent, as they did during the discussion of racially restrictive covenants mentioned earlier. White women experiencing gendered ideological dissonance were more likely to make their positions known, as when, for example, Professor Santana asked students to raise their hands if they believed, counter to the existing legal rule, that future professional earnings should always be considered community property to be divided upon divorce, and about half the women in the class raised their hands (while very few of the men did so.)

Because ideological dissonance was easiest for students to express, I occasionally heard students with nonvisible depriviliging identities giving voice to it. For example, Rudy went up to Professor Tate before the beginning of class to comment on a case, discussed during the previous meeting, with a holding intended to deter epileptics from driving automobiles. Reddening and in an anxious tone of voice, Rudy came out to the professor as an epileptic and tentatively complained, "Because we are under a doctor's care, it is assumed that we pose more of a risk than, say, senior citizens." Professor Tate retained his bantering, insensitive demeanor, responding unsympathetically, "So are you saying we ought to get all the old folks off the road for parity's sake?"

When students had obviously perceptible disabilities, I was also able to observe their habitus difficulties. On the same day that Rudy approached Professor Tate, the professor had informed Beverly, a deaf student, that she would be called on. He asked her to recite the fact of *Jones v. Young*, which she was able to do orally, because, having been hearing as a child, she had retained good oral speech skills. But when Professor Tate began to question Beverly Socratically, she had difficulty reading his lips and was forced to lean awkwardly over the shoulder of her stenographer to read a time-delayed transcription of his questions. The questions he asked her were all straightforward, however, and she answered them easily. Professor Tate then went off on a long tangent, and Beverly relaxed, believing he was done questioning her. When the professor then directed another question at her, Beverly did not realize it for several awkward seconds, until the question came up on her screen and she started and blushed.

Another group whose dissonance I could occasionally observe were closeted lesbian, gay, and bisexual law students. For example, Jaspreet, a South Asian woman wearing a T-shirt and jeans, ran up to the blackboard before class one day to dash out a meeting notice. This was a common practice, but her notice was uncommon: "Girls Night Out! Lesbian Bar Review. All are welcome. 9 PM at the White Horse." Full of nervous energy after her transgressive act, Jaspreet bounded back toward her seat, but she stopped on the way to ask Emily if she would come. Emily smiled politely but shook her head vehemently, literally pushing back into her seat away from Jaspreet as she made her excuses. Clearly, Emily had no interest in being publicly identified at the Law School as the kind of woman who would attend a lesbian event.

A final pattern of dissonance I was able to observe at the Law School pertained to women of color. After the first couple of weeks of class, women of color began to stand out as having a more feminine appearance than their white female peers had. Women of color wore much more makeup, and by midsemester most of the women with long hair were Asian, Latina, or mixed African American. The androgynous ideal that white women held to was also generally displayed by the women of color who volunteered most often, but the majority of women of color did not adopt it. I infer that they faced more cultural pressure to display feminine beauty signifiers than did their white compatriots. As a result, the white women tended to look more streamlined, efficient, and high-powered than did their peers of color.

At the School of Social Welfare, the patterns of dissonance I observed were not what I had expected. After a few weeks in the field, as I got a good feel for the professional roles as they were conveyed by the professors, I found in a classic example of "he said, she said" miscommunication a metaphor that helped me frame the difference between attorney and social worker roles. The example involves a man and a woman on a drive; the woman, feeling hungry, asks the man, "Do you want to stop for lunch?" and the man replies, "No," and keeps driving. What I had come to understand through my ethnography was that, at the Law School, the woman in this example would be considered to have stated her case poorly, while at the School of Social Welfare, it would be the man who would be considered in the wrong, for lacking rapport or missing cues. A student who acted like the party considered "wrong" at either school would need to alter his or her habitus or face identity dissonance.

Now, the classic example involves a man and a woman with traditionally gendered habits. Based upon this example, I assumed that I would find many women at the Law School and many men at the School of Social Welfare with habitus problems. But while the prediction was borne out for women at the Law School, I did not find it to hold true for men at the School of Social Welfare. Instead, heterosexual white men at Haviland Hall demonstrated identity dissonance at rates no higher than those of their fortunate counterparts at Boalt Hall. This glass-elevator effect was enabled by the fact that none of the men I encountered at the School of Social Welfare ever missed cues or lacked rapport like the man in the classic hypothetical. If a random batch of American men were scooped up and deposited at Haviland Hall, I believe I would observe habitus dissonance in many of them, but the men who chose to pursue an MSW were not average American men—they were more sensitive and more empathetic.

It was other students at the School of Social Welfare who developed habitus dissonance problems, and these were of particular concern to them when they began their placements. Mei Fong, a Chinese American woman, spoke anxiously to her Foundations of Practice class about the problem she was having with her older male Asian clients, who were not respecting her authority. Luis, the sole man of color placed in an agency staffed by white women, uncomfortably described his placement as "weird." And Nora, a white woman, complained:

> So you know my agency office was actually in the high school of the kids I worked with. One of the things I really liked about it is . . . that I could wear the kind of clothes I like and feel comfortable in, like a pair of old overalls, and it would actually help—it would increase rapport with the students; they didn't feel like I was some sort of authority figure who would come down on them. But then I ran into this problem, which is that I look young, and I was dressed a lot like the students, and I would get stopped in the hall and asked for my hall pass by the teachers. But then if I dressed up in dressy professional-looking clothes to meet with a teacher and get their respect, the students wouldn't feel rapport for me, and plus I would feel stiff and just not like myself.

MSW students who were women, people of color, or both often reported feeling out of place, or disrespected, or caught in a double bind. (My impression was that the race and gender effects were interactive, and that women of color experienced the highest rates of habitus dissonance.)

Emotional dissonance was hard for me to observe at the School of Social Welfare. This was because professors usually allowed students wide latitude to express their feelings and also reacted positively to students who made rational, unemotional comments. I had to learn to react to more subtle cues than I received at the Law School, where emotional dissonance was revealed by professorial contempt. After I learned how to listen carefully, I could hear emotional dissonance being voiced largely by women, often when they were unwilling to absorb professors' efforts to socialize them because their feelings conflicted with the professors' efforts. For example, after Professor Dunn had his class break into groups and engage in an exercise on managing homelessness, several students raised their hands to offer feelings-based criticisms of the exercise. Luz said, "I'm worried that having all these various communities meeting together isn't a good setup because it won't let each community feel ownership over the situation"; Sheila fretted, "I feel a little concerned that even if we help this current batch of the homeless, since we're not trying to solve the larger problems, a new crop will be on the streets in a few years."

I observed little ideological dissonance demonstrated by straight white men at Haviland. Students of color and LGBTI students were most likely to exhibit ideological dissonance. For example, I overheard two gay white men discussing how mortifying it had been to read their textbook's definitions of "faggot" and "butch," and I listened to Paula, a Pueblo student, give a long disquisition on the stereotypes that comprised the "cultural competence" readings on Native Americans.

In sum, at both the Law School and the School of Social Welfare, I observed low rates of identity dissonance in straight white middle-class men. Men did not demonstrate higher rates of identity dissonance at the School of Social Welfare; on the contrary, I received the impression that, if anything, they suffered *less*. Students who were of color, female, working class, LGBTI, or disabled were more likely to appear to be identity dissonant, and there seemed to be an interaction among personal identities, so that to be demographically underprivileged in more than one way led to more identity dissonance than did being on the unprivileged end of only a single pole of identity. The interaction effect I was most easily able to observe was that between gender and race. I observed women of color exhibiting identity dissonance at higher rates than did white women or men of color.

## Stress

For all the students I observed, but particularly for the identity-dissonant students, stress was endemic to the first year of professional school. This was revealed in a number of ways. First, students regularly complained about feeling overworked and pressed for time. For example, after the students in the Gerontology Practicum had finished exuding competence and confidence in their Dr. Kildare show of professionalism, they immediately switched to radiating nervous anxiety in a discussion of upcoming paper deadlines and their lack of time. And in another constant signifier of stress, there were always students who appeared exhausted, sporting bags under their eyes and periodically yawning.

At the Law School, high levels of stress were implied by the amount of licit drug consumption that regularly took place during class. As the semester went on, an ever-growing percentage of students came to class with a can or cup of caffeine—a latté, espresso, cappuccino, iced coffee, chai, or the ever-popular Diet Coke. One day about six weeks into the semester, when I did a visual survey of Professor Tate's class, one in five students had a Diet Coke on his or her desk. The man seated beside me sported a "Quick Slam 20 Ounce Mountain Dew." Other substances were abused more privately, and I rarely observed students' use of them, with the exception of the case of Olivia, who sat directly in front of me in Professor Santana's class. I first noticed that Olivia seemed to be using a lot of Nicorette gum one September day when she consumed two pieces during class (while also maintaining a low profile and avoiding any potentially cold call–inducing eye contact with Professor Santana). A month later, she was using Nicorette constantly, spitting out the old piece and popping in a fresh one every fifteen minutes or so. I do not think Olivia's substance abuse was unique (although her choice of vector may have been), because I know from my interviews that law students were regularly drinking alcohol and smoking marijuana to relax. Alternately, they were popping caffeine pills, ephedra, and other stimulants in an attempt to enhance their academic performance.

Students at the School of Social Welfare did not demonstrate or report abusing substances to self-medicate as the law students did. This was due, not to a lesser degree of stress, but to the health-enforcing norms of the profession, which led them to avoid or conceal such behavior. I am certain the social work students were under a good deal of stress, because they frequently called me to cancel scheduled interviews; during one week in November alone, three social welfare students canceled, apologetically informing me that they had too many academic obligations to attend to. Feeling a great deal of stress, these students cut out all nonessentials, including me. But instead of turning to alcohol, tobacco, marijuana, speed, and caffeine, social welfare students apparently turned to medical psychopharmacology. A substantial number reported to me that they were using antidepressants, and a few acknowledged using antianxiety medication. If Boalt students used such drugs, they did not confess it to me, but the therapeutic ethos at the School of Social Welfare made such admissions an acceptable demonstration of responsible self-care.

As the first year progressed, students who enjoyed the consonant internalization of appropriate professional identities saw their levels of anxiety decrease. This is not to say they enjoyed a stress-free academic life; professional schooling involved too much work for many students to feel peaceful and relaxed. But the relative difference was notable: students who established consonant professional identities saw their stress levels decline, while students who suffered from identity dissonance endured levels of anxiety that failed to decrease and that often in fact rose over time. This anxiety fed back into the identity-dissonant students' academic challenges. During the first-semester finals period, I noticed that many students developed persistent colds and coughs—and I remarked in my field notes that the students exhibiting the most obvious identity dissonance "seem particularly illness-prone, as if identity dissonance were literally sickening." This is in fact plausible, given the commonly noted medical association between stress and illness (see, e.g., Sarafino, 2002). And being sick during finals period did not improve students' chances of achieving good grades.

## Statistical Patterns

I observed identity dissonance patterned in many ways in my qualitative analysis. But every ethnographer would like to provide objective support for her qualitative analysis. I therefore decided to supplement my content analysis with a quantitative analysis of my interview data. I did this by codifying my interviews so that I could compile frequencies of identity consonance, positive dissonance, and negative dissonance according to the personal identities of the students.[14] It is important to note that while seventy-two interviews represent a healthy number, it is not a large number for purposes of statistical analysis. Nevertheless, it is sufficient for a basic correlational analysis, and I did find correlations between personal identity variables and positive or negative dissonance that were statistically significant at $p<.05$ for gender, race, class, strong religious commitment, strong political commitment, disability, and family status (having a spouse/domestic partner or child). The correlation coefficients are summarized in Table 7.1. You can see that except for the case of sexual orientation (for which I had only twelve LGBTI students), significant correlations appear between each axis of personal identity and identity dissonance. (Note that some students experience both positive and negative dissonance along different axes of their identities.)

In addition to doing a correlational analysis, I graphed some simple frequency analyses of the number of interviewees with various characteristics at each school who were experiencing identity dissonance. I wanted to see if these data could confirm or perhaps elaborate on the patterns that emerged via qualitative analysis of my ethnographic data. In fact, a striking pattern did emerge repeatedly, and I took to referring to this pattern as my "normal distribution." The normal distribution confirmed my ethnographic observation that patterns of identity dissonance replicated patterns of social stratification.

The normal distribution I found was that for any axis of identity, if I compared rates of identity dissonance (both positive and negative) at the two schools, there was an interaction between the personal identity effects and school effects such that the rate of dissonance would be highest for law students at the unprivileged pole of the personal identity variable, and low-

## Table 7.1. Correlation Coefficients

|                        | Positive Dissonance | Negative Dissonance | Any Dissonance |
|------------------------|---------------------|---------------------|----------------|
| Gender                 | .3764[a]            | .2502[b]            | .3185[c]       |
| Race/Ethnicity         | .3444[d]            | .3328[d]            | .3604[d]       |
| Class                  | .3615[d]            | .1489               | .2548[b]       |
| Religious commitment   | .4192[a]            | .2398[b]            | .2018          |
| Sexual orientation     | .0146               | .0621               | .0250          |
| Political commitment   | .1123               | .3301[d]            | .2819[b]       |
| Disability             | .1487               | .3444[d]            | .1992          |
| Familial status        | .1123               | .3444[d]            | .1550          |

a. p<.001 (two tailed)
b. p<.05
c. p<.01
d. p<.005

est for the social work students at the privileged pole of that identity. Thus, for example, the rates of combined positive and negative dissonance by gender and school were arranged like this:

> Law School women's rates > Social Welfare School women's rates >
> Law School men's rates > Social Welfare School men's rates.

Similarly, the rates of combined positive and negative dissonance by race/ethnicity and school were arranged like this:

> Rates of Law School students of color > rates of Social Welfare School students of color > rates of Law School white students > rates of Social Welfare School white students.

Thus, in the normal distribution it becomes clear that the effect of personal identity variables was more powerful than the school effect, but that rates of identity dissonance were higher at the Law School than at the School of Social Welfare. The impression I had gathered that the Law School was a harsher place that produced high rates of identity dissonance was confirmed by the frequency analyses (for an overview of the frequency analyses, see www.uwm.edu/~costello).

Looking over my qualitative and quantitative analyses of patterns of identity consonance and dissonance, very clear patterns emerge from the matrix of interactions between selfhood and schooling. Patterns of social stratification are reinscribed, as those with humble class origins suffer higher rates of identity dissonance than those with loftier class backgrounds, those with disabilities suffer more identity dissonance than those without them, and so forth. Intentional discrimination may contribute to these patterns, but even in the absence of any overt bigotry these patterns of dissonance emerge, augmenting the tendency for the privileged to outperform the underprivileged at professional schools. What are the ramifications of this finding for us as individuals and as a society? And why does this happen? We turn to these questions in the concluding chapter.

# 8 Conclusion
## Disparate Impacts, Disaffection, and Strategies for Reducing Identity Dissonance

Why is it that students of various backgrounds all enter professional school with superlative qualifications, yet the distribution of academic approbation and career rewards is demographically stratified? Some argue that this stratification is merit-based and due to the differing intellectual capacities of various subgroups of professional students. But my observations contradict this assertion: students of all backgrounds demonstrated an impressive capacity to absorb and recount the factual information conveyed to them. In fact, subgroups of students who were underperforming could be more willing than were their consonant peers to demonstrate their mastery of the substantive knowledge base of their professions; this was illustrated by the rush of female law students to volunteer when professors solicited factual information.

Others have argued that the unequal distribution of rewards results from a conspiracy to discriminate on the part of biased professional authority figures. In the course of my research, I did observe disparate professorial treatment of students with similar performances, but these incidents were insufficient in number to explain the widespread underperformance of women, people of color, religious minorities, and other underprivileged groups.

What this book has demonstrated is that disparate outcomes can be explained by the patterns of identity consonance and dissonance which emerge when students with varying personal identities attempt to internalize professional identities. During their previous academic experiences, these students could perform similarly because there was no professional socialization component to their education. Having achieved success, women, people of color, individuals with disabilities, and other such students reasonably assumed that if they worked hard, they would continue to excel, as did their more privileged counterparts. But while privileged students generally had their identities as academic overachievers confirmed and their self-esteem buttressed, less privileged students often suffered a crisis of identity and a loss of self-esteem when they encountered identity dissonance and the negative impacts upon academic performance it produced. That is, professional socialization through consistent professorial treatment led to disparate impacts upon individuals with different personal identities.

## Professional Socialization Revisited

This book has explored at length the socializing messages sent to professional students by the architecture, upkeep, and decor of the school setting, by the pedagogic styles employed, by the professors and staff that serve as their role models, and by their peers. Many of these messages were small and subtle, but their cumulative effect was powerful. From the rare straightforwardly didactic messages, such as a class discussion of professional dress, to the most subtle and oblique cues, such as the beverages students consumed (cantaloupe-carrot smoothie? espresso double shot?), they conveyed information to the students about the professional roles they would need to internalize in order to become successful practitioners.

Boalt and Haviland Halls themselves sent numerous socializing messages to the students within them. The rich materials with which Boalt was constructed and the regular new construction there spoke to students of high prestige and growth, while the stained linoleum and chipped paint at Haviland Hall conveyed messages of low prestige and decay. From the very shapes of the classrooms, students at the two programs gleaned different socializing messages about their professions. The amphitheaters of the Law School lecture halls were shaped to instill hierarchical authority. The social welfare classrooms, with their movable desks and chairs, taught greater shared authority and mutual surveillance. For students who quickly felt comfortable with their professional school facilities, the very classrooms, corridors, and libraries enhanced their sense of being integrated into their chosen professions. But for those who were subtly made to feel awkward or unwelcome, identity dissonance and professional disaffection were likely to result.

Professors serve as the classic role models for professional socialization, and the demographics of the faculties of the two programs sent socializing messages. At the Law School, most faculty members were white and male, sending a clear message about whom the profession considered authoritative. At the School of Social Welfare, many instructors were female; however, men constituted the majority of the professoriate, with women holding the majority of the lower-status lecturer and field-consultant positions. Most members of the social welfare faculty were white, although there was a greater proportion of people of color than among the Law School professors. Although the faces of the faculty in Haviland Hall were more diverse, the division of authority among them continued to send socializing input that privileged white men.

The faculties' styles of dress sent additional messages. At the Law School, the style was formal and country clubbish, with blazers and slacks being the norm. Male law professors who were young or of color dressed to an even higher standard, and women took great pains with their dress, attempting to achieve an androgynously attractive, expensive look. Certainly sartorial authority seemed to come more easily to the white male faculty. At the School of Social Welfare, where "calculated casual" standards reigned, clothing was less formal, and male social welfare professors typically wore comfortable-looking outfits of slacks and oxford-cloth shirts. Female social welfare faculty, however, needed to take much greater pains with their wardrobe in order to look put together yet sensitive. Students at both schools were sent messages through their professors' dress that conveyed it was easiest to be a white male.

Professors' general demeanor sent additional messages. At Boalt Hall, the typical professor had a habitus characterized by arrogant self-confidence, authoritative control, remarkably hyperarticulate loquacity, a light, bantering style, and a disdain for emotional sensitivity. They favored the strong and admired the confident. At Haviland, the professors were serious and sensitive in their comportment, with self-presentations that were more reminiscent of white middle-class parents than of upper-crust schoolteachers. They had a more complicated relation to power, seeking to guide without being seen as authoritarian, yet still to be seen as authoritative. They sought to empower, yet they admired demonstrations of self-confidence and rational problem solving. Again, students who responded well to their professors' habitus were likely to achieve cathexis and consonance, while those who found their professors' styles alienating were likely to remain disaffected and identity dissonant.

Professional students also looked to their peers as yardsticks against which to gauge their behavior. At the Law School, the successful students' demeanor was congruent with white heterosexual male upper-middle-class culture. This was interesting because, unlike the faculty, half the law-student population was female, and, compared to the faculty, the student population included more people of color. The long dominance of the legal profession by WASP men of privileged class backgrounds had persisting effects upon the valorized student habitus. While other students—women, people of color, gay men and lesbians, students with less lofty class origins, and so on—tended toward self-presentations that were unusually congruent with white heterosexual male upper-middle-class culture, this habitus unsurprisingly came most naturally to privileged white men.

The law students I encountered were filled with a nervous desire to be taught rules and to be prepared for examinations. They learned from the 2Ls and 3Ls that classroom discussion wasted on "politics"—broadly defined to include any talk of morality or social justice—would endanger their success, and many (particularly those who were most focused on personal success) resisted such diversions. Students concerned with social change or with protecting the disempowered therefore often came to feel alienated from their consonant peers, and alienation impedes socialization.

The typical social welfare student's habitus (like the typical social welfare student) was middle class, feminine, and Anglo in character. Social welfare students tended to be more empathically oriented and politically sensitive than were their professors, which meant that students who were atypically rational received more professorial approbation than did their normatively emotive peers. Social welfare students also distributed and withheld approbation via affirmative listening and shunning; the factors they rewarded did not include rationalism, but rather communalism, politically sensitive language, and emotional openness. These differing criteria meant that men received disproportionate amounts of positive feedback from professors, while middle-class white women received disproportionate amounts of positive feedback from peers. Thus men of all ethnicities and white women were both likely to enjoy identity consonance. The influence of professors apparently being greater than that of peers, however, white women's identity-dissonance rates were significantly higher than those of most males, who rarely endured dissonance at the School of Social Welfare.

When most people think of professional socialization, they focus on professional pedagogy, and certainly pedagogy has a strong influence on the socialization process. Yet this influence hardly flows from explicit discussions of professional roles or professional socialization—such discussions were infrequent at the School of Social Welfare and even rarer at the Law School. Students instead absorbed messages about professional roles indirectly through the pedagogic methods employed, and via the humor, metaphors, and cautionary tales professors favored.

At the Law School, students had to endure the hazing ritual of Socratic inquiry, panoptically arrayed before a professor who might cold call them at any time. They fared well only when they displayed a habitus similar to that of their professors: self-confident, vocally dominant, sadistically witty, and inclined toward prolixity. Students with other dispositions faced the humiliation of a scrub before a large body of witnesses. These dissonance-prone students might make attempts at "making it by faking it," but conscious role play was rarely as successful as the nonconscious authenticity produced by identity consonance. Students who scrubbed were likely to be distracted by rehashing behavior, to suffer academically therefrom, and to attempt to protect themselves through alienation. This alienation served only to prolong their identity dissonance by impeding their professional socialization.

At the School of Social Welfare, the hierarchy of professor-student relations was much reduced compared to that at the Law School, as instruction proceeded via class discussion and the professor sat within a circle of students. Yet authority in the social welfare classroom was not reduced but diffused, and hence its sources multiplied, as every student became a potential source of discipline for his peers. The social welfare professors, champions of affirmative listening techniques, denied that surveillance and power operated in their classrooms, delegitimating their students' sense of being observed, evaluated, and controlled. Facing the nods and smiling faces of their surveillors, it was hard for identity-dissonant students to object but easy for them to become disaffected.

Although the same socializing forces were arrayed against all the students in each professional school, factors such as pedagogic style had disparate impacts upon students with differing personal identities. Students who were upper-middle-class politically and religiously moderate heterosexual white males without children or disability did not experience identity dissonance at either of the schools I studied. The circle of students likely to join these privileged individuals in identity consonance was much larger at the School of Social Welfare than at the Law School, but some students were usually excluded from the consonant circle at both schools, including students with visible disabilities, mothers, students with strong religious or political commitments, and women of color.

Students experiencing identity dissonance faced a number of difficulties that their identity-consonant peers did not encounter. First, they faced an identity crisis that was distracting and distressing, and that often led them to become alienated from their significant others and communities of origin. Positively dissonant students paid this painful price willingly, but their more numerous negatively dissonant peers did not. The identity crisis and its sequelae distracted dissonant students from their studies, which negatively impacted their performance. In addition, the academic performance of identity-dissonant students was directly impaired by their failure to display the attitude and ideology that were considered professional. Over time, as professional socialization progressed, some students achieved consonance—but others, who withdrew from the painful stimuli they faced at professional school and shielded themselves in a shell of alienation, continued to experience prolonged identity dissonance. Some of these disaffected students might never achieve identity consonance, and their professional careers would suffer.

## Patterns of Identity Dissonance

Under the influence of the socializing input just recapitulated, I observed identity consonance and dissonance emerge during the first days of professional school. For example, by the second week of the fall semester, certain students at both schools were frequently volunteering to speak in class, because the pedagogic styles suited their habitus. These students were disproportionately white and male at both schools (although, because men constituted a minority of the social welfare students, male voices did not dominate class discussion as they did at the Law School).

The patterns of identity dissonance at the professional schools I studied varied over the course of the year. For example, negative dissonance rates rose for the gender nontraditionals (women at Boalt Hall and men at Haviland), while it fell for the gender traditionals. For many students, identity dissonance resolved—after weeks, months, or even years—but for others, it persisted throughout their professional school careers. For example, I had a long conversation with Wei, an Asian American third-year law student, about a month before he was to graduate. Wei said of Boalt, "I hate this place," and he was clearly experiencing negative identity dissonance. He described the professors as "arrogant assholes" who got sadistic pleasure out of their "power trip," and who were oblivious to social justice. Wei demonstrated that he employed the dissonance-management technique of maintaining an alienated distance when he told me, "I avoid hanging around this place, and try not to let it get to me." He also relied on solidarity, spending his time away from campus in the company of non–law students or Boalt students "who aren't really the law-school type, like me." Despite having been exposed to three years of socialization at law school, Wei was not integrated into the profession.

Broad patterns of identity consonance and dissonance emerged through both my interview and my observational data. In general, for any axis of personal identity, students who identified with the pole that was socially depriviteging had higher rates of identity dissonance than did students who identified with the privileged pole. That they experienced identity dissonance at higher rates was not always perceived as negative, however, because students with nonprivileged identities experienced higher rates of positive dissonance as well as higher rates of negative dissonance. That is, students with nonprivileged identities were more likely to feel as if they were finding themselves at professional school, as well as more likely to feel as if they were losing themselves, than were their socially privileged peers, who felt that they were merely going to school.

Another broad pattern that emerged was the schools' effect upon rates of identity dissonance. For any given subgroup of students, combined rates of identity dissonance were usually higher at the Law School than at the School of Social Welfare; the professional socialization process was stronger and harsher at the School of Law. The school effect combined with particular personal identity effects to produce what I termed the "normal distribution" of identity-dissonance rates. In the normal distribution, personal identity effects were stronger than school effects. Thus, for example, the rates of identity dissonance by gender and school were arranged like this: rates of Law School women > rates of School of Social Welfare women > rates of Law School men > rates of School of Social Welfare men. It is plausible that a similar pattern would emerge if my research were repeated in other professional school settings: schools with harsher socialization climates (e.g., medical schools) are likely to produce more identity dissonance than schools with gentler ones (e.g., divinity schools).

## Why and Wherefore? Hypothesizing Explanations for the Patterns of Dissonance Revealed

Why do patterns of identity consonance and dissonance recapitulate patterns of social stratification? Scholars have posited a number of explanations with regard to various axes of identity (although few have attempted to hypothesize a global theory to explain multiple dimensions of stratification simultaneously). Let us consider some of the more popular explanations for disparate professional success among different demographic groups.

## Theories of Gender and Professional Identity

**Self-Selection Theory:** One theory regarding gender and the professions is the self-selection theory, which posits that individuals who are gender nontraditionals within their chosen professions self-select to enter these professions because they do not have traditional gender identities. That is, women who choose to join the military are believed to do so because they are unusually masculine, while men who choose to go to nursing school are thought to be atypically feminine in their gender identity. Hence, the self-selection theory would predict low rates of professional identity dissonance according to gender. Once a popular theory, the self-selection hypothesis is generally held to have been discredited, because women in masculine professions have been found to have typically feminine gender identities (see Lyson, 1984). Among the professional students I studied, while women at the Law School generally had a typically gender habitus, men at the School of Social Welfare were more atypical in their gender habitus—and the Law School women suffered much higher rates of identity dissonance than did the social welfare men. Why might this be so?

One possible answer is that students who attend the School of Social Welfare are a more highly self-selected group in general than are individuals who attend the School of Law. Most MSW admittees have prior work experience with social service agencies, and although this is typically in a paraprofessional or volunteer capacity, they are still more familiar with the requirements of professional practice than are their Law School counterparts. Most law students, on the other hand, have no prior legal experience. In fact, many of the law students I studied chose to apply to law school knowing very little about the world of law; "attend law school" was a sort of default decision for students with liberal arts backgrounds who were seeking financial security or who simply did not know what else to do. Thus, a man with a brusque, insensitive mien was unlikely to apply to the MSW program, because he would not have done well enough working with a social service agency to think this would be a good choice and would self-select out. A woman with a sensitive, deferential demeanor, on the other hand, could be unaware that she would run into trouble at law school and might well believe that her good college grades and high Law School Aptitude Test (LSAT) score ensured that she would excel.

Another possible reason that the men at Haviland Hall had an atypically feminine habitus while the women at Boalt were not particularly masculine has to do with the relative prestige of law and social work as professions. Law is a high-status profession, while social work has lower prestige. The individuals who apply to train for either profession generally have good credentials and could choose to pursue other careers. They might find a career path with greater remuneration and prestige than social work, but they are not likely to find a career path with greater remuneration and prestige than law. If we agree that people are more likely to carefully consider a step which could reduce their potential status than to hesitate over a status-enhancing step, this would help explain the greater rates of self-selection by social welfare men than law-school women.

A final possible explanation for the greater rates of self-selection by social welfare men than law school women might lie in popular conceptions of the professions of law and social work. The popular conception of a social worker seems to be more consolidated than is that of the lawyer. On the one hand, most Americans conceive of a person with an MSW as one with good people skills who can empathize with the needy or counsel those in crisis.[1] On the other hand, as a society we have conflicting images of lawyers: we imagine rational, cold, ruthless litigators, but we also imagine impassioned champions of justice who fight for the rights of the downtrodden. Given our more consolidated conception of the social worker, a person lacking empathy and good people skills would not be likely to consider a career in social work. But given our unconsolidated vision of the lawyer, women (and men) with empathetic orientations and sensitive natures might imagine that they would do well at law school.

**Feminist Psychoanalytic Theory:** According to feminist psychoanalytic theory such as that proposed by Nancy Chodorow (1978), because children are generally cared for by women, girls develop strong gender identities, since they do so in identification with their caretakers, while boys develop weaker gender identities against identification with their caretakers. To maintain their masculine gender identities, males are said to need constantly to prove that they are not feminine (Coltrane, 1996). Hence, predictions are that men in feminine professions will suffer more identity problems than will women in masculine ones, because the men but not the women would face a threat to their gender identities (Williams, 1989).

This prediction was not borne out by my findings. It was the women at the Law School who experienced the greater levels of identity dissonance. However, the feminist psychoanalytic prediction might hold true if individuals were randomly selected to attend a JD or MSW program, so that the men in a school of social work would not have atypically feminine gender identities, as my study subjects did. As it was, the self-selected pool of men who chose to attend the social welfare program did not demonstrate gender-related identity dissonance.

I should point out that although the male social welfare students I studied had an atypically feminine flavor to their gendered deportment, they were still fairly masculine; for instance, they were more likely to engage in debating behavior and to focus on rational approaches to understanding client behavior.[2] I believe that the men at the School of Social Welfare, with their rather androgynous gender habitus, conformed more closely to the social work role as demonstrated by their professors than did their generally more highly empathically oriented female peers, which contributed to the men's high rates of identity consonance.

**Proportionate Theory:** According to the proportionate thesis, members of any group that constitutes a minority of a body of socializees should have more identity problems than do members of the dominant group. Hence, the proportionate theory would predict that at the Law School, men and women should experience roughly equal rates of identity dissonance, while at the School of Social Welfare, men should experience higher rates of identity dissonance than women, being a numerical minority.

My findings contradicted these predictions. Men, the numerical minority at Haviland Hall, experienced the lowest rates of identity dissonance of any gender/school group. It is true that some demographic groups that had little representation at the professional schools I studied, such as people with visible disabilities or strong religious commitments, experienced high rates of identity dissonance, but their underrepresentation is not sufficient to explain these high rates. Underrepresentation may exacerbate the alienation experienced by minority students with nonprivileged identities, but for the privileged students who constituted a numerical minority, underrepresentation did not have a negative impact. In fact, being a big fish in a small pond may have increased social welfare men's feelings of competence and confidence, allowing them to enjoy their ride on the glass elevator to the top of their class (Williams, 2002).

**Patriarchy Theory:** According to the tenets of patriarchy theory, men are accorded disproportionate privileges in our society; for example, for years they not only dominated the professions but successfully excluded women from them (see, e.g., Strom, 1992). Theorists of patriarchy state that men's privilege should allow them to feel comfortable and to succeed in any context, including "women's" professions. My findings that men have lower rates of identity dissonance than women in both the "masculine" and "feminine" professional schools are consistent with patriarchy theory.

**Class and Social Power Thesis:** The Gramscian class and social power thesis posits that the greater the power granted to a profession, and hence the greater the potential for members of that profession to effect social changes which would disrupt domination by the ruling class, the more will novices being trained for the profession be subjected to socializing forces intended to ensure that they internalize the values of the ruling class. Thus, high-status professions are predicted to resemble more closely fascistic "total institutions" (Goffman, 1968), which should lead to higher rates of identity dissonance.

My data are also consistent with the class and social power thesis. Rates of identity dissonance are proportionately higher for both genders at the Law School, where socialization is more stringent, than at the School of Social Welfare. Dissonance rates are particularly high for women, who, compared to men, are considered more of a threat to the hegemonic order in those versions of the class and social power theory that incorporate patriarchy theory. In addition, students who enter law school with the specific goal of effecting social change suffer very high rates of identity dissonance.

**The Commonsensical Theory:** According to the American commonsensical theory as it relates to gender, "women are from Venus and men are from Mars." In other words, the sexes are separate but equal, and women at the Law School or men at the School of Social Welfare should suffer equally for landing on the wrong planet.

My findings clearly do not comport with the commonsensical thesis.

## Theories of Race and Professional Identity

**Self-Selection Theory:** A theory which posited that self-selection should be higher in general at the School of Social Welfare than at the Law School because of social work's relatively low status would predict that rates of racialized identity dissonance should be higher at Boalt Hall. My data are consistent with this prediction, but in a highly gendered manner. For men of color, the rates of identity dissonance are dramatically higher at the Law School: two-thirds of my male interviewees of color at Boalt were experiencing identity dissonance, as compared to none of the male interviewees of color at Haviland Hall. But for women, the difference was less dramatic: four-fifths of my female interviewees of color at the Law School were experiencing identity dissonance, compared to three-quarters of my female interviewees of color at the School of Social Welfare. My data do not support the argument that differences in levels of self-selection alone can explain the differences in rates of identity dissonance.

**Psychological Theory of Fragile White Identity:** Related to the feminist psychoanalytic theory of gender identity is the psychological theory which holds that white racial identity is much more fragile than other racial identities because a white identity is defined negatively against other racial identities (Clark and O'Donnell, 1999). Usually this negative definition is not problematic for white individuals, because of their racial privilege (Vargas, 1998). But in situations where their privilege is called into question, this theory holds that white individuals should experience high rates of identity dissonance. Since white privilege is intact at the Law School, this theory predicts that white law students should be fine; at the School of Social Welfare, where professional norms require that white privilege be questioned, this theory predicts that white students should experience elevated levels of identity dissonance.

I did not find the levels of identity dissonance among white students at the School of Social Welfare to be elevated in comparison to those of their peers of color. However, I did notice a marked tendency among social welfare students to avoid identifying themselves as "white." Instead, they often chose to identify as members of non-WASP ethnic groups. For example, Jewish students, who almost always identified as "white" at the Law School, identified themselves on the interview volunteer sheets I distributed at the School of Social Welfare as "Jewish" or even "Semitic." A student with some Portuguese ancestry identified herself to me as "Hispanic," and a student who had a Jewish grandparent with some reputed Mongolian blood referred to herself as "part Asian." These data lend a certain credence to the theory that white identity is fragile when deprivileged.

**The Racism Thesis:** According to the racism thesis, white students should enjoy higher rates of identity consonance in any professional context, because white privilege is pervasive. White consonance levels may be higher in professional contexts in which white privilege goes unchallenged, but they should be higher than the rates of consonance of people of color even in professions, such as social welfare, where white privilege is said to run counter to professional norms. My data are consistent with these predictions, supporting them especially for women.

**Class and Social Power Theory:** Since class and social power theory predicts that rates of identity dissonance should be higher in general at the School of Law because of the great deal of social power which attorneys are granted, it predicts higher rates of dissonance among people of color at the Law School than among people of color at the School of Social Welfare. My data accord with this prediction. People of color at the Law School have the highest rate of identity dissonance among the four race/school groupings, suggesting an interactive effect with the racism thesis.

**A Note on Positive Dissonance:** Professional students of color experienced high rates of dissonance, and among women of color the rates of identity dissonance were very high indeed. But it should be borne in mind that women of color also experienced more positive dissonance than did any other subgroup. Women of color may have been cursed with low chances of experiencing the confidence of identity consonance, but they were blessed with the greatest chances of feeling that they were "finding themselves" at professional school, and becoming better and more powerful people.

## *Class and Identity Dissonance*

The tendency for my data to accord with the predictions of the self-selection theory, a bias thesis, and the class and social power theory continued along the axis of class. Rates of identity dissonance among students with underprivileged class backgrounds were generally higher than the rates experienced by their peers with middle- or upper-class backgrounds, as the classism thesis would predict, and among students with underprivileged class backgrounds, rates of identity dissonance were highest at the Law School, as the self-selection and social power theses would predict.[3]

Class had little impact on two groups of students. For white students at the School of Social Welfare, dissonance rates were low no matter what their class origin; for students of color at the Law School, however, the inverse was true—their dissonance rates were high no matter what their class origin. In other words, there was a strong interaction between race and class effects.

Positive dissonance rates were higher among students with lower-class backgrounds than among those with middle- and upper-class origins. Positive dissonance rates were especially high among women of color with underprivileged class origins. Thus, identity dissonance was most likely to be experienced as empowering by those with the least race/class/gender privilege—almost as if they had the least to lose.

## Religious Commitments and Identity Dissonance

The pattern of identity consonance and dissonance that emerged with respect to religious commitments was unusual, because only the women students I interviewed demonstrated strong religious commitments. (A fair number of men mentioned worshiping regularly, and a few even told me they felt called to their profession, but none spontaneously described religion as a primary identity, and none spoke of religion as shaping their decision making and daily lives in the way women did.)

For women who had strong religious commitments, rates of identity dissonance were high. In the rational world of the professions, religion was considered irrational—acceptable to practice in private, but inappropriate if allowed to influence professional decision making—which led the strongly religiously committed toward identity dissonance. Particularly at risk in my sample were evangelical Christian women who used a "what-would-Jesus-do" standard to guide all of their behavior and decisions, but students from other religious backgrounds whose religious dictates took precedence over other commitments could also be at risk.

## Political Commitments and Identity Dissonance

Students who had political commitments that were strong compared to those of their peers also experienced heightened rates of identity dissonance. Being seen as a radical was by far the greatest source of identity dissonance among white men at the Law School. Except among men at the School of Social Welfare (whose gender privilege apparently overwhelmed the effects of any other personal identities that generally produced dissonance), most students with strong progressive or conservative political commitments were experiencing identity dissonance. Among my interviewees, every woman and School of Social Welfare student of color with strong political commitments was experiencing identity dissonance, as were three-fourths of the Law School men with strong political commitments. Within the professions, an ethos of moderate centrism was normative, and strong political commitments, like strong religious commitments, came across as irrational and discrediting. This accords with the Gramscian class and power theory, which predicts that the power of professionals to transform society will be culturally restrained (in my research, by the preservation of a specific professional habitus)—and the greater the social prestige of the professional school, the greater the restraint will be.

### Familial Identity and Identity Dissonance

In general, rates of identity dissonance were higher among students who identified as being a domestic partner or parent than among their peers who did not identify themselves to me as having a partner or child. As Arlie Hochschild points out in her book *The Time Bind* (1997), individuals who seek to combine family with career typically find that they have too few hours in the day to take care of all their responsibilities to the career, family members, and themselves. Among those I studied, the students with families led harried lives, often getting by on reduced sleep, reduced standards of cleanliness, and reduced time with significant others. But the time pressure students and their partners experienced was shaped by another factor, identified by Hochschild in *The Second Shift* (1993): the tendency for working women to do more of the domestic labor than do their working male partners.

Of the students I interviewed who lived with partners, in every case female members of couples significantly increased the total number of hours they spent working at home and "on the job" at the outset of their partners' or their own professional schooling.[4] And in many cases, male members of couples, whether they were professional students or their partners, picked up little or none of the slack. In heterosexual couples, the male partner approached the woman's becoming a professional student as her "not having a job" and thus being free to do chores, but when it was the male partner who became a student, his studies were portrayed as his all-consuming and vital work.

This patterning of time binds produced four groups of students. Most of the female professional students with families resented their partners for not picking up more of the slack and had to cope both with the bulk of the domestic labor and with their resentment toward partners who did not seem to be taking their professional school responsibilities seriously. On the other hand, a few female professional students with families were proud of having to do more domestic labor than did their single female peers; they felt self-defined by their dutiful attention to domestic chores, as did Susan, who described herself as a "housewife wanna-be." Whichever group they fell into, female professional students with families were likely to be identity dissonant.

The men I interviewed who had domestic partners (all female, mostly wives) were doing little domestic labor. These men asserted to me with absolute certainty that their professional school training was more important than domestic chores such as dishwashing, and they wanted to avoid being distracted from their work. The two groups of professional student men that emerged, then, were those whose partners accepted the burden of domestic chores stoically, and those whose partners raised a stink.[5] Many professional student men were lucky enough to have partners who fell into the stoic camp and did most of the chores without burdening their mates with complaints or "nagging" for assistance. (I was sometimes amazed by what the female partners of professional students were willing to take on; the wife of Michael, a law student, for example, was a doctor, and not only did she do most of the domestic labor, but also she had a baby during the course of Michael's 1L year and assumed all the care for the child, letting Michael get his nighttime sleep.)[6] But a few men I interviewed had partners who felt they were being taken advantage of and not paid attention to, and who made their feelings known quite clearly. In response, the male students did not increase their participation in domestic labor but resisted, which led to the breakup of Carlos's engagement and almost led to divorce for Tsong-Min.

It was remarkable how rarely familial status seemed to lead to identity dissonance for men. Those of my male interviewees whose partners stoically took responsibility for the domestic work were happy with the arrangement and felt that their relationships were an asset to their professional school careers. Even those whose partners did the labor kicking and screaming and threatening to leave did not necessarily feel identity dissonance. Carlos felt that his breakup was all for the best, and that avoiding his nagging fiancée improved his study habits. Only Tsong-Min was experiencing negative dissonance related to his familial identity. When it came to familial identity, men certainly did appear to have been dealt the winning hand.

## Sexual Orientation and Identity Dissonance

I had difficulty obtaining a suitable sample of nonheterosexual students because so few professional students were willing to identify themselves to me as bisexual, lesbian, or gay on the interview sign-up sheets, particularly at the Law School. At the School of Social Welfare, where a substantial plurality of the men I interviewed self-identified as queer, I could see a strong sexual identity effect: half these men were experiencing identity dissonance, as compared to none of the heterosexually identified men. At the Law School, half the sexual minority students I interviewed were also experiencing identity dissonance, but this amounts to a mere two out of four LGBTI interviewees. Still, the high rate of closeting and incidents such as Eliza's agitated withdrawal from Jaspreet when Jaspreet invited her to the Lesbian Bar Review lead me to believe that a strong association probably exists between sexual orientation and identity dissonance at both schools, comporting with a homophobia thesis, which posits a heterosexist bias.

### Disability and Identity Dissonance

The number of students I interviewed who identified as people with disabilities was small—seven. Of these, six were experiencing identity dissonance. Because such a small proportion of the individuals admitted to professional schools are people with disabilities, I can say little more than that there is a significantly higher rate of identity dissonance among students with disabilities than among their nondisabled peers, as an ableism thesis would predict. Disabilities operate at the level of the body, and bodily hexis is a substantial component of habitus, making it especially difficult for professional students with disabilities to internalize and display an approved professional identity.

## Predictions for Professional Practice

Since the students who were identity dissonant were underachieving at professional school and were receiving lower grades from professors and less positive reviews from their clinical placement supervisors than were their peers, their chances for securing high-status plum jobs were lower than were those of the consonant students with their high grades and glowing reviews. And since the prestige of the entry-level job or clerkship that a professional student secures affects the prestige of the next position, this could set off a chain reaction in the professional student's career path. Even for those who do secure high-status, high-paying jobs as new graduates, it is likely that identity dissonance will allow those with privileged characteristics to reap greater rewards from this placement than those with less privileged characteristics. (This prediction is supported by the statistic that one of the venues in which women have the lowest odds of serving as managers when compared to male colleagues is nursing-care facilities [Equal Employment Opportunity Commission, 2002].) Identity dissonance reproduces patterns of social stratification in student grades, and thus leads to social inequality in first jobs secured, with long-term impacts on professional success.

Another prediction I can confidently make is that some students will complete professional school without resolving their identity dissonance. (Certainly negatively dissonant Chinese American 3L Wei was unlikely to resolve his identity dissonance in the month between the time I spoke with him and his graduation date.) Individuals who enter professional practice without having internalized the appropriate professional identity are likely to face difficulties. Their coworkers may not respect them, clients may avoid them, and they may face years of dealing with an ongoing identity crisis that negatively affects their job performance, raises, and promotions. (This prediction is supported by government statistics showing that men who secure jobs at large law firms are more than twice as likely to be promoted to partner as are women hired by those firms [Equal Employment Opportunity Commission, 2003].)

I also predict that upon completing their training and beginning professional practice, neophyte attorneys are much more likely to face a problematic resocialization than are novice MSWs. There are several reasons I believe this to be true. First, social work students are required to engage in supervised clinical practice with actual clients, while students at prestigious law schools need do no more than engage in a first-year moot court trial simulation.[7] Second, while social welfare students take classes specifically geared to the demands of clinical practice, at the Law School the students' energy is completely focused upon academic performance, and professors are dismissive of questions about the "real world". And finally, the fact that, when interviewing for jobs, the women at the Law School adopted a very feminine self-presentation instead of their usual androgynous self-presentation leads me to suspect that they had a resocialization lying ahead of them. If, as I predict, the identities that law students and attorneys must internalize are not identical, then the higher rates of identity dissonance law students experience in comparison to their social welfare counterparts will be followed by higher rates of professional identity dissonance for new lawyers than for new MSWs.

My final prediction is that, just as disaffection leads to identity dissonance, identity dissonance leads to increased disaffection, and that prolonged disaffection in professional careers leads people to suffer depression, anxiety, relationship problems, and the like.[8] As a result, I believe that people who suffer prolonged identity dissonance are at risk for giving up their professional careers. (This could help explain why a large percentage of women leave legal practice within ten years [Hagan and Kay, 1995].)

# Implications of the Patterning of Identity Dissonance

My research shows that the privileged are more likely to enjoy success at professional schools than are their underprivileged peers. Women underperform when compared to men, students of color lag behind white students, students from impoverished backgrounds do less well than students from financially privileged backgrounds, and so forth. While my study was limited to a school of law and a school of social work, there is no reason to believe that identity dissonance is not equally a problem in other professional schools, such as schools of medicine and nursing, MBA programs, architecture programs, and divinity schools. What does this mean for us, as individuals and as a society?

## *Social Implications*

The main implication of my findings is that the great American ideology of pulling oneself up by one's bootstraps is more uplifting myth than surety. The belief that anyone with sufficient will and determination can succeed has long been a part of the U.S. worldview and persists despite an equally long tradition of criticism of that belief.[9] If anyone should be capable of achieving the heights of social success by applied hard work, it is those from challenging backgrounds who, despite the odds stacked against them by poverty, prejudice, medical difficulties, family responsibilities, and the like, have managed to accrue the college grades and impressive resumes that allow them to be admitted to professional schools.

That disadvantaged professional students underperform compared to the more privileged members of their cohort is particularly distressing because professional schooling is often viewed as a main route into the ranks of the "respectable" upper middle classes. Some students, such as Charmaine (introduced in Chapter 1), voiced this tenet of American faith quite clearly. Charmaine, who became a mother at seventeen and had been a client of social workers, described her own mother as "ecstatic" when she heard that Charmaine was admitted to an MSW program, because this would secure the life that her mother had always dreamed of for her. But Charmaine found negotiating the social welfare program difficult and frustrating, and the identity dissonance she suffered hindered her professional school success. Despite feeling that she was "finding herself" and growing as a person—that is, despite experiencing the positive form of identity dissonance—Charmaine was unlikely to achieve the level of success in the social work profession that the identity-consonant star students, with their superior grades and evaluations, would likely enjoy. For Charmaine and the many others like her, the belief that social and financial security would be guaranteed by admission to professional school was overly optimistic.

Another implication of my findings is that our narrative of what it takes to succeed is unduly simplistic. According to American ideology, the only necessary conditions for success are hard work and protection from acts of malicious bigotry. If no repugnant, bigoted acts are discovered, then people's success or failure is held to turn on their merit and dedication. U.S. commentators tend to look askance at claims of more subtle prejudice—which is perhaps understandable, since such claims are often amorphous, with their mechanism unspecified. But my research findings make it clear that there are other phenomena that determine success or failure, including the internalization of an appropriate identity. So long as the problem of identity dissonance goes unacknowledged, social disparities will continue to be reinscribed, while debate on the persistence of these disparities will fruitlessly focus on whether this is due to lesser merit or intentional discrimination.

## Implications for Prospective Students

Individuals who contemplate applying to professional programs could benefit from understanding the problem of identity dissonance—but only to a degree. Because so much of identity is located in nonconscious habitus, much of a person's identity is opaque to her, making it hard for her to predict what problems she is likely to encounter. Furthermore, even when an individual is made aware of a problem, he cannot alter a problematic disposition simply by consciously trying to do so. Recall the students in my Sociology of Gender class trying gravely to walk with the gait of the opposite sex and failing miserably.

The information that could most benefit prospective professional students is this: identity matters, and it matters a great deal. Prospective students should be made aware that identity is of greater salience at professional school than at college. Certainly, one's identity is significant at college—a quick look at college dropout rates shows persistent race, class, and gender differences (see, e.g., Frehill, 2000) that are no doubt related to this phenomenon. But there is no consolidated collegiate identity students must internalize as a condition of success at college equivalent to the professional identities they must take on in professional school. This means that a student who spent his childhood in poverty, or who uses a power wheelchair, or who speaks English with a pronounced Jamaican accent may get a false impression from succeeding at college that he will enjoy equal success at professional school. Understanding that this is not necessarily so would be helpful.

If a prospective professional school student hails from an underprivileged background, it would behoove him to anticipate problems with identity dissonance. This will not prevent identity dissonance from occurring, but will at least help him understand that his failure to excel is not due to insufficient time spent studying, or to intellectual inferiority. This awareness could reduce some of the anxiety and loss of self-esteem that are common among identity-dissonant students.

What a prospective student must most carefully contemplate before making the decision to attend professional school is that to succeed, she may have to change things that are fundamental to her sense of self. Perhaps she is drawn to professional service by a strong sense of empathy. If she will have to curtail this impulse—as is likely not just in traditionally masculine professions like medicine and law, but even in the social services—will she lose her sense of calling and find her professional life uninspiring? Perhaps a student is driven to apply to professional school to improve the lives of his fellow residents of public housing projects, or Southeast Asian immigrants, or missionaries of the Church of the Nazarene. Does it make sense for him to apply if he is likely to lose his sense of connection to his community while undergoing professional socialization? Prospective students should give these questions soul-searching consideration and avoid the temptation to believe that they will be the exception, finding professional success without altering their nontraditional identities.

## What about Affirmative Action?

An argument periodically aired is that the underperformance of students of color at professional schools is proof that affirmative action is inappropriate. For example, Richard Sander recently argued in the *Stanford Law Review* that affirmative action is against the best interests of African American law students. Like all who make such arguments, Sander presents evidence that black law students get significantly lower grades than do their white peers and are much less likely to pass the bar exam, and then he asserts that these results must be due to African Americans being boosted by affirmative action into schools too intellectually challenging for them. Without affirmative action, Sander states, a black student would be admitted to "a less competitive school" and "might well thrive because the pace would be slower, the theoretical nuances would be a little less involved, and the student would stay on top of the material" (2005: 450).[10]

What Sander commits, as do others who argue as he does, is the classic logic error of assuming that correlation equals causation. Because being African American is correlated both with receiving affirmative action and with low performance, Sander asserts that the affirmative action causes the low performance. But this argument is faulty in the same way that it would be illogical to conclude that since ice cream consumption and shark attacks are correlated, the former causes the latter. Instead, ice cream consumption and shark attacks rise and fall together with the temperature. Affirmative action and lesser professional success are correlated, but not because the former causes the latter. In fact, Sanders's own data provide evidence that African American underperformance exists in the absence of affirmative action: his charts show that African American students with superlative LSAT scores and college grades who are admitted to elite law schools without any affirmative action are nonetheless more than twice as likely as their elite white peers to fail the bar exam (2005: 446).

What my research makes clear is that we cannot blame affirmative action for the fact that professional students who are members of underrepresented minorities tend to receive lower grades and professional rewards. Asian students, who are considered an overrepresented minority and are not eligible for affirmative action, also often underperform during professional schooling, despite exemplary college grades, because they suffer from identity dissonance at professional schools. Groups such as women, religious evangelicals, and sexual minorities suffer the same sorts of underperformance problems as do African Americans, Native Americans, and Latina/o students in the absence of affirmative action. Thus, affirmative action neither produces nor reduces the underperformance caused by identity dissonance. Eliminating affirmative action would reduce diversity among professional student populations, which would be unfortunate. However, the existence of affirmative action is not enough to produce racial equality in the professions—to ensure equality in professional rewards between all demographic groups, something must be done to address the problem of identity dissonance.

## Strategies for Reducing Identity Dissonance

Unfortunately, identity dissonance cannot simply be litigated or legislated away. Professional identities are shaped around professional roles, which exist at a societywide level, change very slowly, and are created though interpersonal interactions rather than legislative fiat. The level of micromanagement that would be required to regulate identity dissonance away is unimaginable. It is easy enough to ban racist jokes in the classroom, but can you imagine the American Bar Association writing a series of regulations banning all varieties of humor with a sadistic edge, out of deference to people with empathetic orientations? And even if that were to occur, it would not put an end to emotional dissonance—after all, the professors at the U.C. Berkeley School of Social Welfare abjure insensitive humor, and emotional dissonance arises there nonetheless.

But if the disparate impacts of professional socialization cannot be banned by decree, they nevertheless can and should be reduced. The simplest and most important step is to acknowledge that the problem of identity dissonance exists. Identity dissonance causes such persistent problems for students being socialized in professional schools precisely because it goes unrecognized, leading professors and employers to believe that students who underperform are either less intelligent or less diligent than their peers—blaming the victim. The underperforming students themselves, having no other explanation available, engage in self-disparagement, and their self-esteem suffers. And the solution suggested by professors, parents, partners, and the students themselves—to study harder—is ineffective.

The first step that could be taken to address the problem of identity dissonance directly would be to require schools to gather and make public information that would allow prospective students to estimate the likelihood that they would experience identity dissonance should they attend. Professional schools already routinely inform potential applicants of the demographic breakdown of their student population and information such as the average admission-test scores. One way in which levels of identity dissonance could be roughly estimated would be to compare the college GPAs and admission-test scores of demographic subgroups of newly admitted students to their GPAs after one year of professional school, producing a ratio for each subgroup.

Having to calculate a differential performance ratio every year would raise the consciousness of professional school faculties and administrations as to the disparities which arise under their stewardship. Being forced to calculate the effects of identity dissonance might prod professors and administrators into trying to ameliorate the problem. The disparate patterns of identity dissonance could not be eliminated completely without taking unlikely, heroic measures, such as hiring new faculties with different personal identities and making existing professional role models alter their habitus. But a simple, if only partly effective, first step that all professional schools could take would be to add a formal component to informal professional socialization. A course on professional identity and professional socialization could be required for all students; in this class, students could be made at least partly aware of whether they were experiencing identity dissonance, and if so, from what source(s) that dissonance was arising. This might be difficult, because the sensation of identity dissonance is a rather inchoate one—an unlabeled feeling, rarely if ever described by those suffering it—but I have found that once I explain it, people often immediately label it as something from which they have suffered, leading to the liberatory hope of consciousness raising.

Of course, while being able to identify his or her identity dissonance problem is an important first step for any student, merely establishing such a professional identity course requirement does not address the truly contentious problem: what must be changed in order to eliminate identity dissonance. When professors discover that many students of color are suffering the effects of habitus dissonance arising from their ethnic patterns of cultural behavior, will they instruct these students to alter their vocal inflections, their musical preferences, their gestural repertoires, and the like until they are mimicking the demeanor of their middle-class white peers? According to psychologists of race, this constitutes a retreat to the most infantile stage of racial identity for people of color (Cross, 1991), and the advocacy of such actions would be deemed inappropriate by such experts. What do you imagine would be the response of students with strong religious or political commitments if they were told by their professors that to get high grades and secure plum jobs, they must abandon their atypical belief systems? Surely, at this juncture, cries of discrimination would ensue.

And yet, the advice that professors would be unwilling formally to give lest they be accused of discrimination would be *good* advice, at least with regard to professional success in the context that exists today. In a world where the barriers of formal discrimination within the professions have been greatly reduced, disparate patterns of professional success continue to persist because professional roles were constructed around the personal identities of past practitioners. If a student with a conflicting personal identity wishes to become fully integrated into the professions, he must do so at the cost of losing himself, for an individual can change himself but not a role.

What I suggest, if this situation is to be altered, is that professional students and practitioners turn their attention toward a long-term group effort to alter professional roles. Rather than engage in ineffective practices such as putting in more and more hours at work, or maintaining a protective, alienated distance, or seeking to convince unsympathetic courts or administrations that their identity-dissonance problems are the result of widespread intentional discrimination, those who have suffered from professional identity dissonance should gather their supporters and agitate to change what it means, identitywise, to be a lawyer or social worker, a doctor, professor, or rabbi. Armed with statistics and anecdotes comparing earlier academic performance to later professional school performance or salary differentials, reformers should raise the issue of professional roles at meetings of their professional associations.

Professional associations cannot be expected to regulate away identity dissonance via micromanagement. However, just as professional associations have adopted formal codes of ethics, they could develop codifications of professional role requirements and nonrequirements. This would at least force the professions to debate openly issues such as whether a lawyer should be expected to dominate others verbally or whether a social worker may not allow religious sentiments to influence her professional life. In addition, professional associations could address the issue of the disparate impact of professional socialization upon various demographic groups. They could adopt resolutions against allowing patterns of grade stratification to develop, and they could ameliorate disparate impacts upon salaries by encouraging demographically proportionate hiring and promotion policies.

None of these top-down resolutions would eliminate patterns of identity dissonance, but they would constitute a good start. Ultimately, it will take time for professional roles to shift, but the speed of their shifting could be increased from glacial to merely slow if students and practitioners were to agitate on the issue. Until professional roles shift to become more compatible with diverse bodies of professional school matriculants, the best we can hope for is that professional students, professors, and practitioners become more aware of the genesis and sequelae of identity dissonance.

# Notes

## Chapter 1

1. Some important resources for those interested in exploring patterns of social inequality produced by the workplace include Amott and Matthaei, 1996; Reskin and Padavic, 1994; and Browne, 1999.
2. My own research provides evidence that the underperformance of professional students of color occurs with or without the presence of affirmative action policies. I found evidence of substantial underperformance of professional students of color at U.C. Berkeley after affirmative action policies were canceled and students were admitted without racial consideration.
3. I interviewed seventy-two students and observed more than three hundred more.
4. Brian was financially conservative but advocated the decriminalization of recreational drugs, a classically libertarian position.
5. One of the factors which revealed Charmaine's changing style was her pattern of speech, with its swift fluctuations between formal, professional phrases and the sort of informal "street" phrasing professionals might deem ungrammatical.
6. I interviewed Charmaine early in her first year, so she had not yet received significant grades, but most of the students I encountered who had experiences similar to hers were underperforming academically.
7. In Peter's class there were sixteen students in the management track, nine of them male and seven of them female.
8. One of the reasons that Peter was not feeling time pressured was that he had turned over many of his domestic chores to his wife (who had a full-time job of her own). Peter said that they both saw his reduction in domestic duties as necessary, and "I don't feel that she objects."

## Chapter 2

1.  In fact, while I worked in food service I did develop a working-class identity, because I was a member of a vocal union and involved in a strike. But this was a class identity and not an occupational identity.
2.  Transsexual people try to reduce this discomfort by altering their genitalia to conform to their self-identification, but this is only partly successful, as it results in a gender-determines-genitals maxim not equivalent to the standard converse genitals-determine-gender rule.
3.  I must acknowledge that several other scholars have used the phrase "identity dissonance" in their work (Babcock, 1977; Elsback, 1996; Knefelkamp, 2000; Thumma, 1991; Tsuda 1998). Each uses the term to refer to people's subjective discomfort with their consciously acknowledged conflicting identities. My usage of the term is much broader. Many of the students I studied were suffering without having any notion of the source of their problem, because their identity conflicts were at the nonconscious level of habitus.
4.  While the concept of identity is currently well received in academia, the related concept of role is in disfavor. The concept of role is typically criticized because roles have often been reified by theorists--that is, treated as if they have an objective existence outside people's heads. Role theorists have also been criticized for treating roles as monolithic constructs, as if each social group did not hold different concepts of what it means to fulfill, for example, the masculine role. While I agree with these criticisms, I believe it is counterproductive to throw the baby out with the bathwater and reject the concept of the role. A man does not develop a masculine identity in a vacuum but in relation to larger social understandings of what it is to be a man: the masculine role as understood in his family, his ethnic culture, his generational cohort, the larger popular culture, and so on. This is socialization: the internalization of sociocultural roles as identity. If we dispense with the concept of role, we are left with a socially unanchored conception of identity.
5.  Note that identity dissonance does not develop until the student begins to internalize the professional role as identity. Identity dissonance is a subjective, phenomenological experience related to objective role conflict ("role strain") but not equivalent to it.
6.  The phenomenon of cognitive dissonance was first identified and named by Leon Festinger in 1957. For a contemporary treatment, see Harmon-Jones and Mills, 1999.
7.  Approximately one-quarter of first-time college students fail to return for their second year (National Information Center for Higher Education Policymaking and Analysis, 2002), while the retention rates at the professional schools I studied were well over 90 percent.
8.  In other words, students can attempt to pass as properly socialized members

of their chosen professions. As Robert Granfield put it, such students aim at "making it by faking it" (1992). As in all passing situations, this strategy involves constant anxiety about making performance errors and being revealed as a fraud.

9.  I have observed that students living in a state of denial regarding their identity dissonance must devote significant energy to maintaining that denial: denial is not an easy or passive dissonance-management strategy.

10. Social science researchers engage in socioanalysis, which allows them, like psychoanalysts, to gain insight into processes to which subjects to not have conscious access, and, like historians, to perceive processes of which subjects are consciously aware. When exploring processes that operate below the level of conscious awareness, sociologists, like psychologists, have the honor of being able to give subjects the gift of insight into these processes.

11. It is essential to acknowledge how nonmonolithic roles are without dismissing the power they have in people's lives. For example, consider the dissensus over the role of the "good mother": it is conceived quite differently in Victorian culture and twenty-first-century feminist culture, and among people of various racial and ethnic backgrounds (not that "race" is monolithic—it too is a role variously interpreted). Despite this great disparity in understandings, to be cast in the role of a "bad mother" has enormous consequences in each of these contexts.

12. Structural functionalist approaches to identity have had a renaissance in what is termed "structural symbolic interactionism" (Hoelter, 1983: 140). Researchers employing this framework merge roles and identities into a single phenomenon: a "role-identity" (Spenner and Rosenfeld, 1990: 267). This trick allows the researchers to easily operationalize identity for quantitative study, but it recapitulates the original errors of structural functionalism, ignoring diversity and agency (see, e.g., Burke and Reitzes, 1981; Callero, 1985).

13. Students who did employ this "rebellious" strategy were disproportionately male. Professional students who were "multiply nontraditional," such as strongly religious women of color, were extremely unlikely to employ this defiant strategy, contrary to the urgings of identity-politics theorists.

14. This balancing of identities is a particular focus of scholars who study people in bicultural or multicultural settings, where the ability to find a personal accommodation to multiple identities is deemed necessary (e.g. Oyserman, 1993).

## Chapter 3

1.  I did not make observations in the men's bathrooms. Every researcher encounters her limits.

2. Because it is impossible for me to conceal the identities of the schools at which I did my research, since I describe their settings in detail, I conceal the exact years during which I conducted my research to help preserve the confidentiality of the study subjects.

3. LGBTI is an accepted acronym for "lesbian, gay, bisexual, transsexual, or intersexed."

4. This quote is attributed to Benjamin N. Cardozo, associate justice of the U.S. Supreme Court, 1932–1938.

5. The difference between the linoleum floors at the two professional schools is emblematic of the schools' differences generally. At the Law School, decorators transformed linoleum into an elegant surface by crafting it into glossy parqueted checkerboards of black and white, while the floors at the School of Social Welfare displayed linoleum to its worst advantage: brown and beige tiles with off-white speckles were used functionally to conceal dirt, but their scuffed and scratched surface left them appearing constantly dirty anyway.

6. All the names used in this book have been changed to protect the confidentiality of those I studied to the greatest extent possible. Because the identities of the schools have not been concealed, it may be possible for those familiar with the schools to identify the professors despite their aliases. I have taken special care to disguise the identities of the students I studied, conceivably a vulnerable group. While professors are a less vulnerable population, they are also more easily identifiable. I therefore offered certain professors the opportunity to conceal their identities and/or select their own pseudonyms.

7. For the curious, I went to Harvard Law School, also ranked in the Top 10.

## Chapter 4

1. Professors at the School of Social Welfare did occasionally speak of their function as "role models," conceived of in ideological terms rather than on the level of emotional identity or habitus. As Americans popularly speak of children's need for role models to grow up with appropriate moral values, some of the social work professors I studied believed that they or their peers had a duty to engage in public service in the interests of the poor, and thus model to students that social workers should not limit themselves to comfortable practice among the middle class.

2. For example, he invited each student to schedule a lunch with him so that they could get to know one another.

3. The level of dress adopted by the Law School's female faculty was so high and rather stodgy that first-year students could not imagine themselves emulating it. For example, one student, speaking of Professor Hilliard to me, described her fussy scarves as "the kind you see in Macy's and say, 'Who buys those?'"

4. Male professors at the School of Social Welfare were much more likely to sport facial hair than were those at the Law School. My impression was that the intent was to make the men look more liberal, whereas law professors went for the conservative, clean-shaven look.

5. The use of Latin at the Law School struck me as particularly ironic, because professors periodically mocked courts or commentators for trying to cover up weak reasoning by magically invoking Latin phrases of power. Professors regularly told students that their legal writing should be in clear, plain English, as free as possible from stilted formalism. Nevertheless, professors continued to sprinkle their speech with Latin phrases and were universally admired by students for their ability to do so. The advocacy of the use of simple, clear speech by legal educators was ineffective, because the use of Latin phrases and convoluted, formal speech served a function for professors and students: it conveyed authority.

6. One way in which social welfare professors' authority was evident lay in students generally referring to them as "Professor Alverson" or "Professor Dunn" while class was in session. However, that the authority of the social welfare professors was less than that of the law professors was evinced in students' private conversations about a professor with one another outside class, when they often referred to the professors by their first names, for example, "Marjorie" or "Bob." I never heard a law student call a professor by his or her first name under any circumstances; instead they would drop the title, speaking of "Hoffert" and "Tate," which did not diminish the professors' authority.

7. Professor Alverson said this in a joking tone to a student who came to her during a class break with an ethical dilemma; Professor Hennings, whose class I visited once, said it as a warning to the entire class while exhorting them to turn in assignments in a timely fashion.

8. I wrote in my notes of the "Ally McBeal phenomenon": the presence of a significant number of women wearing jackets, miniskirts, chunky high-heeled shoes, and even hairstyles carefully contrived to look slightly disheveled. The presocialization provided courtesy of TV shows was poor preparation for professional school, and the Ally McBeal look did not persist for long in the Law School classroom.

9. This number was large only in the comparative sense—in absolute terms the percentage of students who were members of underrepresented minority groups was modest when I began my research and decreased in the second year.

10. The upper-level moot court competitions also looked quite white and male, as did the law review, where, in "blind" competition, white men were admitted at disproportionate rates until a "diversity" essay was added in 1997, generating much controversy.

11. For a more detailed discussion of dress, see Costello, 2004.

12.    I found myself at the center of a demonstration of sensitivity, awareness, and competence one day when I developed a migraine aura on the way to interview a student. Having never experienced one before, I asked a student for help and soon had a circle of social welfare students gathered around me in the Commons Room, giving me advice, writing a note to my interviewee explaining why I would be canceling, and offering me their assistance in getting to the student health clinic.

13.    Later in the semester, when students' professional identities were more secure, they were not likely to jump into off-topic conversations in this way but remained more attentive to the issue at hand.

14.    For a full discussion of the manipulation of white identity, try Clark and O'Donnell, 1999; Lipsitz, 1998.

15.    I will explain the study of cases using the Socratic method in the next chapter, in the section on pedagogic methods. "Cold-calling" was the term employed for a professor's calling upon students using a seating chart, rather than asking for volunteers.

16.    To give an example from a Civil Procedure class described by legal author Duncan Kennedy, some students discussing a case with an outcome that most people would perceive as unjust "volunteered that the case was just wrongly decided." According to Kennedy: "The teacher referred to this response as 'equity above all,' 'justice no matter what the cost.' It was clear that was inadequate, and implicit that students who proposed it suffered from an excessive, *nonlegal* concern with the particular fact situation" (2004: 9; emphasis in original).

17.    In fact, the students who attempted to act in a professional manner did not seem to be responding out of true identity consonance but rather to be making initial, rather overplayed attempts to act the part of an attorney. An individual with a secure lawyerly identity would not say, "The entire ethics area is a grey area;" this is an unflattering stereotype of the lawyerly worldview. A person with true lawyerly habitus would be more likely to respond by stating that members of the bar adhere to a code of ethics which has been carefully crafted, and that the case under discussion was decided the way it was for a good reason that in fact advances ethical goals.

18.    This framing of social justice concerns as policy was a subtle rhetorical maneuver: it framed substantive justice as a matter for policymakers—that is, the legislature. According to the doctrine of separation of powers, the judicial branch may interpret the texts produced by the legislative branch but must not engage in policymaking itself. Hence, students who are preoccupied with policy matters are engaging in an act that is not only framed as irrelevant to learning the law, but also possibly illegitimate.

19.    As a point of interest, I'd like to note that the valence of good typing skills has switched over the past twenty years. At the law firm where I used to work, many of the partners were older white men who dictated or handwrote their

briefs and relied upon secretaries to type them up. These men were proud of their inability to type—for them, typing was pedestrian women's work, and beneath them. But the majority of students taking notes on laptops at Boalt at this time were men, and for them, good typing skills were a sign of computer literacy and technical competence—qualities generally labeled masculine of which they were proud.

20. Professors were almost certainly aware of when students had stopped taking notes and started fidgeting. It seems likely that professors would experience student fidgeting as a form of negative reinforcement and would limit their lecturing on squeak-inducing topics. Socialization proceeds from the bottom up as well as from the top down.

21. Note that the association of an increase in conformity with the increase in school status serves to ensure that those students who graduate with the most social power and prestige are unlikely to use this power to challenge the norms of the legal role.

22. If identity-dissonant students at the School of Law tended to keep quiet for fear of appearing stupid or of being accused of a preoccupation with policy, social welfare students who were experiencing identity dissonance often kept silent for fear of being shunned.

23. While the students were critical of Lisa's idea, they were careful to demonstrate their empathy for her and their understanding of her fear of the parent.

24. Not all these students were law students; some were undergraduates.

25. From my conversations with Paula, I gather that many students expressed gratitude in classes when she told them about Native American culture and social problems, and that she felt put in a bind by their general ignorance about Native American issues and their gratitude when she enlightened them. After several weeks in the MSW program, Paula felt that she was not being allowed to focus on her own studies because she was being treated as an educator, and she wanted to be treated as just another student instead of as "the Indian." She felt that if students were genuinely interested in Native American issues, they would educate themselves, and that their reliance upon her showed that they were dilettantes. But she felt she might be doing a disservice to clients of Native heritage whom her peers might encounter if she stopped, so she continued.

26. They were helped into choosing this path by their classes all being crowded into a Monday–Wednesday schedule that left little time for a midday lunch break, to leave Tuesdays and Thursdays open for clinical work. Still, students could have eaten between classes or delayed lunch until they were done with classes in the early afternoon.

**Chapter 5**

1. The efficacy of various pedagogical methods has been well studied elsewhere, and I neither replicate nor cite that literature. My interest here is not in how substantive material may be best conveyed, but in the "hidden curriculum" that is imparted by professional pedagogy. (For more on the hidden curriculum, see Margolis, 2001.)

2. This pedagogic consensus sent the message that the legal profession is established, consolidated, hegemonic, traditional, and rigid.

3. In fact, Professor Hoffert actually apologized for the degree of informality imparted by his use of first names in the classroom. He explained his usage of first names by stating that "when I started teaching here, I was younger than most of the students," underlining his own brilliance as he excused his supposed informality.

4. The phrase "cold call" is an interesting one, implying as it does a lack of emotional warmth as well as a lack of warning.

5. Boalt students' central classroom interactions with one another were not in the form of intellectual engagement, which took place directly only between professor and student. Rather, they served as witnesses to one another's intellectual triumphs and tribulations during Socratic performances.

6. The principles included in Dahmer's Discussion Code were similar to those employed routinely at the Law School—such as accepting a burden of proof, making only relevant points, and engaging in rebuttal—with three notable exceptions. The first principle, fallibility, requires the debater to admit at the outset that she could be wrong; the fourth, charity, requires the debater to give the other person the benefit of the doubt; and the fifth, clarity, requires the debater to avoid "linguistic tricks," a phrase never heard at the Law School.

7. At worst, as we saw in the previous chapter, students who made controversial statements might face shunning. But few students had many controversial things to say in the first place, because of their ideological homogeneity.

8. Since professors differed in their preferred classroom arrangements, students often had to rearrange the chairs before class began. As a courtesy, the first to arrive might move all the chairs into the pattern preferred by the professor. For example, Professor Alverson's class was held in a room in which an undergraduate French class was also held. The French teacher arranged the seats into rows, while Professor Alverson wished her class to sit in a horseshoe arrangement, with her desk at the open end of the U. As students had a habit of straggling in, I was often the first to arrive, and I quickly adopted the custom of rearranging the furniture. One of the students in the class used to joke with me about it, saying that in other psychology studies in which she had participated, she had been paid in money, but that here at the School of Social Welfare, the best I could do was move her chair for her.

9.  Note that besides functioning to instruct students in techniques of mediation and of drawing up community-action plans, this exercise was intended to teach future social workers to have empathy with interest groups often framed by grassroots activists as the enemy, such as business leaders and the police.

10. Basically, consideration is the money, act, promise, or other inducement that convinces a party to enter into a contract.

11. My Law School field notebooks bristle with turquoise flags bearing an "H" for humor, while my social work field notebooks contain only five such flags.

12. This is how mentorship is generally understood in the legal profession. For example, Guinier, Fine, and Balin define mentorship as "one-on-one personal contact," an "interpersonal relationship" which occurs outside the classroom. They also say that "many faculty do not view mentoring as part of their job," that mentoring relationships must usually be initiated by students, and that most of the students who do initiate a mentoring relationship are men (1994: 73, 74).

13. Professor Lipman's own survey results confirm that students did enter with the intention to serve underprivileged populations. In 1995, 65 percent of the students entering the U.C. Berkeley MSW program intended to give most of their attention to the poor, while only 35 percent intended to serve people of all classes equally. According to Professor Lipman, this statistic had flipped in values since 1990, which should have given him some cause for optimism.

14. The possibility of students eventually losing cases was never even mentioned at the Law School. (In this refusal to even raise the possibility of failure, law professors acted like sports coaches who refuse to countenance such talk as evidence of a losers' mentality.)

15. This assertion that clients have the power to help themselves, and that the power of social workers lies in enabling clients to tap their own power, presents social workers as partners with clients, standing on equal footing. In the picture painted by law professors, attorneys solve problems for clients that clients cannot understand themselves—a hierarchical, unidirectional picture of professional interactions.

16. Professor Alverson's advice on dress echoed her own calculated casual approach to apparel: she told students to dress "above" their clients "because you show respect for people by your attire"; she also told them that they should be comfortable and "somewhat casual" but "should not wear [their] shorts or tank top."

17. Professor Alverson warned students that defense lawyers in child-abuse cases often tried to win by attacking a social worker's credibility. (Her students shook their heads and tsked.) She also cautioned students about how "technicalities" can cause problems; for example, "getting some piece of information to the other lawyer too late may give the defense lawyer an op-

portunity to block your placement." She warned that if they too often failed to get their reports in on time, a judge could hold them in contempt and fine them or even send them to jail. (The general impression she gave was that lawyers were an impediment to the general effectiveness of social work, and an unpleasant impediment at that.)

18.   This was the only didactic handout I received on professional practice during the course of three semesters of observations at the Law School.

19.   Because Boalt, like other national law schools, imparted abstract knowledge but not practical skills, its graduates were unprepared for unsupervised practice and needed to obtain jobs that were in essence apprentice positions where they would be trained in the craft of lawyering. This is one of the central factors that steered them toward practice in substantial-sized law firms, which could best afford to take on quasi-apprentices. A two-person partnership or cash-strapped public-interest organization could ill afford to pay a fresh Law School graduate a substantial salary when she was unprepared to handle any cases on her own.

20.   Note that far from treating social welfare materials uncritically as seamless documents united by logical rules, Professor Lipman presented them irreverently as mediocre and flawed.

21.   This averages to about three chapters or articles per week of required reading and seven chapters or articles per week of recommended reading per class over the course of the fifteen-week semester.

22.   According to sociologists of the professions, it is for this reason that social workers lack the professional power that lawyers enjoy (Abbott, 1988).

23.   Few and far between are the organizations employing MSWs that could afford to train them on the job the way prestigious law firms train novice JDs.

24.   Whatever exposure most law students did have to actual cases occurred in the course of summer employment, which varied widely from student to student. What students learned during this unsystematic exposure varied equally widely.

25.   The logic behind these incommensurable figures was said to be that for every hour of class law students attended, they needed to do several hours of preparation. While this is true, it is also true that students prepared for their clinical work outside their placement hours.

26.   Professor Lipman, the most academically oriented of the professors I observed, championed in class the value of abstract knowledge. (When class became too theoretical, the others preferred to bring it down to the pragmatic level.) In fact, while Professor Lipman was more likely than the other professors I observed to present abstract knowledge without making clear its pragmatic applications, he too generally related theory to practice.

27.   This raises an interesting possibility to which I will return in the conclusion of this book: that the professional identities internalized by social welfare students at school will need little revision when they transition to profes-

sional practice upon graduation, while the professional identities internalized by law students, being schooling oriented, will need substantial revision when the new graduates transition to professional practice as attorneys.

28.  A smattering of Boalt professors, including Professor Santana, provided other graded evaluation opportunities, mostly in the form of midterms, but even in these classes performance on the final exam largely determined a student's grade. Second- and third-year students had the opportunity to take seminars or legal practice courses in which grades were based on seminar papers or legal practice exercises; still, most upper-level law courses were lecture courses in which final exam performance was all-important.

29.  As Colin expressed it to me, the real problem with Joanna's behavior was that she did not seek the permission of the study-group members before sharing their work with her friend. This point was basically moot, because, according to Colin, another male member of the group would never have granted permission. But to Colin's mind, this was the crux of the matter; he felt that if Joanna had presented her friend's case to him, he might well have granted permission, but by neglecting to ask for permission (which, admittedly, she knew she would not receive with the required unanimity), Joanna had committed a personal offense against Colin.

30.  I later found out that Ellen did fine.

31.  This came across clearly in the interviews. Some students raised an ethic of care almost immediately when answering my first question, which was to describe themselves to me. For example, Pia said: "In terms of me as a person, I think I chose social work because in my family and with my friends, I've always felt like I'm the one people come to. I've always been kind of a helping person."

### Chapter 6

1.  Identity dissonance is a continuous variable: one can be highly or slightly dissonant. In analyzing identity dissonance dichotomously for purposes of this analysis, I included students with any significant dissonance in the identity-dissonant group. The only student whose dissonance I considered too insignificant to bump her from the consonant camp was Josie, whose only dissonance consisted of a little habitus problem with her nails: she was a social welfare student who had her nails artificially lengthened. She was embarrassed about getting her nails manicured and did not brag about it to her peers. This was an actual but very slight dissonance; in all other ways she was consonant.

2.  However, Eric identified himself as "mixed" on the interview volunteer form.

3.  Harmony, a mixed Native American and Welsh social welfare student, was

an exception; she was very conscious of changing. When I asked her to describe herself to me, she said: "My identity is in transition, and I think as a result how I would describe myself is 'in transition'. . . I'm trying to figure out who I am, who is Harmony, or who is my identity, so to speak."

4.  Robert Granfield reported a similar pattern of ambivalent feeling among the Harvard law students he studied who haled from working-class backgrounds (1992).

5.  A point that seemed ironic to me was that many students expressed a desire to finish school so they would have more time. For example, students who had partners or spouses generally stated that they would wait until they were done with school to have children, because they were too busy (and financially strapped) as students. As my own experience as an attorney returning to school brought home to me, the life of the practicing professional is busier and more pressured than the life of a student. My interviewees seemed blissfully unaware that they would jump out of the frying pan and into the fire.

6.  Some students were experiencing both positive and negative dissonance along different axes of their personal identities.

7.  Of course, many students have ideological gripes with particular professors or policies; cognitive/ideological dissonance exists only where there is a conflict between a student's conscious identity and the professional role.

8.  Although I did not interview any female students who employed the strategy of resistance to manage their ideological dissonance, I am certain females can adopt it, because it is in fact the strategy I employed as a law student. Based on my own experience, I had expected resistance to be a more common strategy that my research revealed it to be.

9.  The questions in my interview schedule most likely to elicit demonstrations of habitus dissonance were my initial request for the interviewees to describe themselves; my inquiry into their level of comfort in their program; my questions about whether professional school seemed to be meeting their expectations, whether the interviewees thought they would be good professionals, and whether they thought they looked like lawyers or social workers; queries into the relevance of various elements of identity for them at school; my questions asking them to compare their families, communities of origin, and significant others to those of their peers; questions about recent difficulties in personal relationships; and my question of whether anyone had told the interviewees that they had changed. (You may view my interview schedule at www.uwm.edu/~costello.)

10.  Law students who felt a dissonant aversion to law-student competitiveness were primarily women, but some men, such as Miguel, also deemed the competitive atmosphere "oppressive and unhealthy." (Note, however, that Miguel's habitus was confidently confrontational.) In addition, it was true

that a few social welfare students complained that the school atmosphere was too competitive, as did Kammi, who described her peers as "cutthroat."

11. Michael, who became a father during his first semester of law school, did not share it either; in fact, he was very career focused and was leaving most child-care responsibilities (including all nighttime care) to his wife.

12. Ideologically and emotionally dissonant students also used this alienation strategy, as discussed earlier.

13. For example, Sita did not know the Bengali words for "tort" or "civil procedure" when I asked her.

14. During our interview, Jed revealed that he had become seriously tempted to take a $100,000 per year law-firm job after graduating, which he had once said he would never do, indicating that his habitus *was* changing.

15. In fact, both consonant and dissonant students at the Law School felt dissatisfied by their grades if they had not received HH marks, even when they were doing relatively well. Michael, a consonant student who received all H grades (despite expecting his first child to be born in the middle of the final exam period), was "disappointed," as was Julia, who, with two H and two P grades, was doing well for a student coping with identity dissonance. The difference between the experiences of consonant and dissonant law students was often one of degree of disappointment.

## Chapter 7

1. An exception to this attempt to keep conversations down and to avoid slamming doors occurred whenever a class neared its end. Students would congregate outside the doors, laughing and chatting and acting as a goad to the professor not to go over time.

2. Individuals with these cognitive habits are likely the sort who get told, "You really ought to go to law school."

3. Note that the while the valorized comments were rational and incisive, their subject matter often involved emotions and the provision of social support. The "science of caring" seemed to come most naturally to students who combined rational orientations and social-justice-centered ideologies. I believe that a student who combined a rational orientation with a libertarian ideology would have been treated negatively by professors and would have suffered identity dissonance—but no such individual chose to attend the MSW program.

4. Professor Hoffert's use of the childish "Let's play the game" infantilizes Betsy. I believe this is because, like Lawrence Kohlberg, the (in)famous developer of the theory of stages of moral reasoning to whom Carol Gilligan responds in *In a Different Voice* (1982), Professor Hoffert believed that

particularistic, empathic, relational reasoning is an immature style of moral reasoning, and that universalistic, Kantian reasoning is the mature form.

5. In an example of the swift spread of trends among first-year professional students, two women in Professor Santana's class dressed their hair in French twists on 4 September, and on 5 September, French twists and buns appeared everywhere one looked.

6. That some women apparently dyed their graying hair was somewhat ironic, considering that many women complained in their interviews that they felt they appeared too young for a professional. Women were evidently caught in a double bind, wanting to look mature, yet fearing to look old.

7. It is ironically amusing that status-advertising students can accumulate so many technological devices said to increase efficiency—laptops, cellphones, PalmPilots, iPods, and so on—that they can prove a physical hindrance.

8. According to Nicole, the administrator in charge of class schedules believed Nicole was trying to secure an advantage unavailable to her peers—the ability to select desirable professors—by claiming undeserved disability privileges for a minor medical problem.

9. In fact, black leather jackets were closer to the norm at Haviland Hall than were long, artificially lengthened nails.

10. Note that this antipathy to piercing is true despite Boalt School of Law's location in Berkeley, one of the epicenters from which the body-piercing trend spread. Having a pierced nose (or eyebrow, bellybutton, or lip) was unremarkable among U.C. Berkeley undergraduates; nevertheless, it remained verboten within the conservative Law School milieu.

11. Just a few examples of the law students' jargon: "negligence per se," " the status quo ante," "voir dire," and "prima facie."

12. By the third week of class, I noted that almost no men were taking notes while peers spoke, while half the women continued to do so.

13. White men seemed generally to be the most comfortable in whatever they wore at the Law School—they established the dress code in the first days, were able to wear old comfortable clothes when they wished, and also looked the most comfortable, natural, and authoritative when striding about in their interview suits.

14. Identity dissonance is a continuous variable: one can be somewhat or extremely identity dissonant. For purposes of the quantitative analysis, I converted identity dissonance into a simple dichotomous variable, consonant or dissonant, lumping together all students exhibiting any meaningful identity dissonance. I would have liked to break the dissonance variable into several discrete levels, but seventy-two interviewees were too few for this operation. It would be interesting to do a survey-based research project on enough interviewees to allow a more sophisticated quantitative analysis.

## Chapter 8

1. This conception of the sympathetic social worker holds less true for people from underprivileged class backgrounds who must frequently deal with the large federal and state programs that serve the indigent, and who therefore encounter social workers whose sole purpose seems to be to scrutinize their lives to determine if they truly deserve government aid. When I, as a penurious student, relied on MediCal to provide medical insurance for my infant daughter, I gained an impression of social workers as uncaring and mistrustful rather than as empathic. Still, I and the other clients with whom I chatted while waiting in long lines felt that these social workers were "bad" because they did not live up to the cultural ideal of which we were generally aware.

2. I received the impression that the men in the management track of the MSW program were more rationally oriented than were their male peers in the direct services track.

3. Not that any student identified as having an upper-class background. No matter how privileged they were, students who came from wealthy backgrounds identified themselves to me as "upper middle class." This accords with typical U.S. class(less) ideology, which leads individuals from almost any background to identify with the middle class.

4. All the students I interviewed who were living with partners were either in heterogendered or lesbian relationships, so each couple had at least one female member.

5. Note that whether they complained or not, all the female partners did assume the bulk of the domestic responsibilities.

6. Compare Michael's situation to that of Jackie, a social welfare student who not only was attending professional school, doing most of the domestic chores, and working with her church, but also was mainly responsible for the care of her three biological children and one foster child.

7. While many law students work as summer associates during their summer breaks, this is not a requirement, and in any case, students with unimpressive grades often cannot secure such positions.

8. Studies of the mental health and career satisfaction of practicing attorneys indicate that lawyers do indeed suffer from high levels of depression, substance abuse, poor health, and dissatisfaction (Schiltz, 1999).

9. This of course raises the question of whether my findings will be taken to heart by individuals or institutions that share this belief. While I am an optimist, I have to admit to a pessimistic response to this question. When it comes to a conflict between fact and faith, people do seem to go with dogma most of the time.

10. Sander attributes the "cognitive gap" between blacks and whites to parenting differences, "e.g. time children spend reading with parents or watching

television," and states that the "cognitive gap" disappears when African American babies are reared by white parents (2005: 31n169). While a gap between the grades and salaries of black and white individuals raised by white parents does in fact exist, it is smaller than the gap between black and white individuals raised by same-race parents. I would argue that this is because African American children raised by white parents have a different habitus than those raised by black parents, leading to differing rates of identity dissonance at professional schools.

# Sources Cited

Abbott, Allen. 1988. *The System of Professions : An Essay on the Division of Expert Labor.* Chicago: University of Chicago Press.

Allen, T. H. 1939. "The Recent History of Professionalism." *Canadian Journal of Economics and Political Science* 5(3): 325–340.

Amott, Teresa, and Julie Matthaei. 1996. *Race, Gender, and Work: A Multi-Cultural Economic History of Women in the United States.* Boston: South End Press.

Atkinson, Paul. 1983. "The Reproduction of the Professional Community." In Robert Dingwall and Philip Lewis, eds., *The Sociology of the Professions: Lawyers, Doctors, and Others*, 224–243. London: Macmillan.

Axtel, Roger E. 1997. *Gestures: The Do's and Taboos of Body Language around the World.* Hoboken, N.J.: Wiley.

Babcock, Ginna M. 1997. "Stigma, Identity Dissonance, and the Nonresidential Mother." *Journal of Divorce and Remarriage* 28(1–2): 139–156.

Baille, Alverson. 1993. *Problems in Personal Identity.* New York: Paragon House.

Becker, Howard S., Anselm L. Strauss, Blanche Geer, and Everett C. Hughes. 1961. *Boys in White: Student Culture in Medical School.* New Brunswick, N.J.: Transaction Books.

Bernstein, Nina. 1996. "Equal Opportunity Recedes for Most Female Lawyers." *New York Times.* 8 January.

Blumenthal, Jeff. 2004. "ABA to Examine Career Paths of Minority Women Lawyers." *Legal Intelligencer* 230(96): 3.

Bosma, Harke A., David J. de Levita, Tobi Graafsma, and Harold D. Grotevant, eds. 1994. Introduction. *Identity and Development: An Interdisciplinary Approach.* Thousand Oaks, Calif.: Sage.

Bourdieu, Pierre. 1977. *Outline of a Theory of Practice.* Cambridge: Cambridge University Press.

———. 1990. "Structures, *Habitus*, Practices." In *The Logic of Practice.* Trans. Richard Nice. Cambridge, Mass.: Polity Press.

————. 1996. *The State Nobility: Elite Schools in the Field of Power.* Stanford, Calif.: Stanford University Press.

Bourdieu, Pierre, and Loïc J. D. Wacquant. 1992. *An Invitation to Reflexive Sociology.* Chicago: University of Chicago Press.

Browne, Irene. 1999. *Latinas and African American Women at Work: Race, Gender, and Economic Inequality.* New York: Russell Sage.

Burawoy, Michael. 1988. "The Extended Case Method." *Sociological Theory* 16(1): 4–33.

Burawoy, Michael, ed. 1991. *Ethnography Unbound: Power and Resistance in the Modern Metropolis.* Berkeley: University of California Press.

Burke, Peter J., and Donald C. Reitzes. 1981. "The Link between Identity and Role Performance." *Social Psychology Quarterly* 44(2): 83–92.

Callero, Peter L. 1985. "Role-Identity Salience." *Social Psychology Quarterly* 48(3): 203–215.

Carter, Ruth, and Gill Kirkup. 1990. "Women in Professional Engineering: The Interaction of Gendered Structures and Values." *Feminist Review* 35 (Summer): 92–101.

Cassell, Joan. 1998. *The Woman in the Surgeon's Body.* Cambridge: Harvard University Press.

Chodorow, Nancy. 1978. *The Reproduction of Mothering: Psychoanalysis and the Sociology of Gender.* Berkeley: University of California Press.

Clark, Christine, and James O'Donnell. 1999. *Becoming and Unbecoming White: Owning and Disowning Racial Identity.* Westport, Conn.: Bergin and Garvey.

Collins, P. J. 2002. "Habitus and the Storied Self: Religious Faith and Practice as a Dynamic Means of Consolidating Identities." *Culture and Religion* 3(2): 147–161.

Coltrane, Scott. 1996. *Family Man: Fatherhood, Housework, and Gender Equity.* New York: Oxford University Press.

Connecticut Bar Association. 1995. "Gender Issues in the Legal Profession." *Connecticut Bar Journal* 69(3): 161–291.

Costello, Carrie Yang. 2001. "Schooled by the Classroom: The (Re)Production of Social Stratification and Professional School Settings." In Eric Margolis, ed., The *Hidden Curriculum in Higher Education*, 43–59. New York: Routledge.

————. 2004. "Changing Clothes: Gender Inequality and Professional Socialization." *National Women's Studies Association Journal* 16(2): 138-155.

Cross, William E. 1991. *Shades of Black: Diversity in African American Identity.* Philadelphia, Penn.: Temple University Press.

"Dahmer's Discussion Code." 1996. Handout, Introduction to the Professions class, U.C. Berkeley School of Social Welfare.

Dalmage, Heather. 2000. *Tripping on the Color Line: Blackwhite Multiracial Families in a Racially Divided World.* New Brunswick, N.J.: Rutgers University Press.

Dankmeijer, Peter. 1993. "The Construction of Identities as a Means of Survival: Case of Gay and Lesbian Teachers." *Journal of Homosexuality* 24(3): 95–105.

Davidson, Julia O'Connell, and Derek Layder. 1994. *Methods, Sex, and Madness.* New York: Routledge.

Derry, Paula S. 1994. "Motherhood and the Importance of Professional Identity to Psychotherapists." *Women and Therapy* 15(2): 149–163.

Drachman, Virginia D. 1990. "Women Lawyers and the Quest for Professional Identity in Late Nineteenth-Century America." *Michigan Law Review* 88 (August): 2414–2443.

Dugan, Hannah C. 2002. "Integrating Women into the Legal Profession." *Wisconsin Lawyer* 75(10): 1–7.

Du Gay, Paul, Jessica Evans, and Peter Redman. 2000. *Identity: A Reader.* Thousand Oaks, Calif.: Sage.

Dunn, Robert G. 1998. *Identity Crises: A Social Critique of Postmodernity.* Minneapolis: University of Minnesota Press.

Durkheim, Emile. 1951 [1897]. *Suicide.* Trans. John A. Spaulding and George Simpson. New York: Free Press..

———. 1984 [1893]. *The Division of Labor in Society.* Trans. W. D. Halls. New York: Free Press.

Elsbach, Kimberly D. 1996. "Members' Responses to Organizational Identity Threats: Encountering and Countering the *Business Week* Rankings." *Administrative Science Quarterly* 41 (September): 442–476.

Epstein, Sandra. 1997. *Law at Berkeley: The History of Boalt Hall.* Berkeley, Calif.: Institute of Government Studies Press.

Equal Employment Opportunity Commission. 2002. "Glass Ceilings: The Status of Women as Officials and Managers in the Private Sector." Retrieved June 2004, www.eeoc.gov/stats/reports/glassceiling/index.html.

———. 2003. "Diversity in Law Firms." Retrieved June 2004, www.eeoc.gov/stats/reports/diversity/law.

Erlanger, Howard S., and Douglass A. Klegon. 1977. "Socialization Effects of Professional School: The Law School Experience and Student Orientation to Public Interest Concerns." *Institute for Research on Poverty Discussion Papers.* Madison: Institute for Research on Poverty, University of Wisconsin.

Festinger, Leon. (1957). *A Theory of Cognitive Dissonance.* Stanford, Calif.: Stanford University Press.

Foucault, Michel. 1979. *Discipline and Punish: The Birth of the Prison.* Trans. Alan Sheridan. New York: Vintage Books.

Freedman, Diane P., and Martha Stoddard Holmes, eds. 2003. *The Teacher's Body: Embodiment, Authority, and Identity in the Academy.* Albany: State University of New York Press.

Frehill, Lisa M. 2000. "Race, Class, Gender, and College Completion: The 1980 High School Senior Cohort." *Race, Gender, and Class* 7(3): 81–107.

Freyberg, Mark, and Ed Ponarin. 1993. "Resocializing Teachers: Effects of Graduate Programs on Teaching Assistants." *Teaching Sociology* 21 (April): 140–147.

Friedson, Eliot. 1994. *Professionalism Reborn: Theory, Prophecy, and Policy.* Chicago: University of Chicago Press.

Giddens, Anthony. 1991. *Modernity and Self-Identity: Self and Society in the Late Modern Age.* Stanford, Calif.: Stanford University Press.

Gilkes, Cheryl Townsend. 1982. "Successful Rebellious Professionals: The Black Woman's Professional Identity and Community Commitment." *Psychology of Women Quarterly* 6(3): 289–311.

Gilligan, Carol. 1982. *In a Different Voice: Psychological Theory and Women's Development.* Cambridge: Harvard University Press.

Goffman, Erving. 1959. *The Presentation of Self in Everyday Life.* New York: Doubleday.

———. 1968. *Asylums.* New York: Penguin Books.

Gold, R. 1958. "Roles in Sociological Field Observations." *Social Forces* 36:217–223.

Goslin, David A., ed. 1969. Introduction. *Handbook of Socialization Theory and Research.* Chicago: Rand McNally.

Granfield, Robert. 1992. *Making Elite Lawyers: Visions of Law at Harvard and Beyond.* New York: Routledge.

Gray, Louis, and Robin van der Vegt. 1997. "Boalt Protesters Arrested during Sit-in." *Daily Californian,* 14 October 1997, 1.

Grove, Kathleen. 1992. "Career Change and Identity: Nurse Practitioners' Accounts of Occupational Choice." *Current Research on Occupations and Professions* 7:141–155.

Guinier, Lani, Michele Fine, and Jane Balin. 1994. "Becoming Gentlemen: Women's Experiences at One Ivy League Law School." *University of Pennsylvania Law Review* 143(1): 1–110.

Hagan, John, and Fiona Kay. 1995. *Gender in Practice: A Study of Lawyers' Lives.* New York: Oxford University Press.

Hall, Stuart. 1993. "Minimal Selves." In Ann Gray and Jim McGuigan, eds., *Studying Culture: An Introductory Reader,* 134–138. New York: Edward Arnold.

Harmon-Jones, Eddie, and Judson Mills. 1999. *Cognitive Dissonance: Progress on a Pivotal Theory in Social Psychology.* Washington, D.C.: American Psychological Association.

Hekman, Susan J. 2004. *Private Selves, Public Identities: Reconsidering Identity Politics.* University Park: Pennsylvania State University Press.

Helms, Janet E. 1990. *Black and White Racial Identity: Theory, Research, and Practice.* New York: Greenwood.

Hochschild, Arlie Russell. 1983. *The Managed Heart: Commercialization of Human Feeling.* Berkeley: University of California Press.

———. 1993. *The Second Shift*. New York: Avon Books.

———. 1997. *The Time Bind: When Work Becomes Home and Home Becomes Work*. New York: Metropolitan Books.

Hoelter, Jon W. 1983. "The Effects of Role Evaluation and Commitment on Identity Salience." *Social Psychology Quarterly* 46 (2): 140–147.

Horrocks, John E., and Dorothy W. Jackson. 1972. *Self and Role: A Theory of Self-Process and Role Behavior*. Boston: Houghton Mifflin.

Hughes, Everett C. [1945] 1994. *On Work, Race, and the Sociological Imagination*. Edited by Lewis A. Coser. Chicago: University of Chicago Press.

Jaimes, M. Annette. 1992. "Federal Indian Identification Policy: A Usurpation of Indigenous Sovereignty in North America." In M. Annette Jaimes, ed., *The State of Native America: Genocide, Colonization, and Resistance*, 128–138. Boston: South End.

Kennedy, Duncan. 2004. *Legal Education and the Reproduction of Hierarchy: A Polemic against the System*. New York: New York University Press.

Kertzer, David I., Dominique Arel, Dennis P. Hogan, Andrew Cherlin, Tom Fricke, and Francis Goldscheider, eds. 2001. *Census and Identity: The Politics of Race, Ethnicity, and Language in National Censuses*. Cambridge: Cambridge University Press.

Kimmel, Michael S. 2003. "Toward a Pedagogy of the Oppressor." Introduction to Michael S. Kimmel and Abby L. Farber, eds., *Privilege: A Reader*, 1–10. Boulder, Colo.: Westview.

Kleinman, Sherryl. 1981. "Making Professionals into 'Persons': Discrepancies in Traditional and Humanistic Explanations of Professional Identity." *Sociology of Work and Occupations* 8(1): 61–87.

———. 1996. *Opposing Ambitions: Gender and Identity in an Alternative Organization*. Chicago: University of Chicago Press.

Knefelkamp, Lee. 2000. "Models of Intellectual and Identity Development." Briefing Paper #8, Association of American Colleges and Universities Greater Expectations National Panel. Accessed at www.aacu.org/gex/briefingpapers/intellectualidentity.cfm.

Kollock, Peter, and Judy O'Brien, eds. 1994. "The Elements and Outcomes of Interaction." In *The Production of Reality: Essays and Readings in Social Psychology*, 127-141. Thousand Oaks, Calif.: Pine Forge.

Law School Admission Council, in cooperation with the American Bar Association and the Association of American Law Schools. 1999. *The Official Guide to U.S. Law Schools 1999*. New York: Broadway Books.

Leary, Mark R., David S. Wheeler, and T. Brant Jenkins. 1986. "Aspects of Identity and Behavioral Preference: Studies of Occupation and Recreation Choice." *Social Psychology Quarterly* 49(1): 11–18.

Linsley, Jeann. 2003. "Social Work Salaries: Keeping Up with the Times?" *New Social Worker* 10(1). Accessed at http://www.socialworker.com/salaries2003.htm.

Lipsitz, George. 1998. *The Possessive Investment in Whiteness: How White People Profit from Identity Politics*. Philadelphia: Temple University Press.

Lofland, John, and Lyn Lofland. 1995. *Analyzing Social Settings: A Guide to Qualitative Observation and Analysis*. Belmont, Calif.: Wadsworth.

Loseke, Donileen L., and Spencer E. Cahill. 1986. "Actors in Search of a Character: Student Social Workers' Quest for Professional Identity." *Symbolic Interaction* 9(2): 245–258.

Lyson, T. A. 1984. "Sex Differences in the Choice of a Male or Female Career Line: An Analysis of Background Characteristics and Work Values." *Work and Occupations* 11:131–146.

Malcomson, Scott. 2001. *One Drop of Blood: The American Misadventure of Race*. New York: Farrar, Straus and Giroux.

Margolis, Eric, ed. 2001. *The Hidden Curriculum in Higher Education*. New York: Routledge.

McDowell, Linda. 1999. *Gender, Identity, and Place: Understanding Feminist Geographies*. Minneapolis: University of Minnesota Press.

McFayden, Ruth G. 1996. "Gender, Status, and 'Powerless' Speech: Interactions of Students and Lecturers." *British Journal of Social Psychology* 35(3): 353–367.

McKeon, John, Alverson Gillham, and Carl Bersani. 1981. "Professional Identity and Interaction: The Case of a Juvenile Court." *Sociology of Work and Occupations* 8(3): 353–380.

Menzel, Peter, and Faith D'Aluisio. 1998. *Man Eating Bugs: The Art and Science of Eating Insects*. Berkeley, Calif.: Ten Speed Press.

Meyer, David S., Nancy Whittier, and Belinda Robnett. 2002. *Social Movements: Identity, Culture, and the State*. New York: Oxford University Press.

Mills, C. Wright. 1959. *The Sociological Imagination*. New York: Oxford University Press.

Moore, Wilbert E. 1969. "Occupational Socialization." In David A. Goslin, ed., *Handbook of Socialization Theory and Research*, 861–883. Chicago: Rand McNally.

Morocco, Maria. 1990. "Law Students on Law School: The Job Chase." *American Bar Association Journal* 76(9): 66.

National Information Center for Higher Education Policymaking and Analysis. 2002. "Retention Rates: First-time College Students Returning Their Second Year." Accessed at www.higheredinfo.org/#.

Omi, Michael, and Howard Winant. 1994. *Racial Formation in the United States: From the 1960s to the 1990s*. New York: Routledge.

Oyserman, Daphna. 1993. "The Lens of Personhood: Viewing the Self and Others in a Multicultural Society." *Journal of Personality and Social Psychology* 65(5): 993–1009.

Parsons, Talcott. 1949. *Essays in Sociological Theory, Pure and Applied*. Glencoe, Ill.: Free Press.

Parsons, Talcott, and Robert F. Bales. 1955. *Family Socialization and Interaction Process*. Glencoe, Ill.: Free Press.

Pierce, Jennifer. 1995. *Gender Trials: Emotional Labor in Contemporary Law Firms*. Berkeley: University of California Press.

Reskin, Barbara, and Irene Padavic. 1994. *Women and Men at Work*. Thousand Oaks, Calif.: Pine Forge.

Rosenberg, Janet, Harry Perlstadt, and William R. F. Phillips. 1991. "Politics, Feminism, and Women's Professional Orientations: A Case Study of Women Lawyers." *Women and Politics* 10(4): 19–47.

Rubin, Lillian. 1981. "Sociological Research: The Subjective Dimension." *Symbolic Interactionist* 4(1): 97–112.

Sander, Richard H. 2005. "A Systemic Analysis of Affirmative Action in American Law Schools." *Stanford Law Review* 57(2): 367–484.

Sarafino, Edward P. 2002. *Health Psychology: Biopsychosocial Interactions*. 4th ed. New York: Wiley.

Sato, Stephanie K. 1997. "Ban of Preferences Yields Mixed Results." *Daily Californian*, 27 June, 1.

Schiltz, Patrick J. 1999. "On Being a Happy, Healthy, and Ethical Member of an Unhappy, Unhealthy, and Unethical Profession." *Vanderbilt Law Review* 52:871–951.

Scott, Joan Norman. 1996. "Watching the Changes: Women in Law." In Joyce Tang and Earl Smith, eds., *Women and Minorities in American Professions*, 19–41. Albany: SUNY Press.

Shapiro, Joseph P. 1994. *No Pity: People with Disabilities Forging a New Civil Rights Movement*. New York: Times Books.

Sills, David, ed. 1968. *International Encyclopedia of the Social Sciences*. New York: Macmillan and Free Press.

Spenner, Kenneth I., and Rachel A. Rosenfeld. 1990. "Women, Work, and Identities." *Social Science Research* 19:266–299.

Strauss, Anselm. 1987. *Qualitative Analysis for Social Scientists*. Cambridge: Cambridge University Press.

Strom, Sharon Hartman. 1992. *Beyond the Typewriter: Gender, Class, and the Origins of Modern Office Work, 1900–1930*. Chicago: University of Illinois Press.

Taber, Janet, Marguerite T. Grant, Manny T. Huser, Rise B. Norman, James R. Sutton, Clarence C. Wong, Louise E. Parker, and Claire Picard. 1988. "Gender, Legal Education, and the Legal Profession: An Empirical Study of Stanford Law Students and Graduates." *Stanford Law Review* 40 (May): 1209–1259.

Tatum, Beverly Daniel. 1997. *"Why Are All the Black Kids Sitting Together in the Cafeteria?": And Other Conversations about Race*. New York: Basic Books.

Telushkin, Joseph. 1991. *Jewish Literacy: The Most Important Things to Know about the Jewish Religion, Its People, and Its History*. New York: Morrow.

Tharp, Marye C. 2001. *Marketing and Consumer Identity in Multicultural America*. Newberry Park, Calif.: Sage.

Thumma, Scott. 1991. "Negotiating a Religious Identity: The Case of the Gay Evangelical. *Sociological Analysis* 52(4): 333–347.

Tsuda, Takayuki. 1998. "Ethnicity and the Anthropologist: Negotiating Identities in the Field." *Anthropological Quarterly* 71(3): 107–124.

Turner, Stephen Park, and Jonathan H. Turner. 1990. *The Impossible Science: An Institutional Analysis of American Sociology*. Newbury Park, Calif.: Sage.

Vargas, Sylvia Lazos. 1998. "Deconstructing Homo[geneous] Americanus: The White Ethnic Immigrant Narrative and Its Exclusionary Effect." *Tulane Law Review* 72:1493–1596.

Wacquant, Loïc J. D. 1990. "Exiting Roles or Exiting Role Theory? Critical Notes on Ebaugh's *Becoming an Ex*." *Acta Sociologica* 33(4): 397–404.Walkowitz, Daniel J. 1990. "The Making of a Feminine Professional Identity: Social Workers in the 1920s." *American Historical Review* 95(4): 1051–1075.

Wijeyesinghe, Charmaine L., and Bailey Jackson. 2001. *New Perspectives on Racial Identity Development: A Theoretical and Practical Anthology*. New York: New York University Press.

Wiley, Mary Glenn, and Mary Crittenden. 1992. "By Your Attributions You Shall Be Known: Consequences of Attributional Accounts for Professional and Gender Identities." *Sex Roles* 27(5/6): 259–276.

Williams, Christine L. 1989. *Gender Differences at Work: Women and Men in Nontraditional Occupations*. Berkeley: University of California Press.

———. 1995. *Still a Man's World: Men Who Do "Women's Work."* Berkeley: University of California Press.

———. 2002. "The Glass Elevator: Hidden Advantages for Men in the 'Female' Professions." *Social Problems* 39:253–267.

Williams, Simon Johnson. 2001. *Emotion and Social Theory: Corporeal Reflections on the (Ir)Rational*. London: Sage.

Willie, Sarah. 2003. *Acting Black: College, Identity, and the Performance of Race*. New York: Routledge.

Witz, Anne. 1992. *Professions and Patriarchy*. New York: Routledge.

Women Physician Congress of the American Medical Association. 2003. "Women Physicians Statistics." Retrieved 5 June 2003, www.ama-assn.org/ama/pub/category/171.html.

# Index